INDIAN TRIBES
AS
SOVEREIGN GOVERNMENTS

SECOND EDITION

INDIAN TRIBES
AS
SOVEREIGN GOVERNMENTS

SECOND EDITION

A Sourcebook on
Federal-Tribal History, Law, and Policy

Charles Wilkinson
&
The American Indian Resources Institute

Cover Art—*About the Artist*

ALLAN HOUSER (HA-O-ZOUS)
(1914-1994)

Allan Houser (HA-O-ZOUS), perhaps best known for his monumental sculptures on display in public venues, museums, art galleries and private collections around the world, was the preeminent American Indian artist of the 20th century. Through his life and art, he gently, but powerfully, touched the world with his profound talent and spiritual energy. Allan Houser (Chiricahua Apache)—the son of Sam Haozous, who was captured in 1886 and imprisoned by the federal government for 27 years along with Geronimo, the great Chiricahua Apache leader—was born a short time after his father was released from captivity and dedicated his life to capturing, on canvas and in stone and bronze, images that reflect the enduring spirit and rich cultural traditions of his people. Allan Houser's impressive career included exhibition of his work at two World's Fairs (New York 1936; San Francisco 1939); receipt of the French Palmes d'Academique (1954); dedication of *Offering of the Sacred Pipe* at the United States Mission to the United Nations (1985); receipt of the National Medal of the Arts (1992); and a retrospective exhibition of his work, in recognition of his unequaled prominence as a Native American artist and his contributions to celebrating Native culture, at the historic opening of the Smithsonian's National Museum of the American Indian in Washington, D.C. (2004).

Buffalo Dance, the Indiana limestone relief depicted on the front cover by permission of Mrs. Anna Marie Houser and the Allan Houser Foundation, is in the permanent collection of the Smithsonian's National Museum of American Art. For more information on the life and art of Allan Houser, contact the Allan Houser Foundation, Santa Fe, New Mexico.

Copyright © 2004
Copyright © 1988

First Printing 1988
Second Printing 1990
Third Printing 1991
Fourth Printing 1993
Fifth Printing 1994
Sixth Printing 1997
Seventh Printing 1998
Eighth Printing 1999
Ninth Printing 2000
Tenth Printing 2001
by the
American Indian Lawyer Training Program, Inc. (AILTP)
319 MacArthur Boulevard, Oakland, CA 94610
www.IndianLawReporter.org

ISBN 0-939890-07-0

*This book is dedicated to
tribal leaders of the past and of the modern era
who have done so much to safeguard and develop
a working tribal sovereignty in Indian Country.*

CONTENTS

PART ONE
FEDERAL-TRIBAL HISTORY, LAW, AND POLICY

PART TWO
HISTORY OF TREATY NEGOTIATIONS
BETWEEN THE UNITED STATES AND INDIAN TRIBES;
SELECTED TREATY AND EXECUTIVE ORDER

PART THREE
SELECTED FEDERAL STATUTES
(Edited)

PART FOUR
SELECTED UNITED STATES SUPREME COURT DECISIONS
(Edited)

FOREWORD

The sovereign status of Indian nations predates the formation of the United States. It is the subject of many writings of our nation's Founding Fathers and the debates of the Continental Congress. In addressing the powers and authorities of the three branches of the national government of the United States, the United States Constitution identifies three, and only three, sovereigns other than the Federal government—the several states, foreign nations, and Indian tribes.

This sovereign status of Indian nations is the fundamental premise upon which a course of dealings between the United States and Indian tribal governments ensued and the foundation upon which hundreds of Federal statutes and thousands of Federal court rulings have been based.

The sourcebook, *Indian Tribes as Sovereign Governments*, is an invaluable resource for those who may not be familiar with the history of the native people of America or the principles of Federal-Indian law and policy. It helps one to understand why, for well over two hundred years, native people have had a different status under the law from those who later immigrated to our shores, and why the federal policies of native self-determination and tribal self-governance have served as the cornerstones of the government-to-government relationship between the United States and native nations.

As a student of history, and as one who has had the honor and the privilege of working with the peoples of Native America, this nation's First Americans, I highly recommend the second edition of *Indian Tribes as Sovereign Governments*.

Senator Daniel K. Inouye
United States Senate

FOREWORD

Among the nations of the world, the United States is unique in its recognition of the inherent right of Indian tribes to govern themselves and their lands. The legal foundations of federal policy toward Indian tribes are established in the United States Constitution and can be traced directly to the laws applied to the relations between the tribes and the colonial powers in the period before American independence.

Indian tribes possess a sovereignty that preceded the formation of our nation and which the Congress and the federal courts have, with few exceptions, recognized and upheld since the earliest days of the nation. Tribal governments play an important and significant role in the system of government established by the United States Constitution.

Federal policies toward Indian tribes have been subject to contradictory swings from time to time. Some of these policies, such as allotment and termination, had profound negative impacts on the tribes, the effects of which are still evident today. Fortunately, the policy tide shifted in the last thirty-five years with the promotion of self-determination, which tribes have embraced. Self-determination enables tribes to more successfully develop tribal programs that best serve their members, lessen dependency on the federal government, and ensure greater participation in the national economy.

Much more remains to be done, as evidenced by unacceptably high unemployment rates on the reservations, the incidence of suicide and the need to improve the quality of educational opportunities and other indicia of social well-being. But, the pride and experience that come with self-determination have proven the success of this policy in the improvement of the day-to-day lives of Indian people.

Indian Tribes as Sovereign Governments is an important reference for all people who want to know more about the history and contemporary role of Indian tribes in our federal system of government. It is essential reading for all Americans.

Senator John McCain
United States Senate

PREFACE

There long has been a need for a short and plain summary of Indian law and policy. The Cohen treatise (*Handbook of Federal Indian Law*), the casebooks on Indian law, and other works all serve vital functions, but they do not meet the requirements of a person seeking a reasonably brief introduction to the field. As such, this overview book is intended for those tribal leaders and employees, federal and state government officials, educators, lawyers, Indian people, and members of the general public who have never had formal training in Indian law and policy; all of them may know a great deal about Indian Country or about law in general but they have never had the opportunity to study Indian law and policy in a systematic way. When the first edition of *Indian Tribes as Sovereign Governments* was released in 1988 our intent was to provide a framework for the concise study of federal-Indian law and policy for the purpose of promoting a clearer understanding of the unique position Indian tribes occupy within the federal constitutional system. Our goal remains the same with the release of the Second Edition in 2004. This volume can be read as a sourcebook, assigned as a text for introductory courses in universities and community colleges, or used as reading materials for two- or three-day policy seminars.

This volume is divided into four parts. Part One is a narrative description of the field, with chapters on the history of Indian affairs, tribal sovereignty, the trust relationship, and tribal resource rights, reservation environments, and economic development. Part Two begins with an overview of Indian treaty negotiations; it also presents an illustrative treaty and representative executive order—the Treaty of Point Elliott of 1855 and the Walker River Reservation Executive Order of 1874—along with a description of historical and legal developments relating to the treaty and executive order. Part Three is a compilation of excerpts of selected statutes dealing with Indian law. Part Four is a collection of some of the leading Indian law decisions handed down by the United States Supreme Court. Each case is condensed greatly and legal citations have been removed. Our hope is that this section will make accessible to the public the words of the Supreme Court in such great cases as *Worcester v. Georgia* (1831) (recognizing the supremacy of tribal sovereignty over state laws in Indian Country), *Winters v. United States* (1908) (upholding tribal reserved water rights), *Washington v. Washington State Commercial Passenger Fishing Vessel Association* (1979) (recognizing Indian fishing rights in the Pacific Northwest), *County of Oneida v. Oneida Indian Nation* (1985) (upholding the land claims asserted by tribes in the eastern United States), and *Minnesota v. Mille Lacs Band of Chippewa* (1999) (recognizing Indian fishing rights in the Great Lakes area).

Ultimately this is a straightforward book that provides basic source materials relating to a great idea—the idea of tribal sovereignty. Tribal sovereignty is an ancient notion, 15,000 years old at least and perhaps far older than that. Yet, in spite of having been tested during dark and treacherous times, tribal sovereignty remains vigorous and vibrant in this modern technological society of the 21st century. We hope very much that readers will be challenged by the study of tribal sovereignty and of the other unique rights possessed by Indian tribes. In the last analysis, rights can be preserved only if they are understood.

We are deeply indebted to a great many individuals who helped create this book. We wish to express our sincere appreciation to Deanna Martinez for editing and overseeing the final production of the Second Edition, as well for her editorial work on the first edition manuscript; to Christine Miklas for her editing work on the first edition; to Reid P. Chambers, Susan M. Williams, Alan R. Parker, and W. Richard West, Jr. for their writing contributions to the first edition; and to Rick Banker for his graphic design and production assistance on the Second Edition. We also benefited from the editorial efforts of several law students and research assistants, including Anna Ulrich, Cynthia Carter, Charles Sheketoff, Todd Smith, and Shannon Work. Finally, we wish to thank the many tribes, in particular the Shakopee Mdewakanton Sioux (Dakota) Community, whose support has contributed greatly to AIRI's efforts to preserve and strengthen tribal sovereignty.

Richard Trudell
Founder and Executive Director
American Indian Lawyer Training Program, Inc.
American Indian Resources Institute

Charles Wilkinson
Distinguished University Professor
Moses Lasky Professor of Law
University of Colorado

April 2004

PART ONE

FEDERAL-TRIBAL HISTORY, LAW, AND POLICY

CHAPTER 1

The History of Federal-Tribal Relations

INTRODUCTION

History is the essential foundation for an understanding of American Indian law and policy. Indian policy is seen by many in the United States as an aberration: how is it that nearly 3 percent of all land in the country is set aside for, and governed by, Indians? Isn't that racism in reverse? Isn't that segregation? These and other modern Indian issues cannot be analyzed properly without an appreciation of history. Many ancient statutes—enacted, for example, in 1790, 1817, 1885, and 1887—control major Indian issues today. Numerous Indian treaties more than 100 years old continue to be at issue in current litigation.

Federal policy is central to Indian affairs because Congress has "plenary" (broad) power over Indians, including the authority to decide who is, or is not, recognized as an Indian under federal law. For more than two hundred years, Congress has vacillated between two conflicting themes: self-government for tribes and assimilation of the reservations into the existing framework of state and local government. The tension between those themes likely will remain.

PRE-CONSTITUTIONAL POLICY (1532-1789)

*[O]ur Indian law originated, and can still be most closely grasped, as
a branch of international law, and ... in the field of international law
the basic concepts of modern doctrine were all hammered out by the
Spanish theological jurists of the 16th and 17th centuries....*
                                        — Felix S. Cohen (1942)[1]

During the 1600s, the administrators of some British and Spanish
colonies in the Western Hemisphere began negotiating treaties with
Indian tribes. Such actions—rationalized by theological, philosophical,
and practical arguments—had the effect of according tribes a sovereign
status equivalent to that of the colonial governments with which they were
dealing.[2]

To the extent that treaties involved cessions of Indian territory or
resolved boundary disputes, they also affirmed recognition by the colonial
powers of tribal ownership of the lands Indians used and occupied long
before Europeans arrived. Such tribal land rights had been asserted a
century earlier by Spanish theological jurists Francisco de Victoria and
Bartolome de las Casas.

Shortly before the middle of the 18th century, the British Crown
appropriated to itself some of the administrative responsibilities in dealing
with tribes that it previously had allowed the colonial governments to
exercise. By this time, the practice of negotiating with Indian tribes
through treaty had been well established.

The Articles of Confederation, which became effective in 1781, were
ambiguous concerning state and federal power over Indian matters. They
gave the federal government "sole and exclusive" authority over Indian
affairs, "provided that the legislative right of any State within its own
limites [sic] be not infringed or violated."

THE FORMATIVE YEARS (1789-1871)

*When the United States gave peace, did they not also receive it? Were
not both parties desirous of it? If we consult the history of the day, does
it not inform us that the United States were at least as anxious to obtain*

it as the [Indians]? ... This relation [in a treaty between the United States and an Indian tribe] was that of a nation claiming and receiving the protection of one more powerful: not that of individuals abandoning their national character, and submitting as subjects to a master.

— Chief Justice John Marshall (1832)[3]

We are assured that, beyond the Mississippi, we shall be exempted from further exaction; that no State authority there can reach us; that we shall be secure and happy in these distant abodes.

— Head Men & Warriors of the Creek
Nation, addressing Congress (1832)[4]

I will fight no more forever.

— Chief Joseph (1877)[5]

The shape of federal Indian law and policy was determined by early comprehensive federal legislation and by three leading Supreme Court decisions. Those opinions, written by Chief Justice John Marshall and referred to as the Marshall Trilogy, are *Johnson v. M'Intosh* (1823),[6] *Cherokee Nation v. Georgia* (1831),[7] and, most importantly, *Worcester v. Georgia* (1832).[8] (For text of the Marshall Trilogy opinions, *see* Part Four.)

Federal Power

The new Constitution lodged broad power in Congress under the Indian Commerce Clause, article I, section 8, clause 3: "The Congress shall have Power ... to regulate Commerce with foreign Nations, and among the several States, *and with the Indian Tribes.*" (Emphasis supplied.) Thus state control over Indians was subordinated to federal power.

The Trade and Intercourse Acts and Tribal Property Rights

Congress immediately implemented its broad powers by establishing a comprehensive program regulating Indian affairs. One of these foundational statutes was the Indian Trade and Intercourse Act of 1790 (often referred to as the "Nonintercourse Act").[9] The Act represented congressional policy to implement the treaties and established the basic features of federal Indian policy. The Act brought virtually all interaction between

Indians and non-Indians under federal control. For instance, the Act broadly regulated commercial trade with the Indians and established penalties for violations by traders. Moreover, the Act provided for criminal provisions for murder and other crimes against Indians in Indian Country.

One of the crucial provisions, which is the basis of many modern eastern land claims, is the requirement that Indian land cannot be sold by a tribe without federal approval.[10] This rule was applied judicially to land sales made before the Trade and Intercourse Act of 1790 was passed. In the first case of the Marshall Trilogy, *Johnson v. M'Intosh* (1823),[11] the Supreme Court concluded that discovery gave the United States the exclusive right to extinguish the original tribal right of possession. (For text of opinion, *see* Part Four.) The Indian right of possession, an unusual but acknowledged form of landownership in the Anglo-American system of property law, is referred to today as "aboriginal" or "original Indian" title. Congress may extinguish aboriginal title without compensation.[12] On the other hand, a taking must be compensated pursuant to the Fifth Amendment when title is "recognized" by treaty or statute.[13]

TREATIES WITH INDIAN TRIBES

> *Brothers, listen.... Your Great Father will give [this land] to you forever that it may belong to you and your children while you shall exist as a nation far from all interruptions.... Peace invites you thus, annoyances will be left behind. Within your limits no state or territorial authority will be permitted. Intruders, traders, and above all ardent spirits so destructive to health and morals will be kept from among you only as the law and ordinances of your nation may sanction their admissions.*
> — President Andrew Jackson, to the Choctaws (1830)[14]

Until 1871, Congress dealt with individual tribes by formal treaties. Early cases clarifying these treaties established the basic elements of federal Indian law:

1. **The trust relationship:** Indian tribes are not foreign nations, but constitute "distinct political" communities "that may, more correctly, perhaps, be denominated domestic, dependent nations" whose "relation to the United States resembles that of a ward to his guardian."[15] This language, in *Cherokee Nation v. Georgia* (1831),

gave birth to the doctrine of federal trusteeship in Indian affairs. (For text of *Cherokee* opinion, *see* Part Four.)

2. **Tribal governmental status:** Indian tribes are sovereigns, that is, governments, and state law does not apply to tribes or tribal members within reservation boundaries without congressional consent. State law normally will not apply to non-Indians within reservation boundaries if it will infringe upon the rights of tribes to make their own laws and be ruled by them.[16]

3. **Reserved rights doctrine:** Tribal rights, including rights to land and to self-government, are not granted to a tribe by the United States. Rather, under the reserved rights doctrine, tribes retained ("reserved") such rights as part of their status as prior and continuing sovereigns.[17]

4. **Canons of construction:** Courts have adopted fundamental rules and principles that govern the interpretation of written documents such as treaties. In legal terminology, these rules and principles are known as "canons of construction." Those that apply specifically to Indian law generally have been developed to protect the tribes. For example, the canons provide that treaties are to be construed broadly in determining the existence of Indian rights, but narrowly when considering the elimination or abrogation of those rights. Most of the special canons of construction dealing with treaty rights also have been applied to agreements,[18] executive orders,[19] and statutes,[20] dealing with Indians.

5. **Congress' plenary power:** Rights established by treaty, or by other documents, can be abrogated by Congress pursuant to its plenary power.[21]

Most, although not all, of the above principles, first developed in treaty cases, have been extended to situations not involving treaties.[22] (For a discussion of the history of treaty negotiations, *see* Part Two.)

REMOVAL

Beginning in the 1830s, many tribes across the country were "removed" from their aboriginal homelands to other lands. Numerous tribes were removed to the "Indian Territory," most of which was later to become the State of Oklahoma. The most famous removal was that of the so-called Five Civilized Tribes (the Cherokee, Chickasaw, Choctaw, Creek and Seminole),[23] but other tribes also were removed to new lands, frequently at great distances from their original homelands. In most of the cases where the United States moved several tribes onto a single reservation, the residents at each such reservation were regarded by the federal government then, and today, as a single tribe, despite the existence of distinct internal divisions.

Some bands, or other portions of tribes, refused to relocate with the main bodies of their tribes. Congress has the power to designate such remnant groups as "tribes" and deal with them in the normal course of the federal-tribal relationship.[24] For example, Congress has exercised this power in regard to the Eastern Band of Cherokee Indians, the Seminole Tribe of Florida, and the Mississippi Band of Choctaw Indians. In some instances, individual Indians from several historic tribes have been located on a single reservation. Such groups also are considered tribes and exercise self-governing power.

THE END OF TREATY MAKING

In 1871, Congress provided that the United States would no longer make treaties with Indian tribes; all rights under existing treaties, however, were protected.[25] (For text of statute, *see* Part Three.) The end of treaty making has had little legal effect, since the United States has continued to deal with Indian tribes in much the same manner through executive orders and agreements enacted as statutes.[26]

THE RESERVATION SYSTEM

Because of the local ill feeling, the people of the States where [Indians] are found are often their deadliest enemies.
— Justice Samuel Miller (1886)[27]

The reservation system, which began during the treaty-making era, continued to expand as later reservations were added by statutes and executive orders. Indian law and policy continues to focus primarily upon the reservation system. Tribal leaders expected that these lands—small remnants of their aboriginal territories—would be protected from the settlers of the westward expansion. Further, the reservation system is the principal means by which "Indian Country" was established. Indian Country is the starting point for analysis of jurisdictional issues and is not limited to land actually owned by Indians but also includes non-Indian lands within the exterior boundaries of a reservation.[28] (*See discussion in* Chapter 2 *at* pp. 30-31; for text of Indian Country Statute, *see* Part Three.)

In carrying out the provisions of Indian treaties, Congress began developing a system of services and benefits for Indian tribes and individuals. These include education, health, welfare, business development, natural resource protection, and other programs. These special programs continue to be directed primarily, though not exclusively, to Indians on or near reservations.

THE ERA OF ALLOTMENT AND ASSIMILATION (1871-1928)

As long as Indians live in villages they will retain many of their old and injurious habits.... I trust that before another year is ended they will generally be located upon individual lands of farms. From that date will begin their real and permanent progress.
> — BIA Agent for the Yankton Sioux Tribe (1877)[29]

The General Allotment Act is a mighty pulverizing engine to break up the tribal mass. It acts directly upon the family and the individual.
> — President Theodore Roosevelt (1901)[30]

THE GENERAL ALLOTMENT ACT OF 1887

Originally, most reservation land was owned communally by the tribe. In some cases, however, land title was lodged with individual tribal members. A few treaties before 1887 provided for "allotments," that is, for some parcels of land to be held by individuals rather than tribes.

Then, in 1887 Congress passed the General Allotment Act, or Dawes Act, one of the most significant federal statutes in the field of Indian law.[31] The Act delegated authority to the Bureau of Indian Affairs to allot parcels of tribal land to individual Indians—generally 160 acres to each family head, 80 acres to each single person over 18 years of age. Each individual allotment would remain in trust (exempt from state property taxes and other state laws) for 25 years, although that period could be shortened or extended. (For text of statute, *see* Part Three.) Indian people lost millions of acres through fraudulent transactions or tax sales after their allotments passed out of trust.

In addition, large amounts of tribal land not allotted were opened for homesteading by non-Indians. As a result of allotment, Indian landholdings decreased from 138 million acres in 1887 to 48 million acres in 1934, a total loss of 90 million acres—an area about the size of Montana. Another effect was the "checkerboard" pattern of land ownership by tribes, individual Indians, and non-Indians, causing serious jurisdiction and management problems. Finally, assimilation and allotment were pursued with vigor in the Indian Territory where tribal governments and landholdings were broken up so that Oklahoma could become a state in 1907.[32]

Allotment was not imposed on all tribes, but it fundamentally altered life on those reservations where it was applied.

ASSIMILATION BY MEANS OF SOCIAL POLICY

The allotment of lands was one of several policies followed during the era that was intended to assimilate Indians into the larger society. BIA boarding schools were established, where Indians were required to abandon their languages, native dress, religious practices, and other traditional customs. Native religious practices generally were stifled, an extreme example being the suppression of the Ghost Dance, which resulted in the 1890 Wounded Knee Massacre. The exercise of governmental authority by tribal governments was discouraged and local BIA superintendents effectively governed the reservations. Under the Major Crimes Act of 1885, the federal government took jurisdiction from the tribes in dealing with certain criminal acts, which further eroded tribal sovereignty.[33]

THE INDIAN CITIZENSHIP ACT OF 1924

Many Indians had become United States citizens upon receiving allotments or by virtue of special provisions in treaties or statutes. As a means both to provide equity and to promote assimilation, all Indians were made United States citizens in 1924.[34]

INDIAN REORGANIZATION (1928-1945)

John Collier was vindictive and overbearing. He tolerated no dissent, either from his staff or from the tribes.... Who can say but that we will succeed in vanquishing the pernicious effects of the Indian Reorganization Act, finally exposing its leader for what he really was, and institute our own independent governments in all the tribes, respected and admired by all.

— Rupert Costo (1983)[35]

Collier's achievement as commissioner was not only to end the forced "atomization" of Indian life, to humanize the Indian administration, and to involve other agencies in the search for remedies to the problems of Indian poverty, ignorance, and despair, but above all to resurrect the "bilateral, contractual relationship between the government and the tribes (the historical, legal, and moral foundation of Government-Indian relations)."

— Wilcomb E. Washburn (1975)[36]

THE MERIAM REPORT

The Meriam Report of 1928 set the tone for a reform movement in Indian affairs. This influential study, prepared by the Brookings Institution, publicized the deplorable living conditions on reservations and recommended that health and education funding be increased, that the allotment policy be ended, and that tribal self-government be encouraged.[37]

THE INDIAN REORGANIZATION ACT OF 1934 (IRA)

The Indian Reorganization Act[38] of 1934 translated into legislation some of the recommendations of the Meriam Report. (For text of statute, *see* Part Three.) A primary thrust of the Act was to stabilize the tribes' landholdings by providing that no new allotments would be made and by extending the trust period for existing allotments. The Act sought to promote tribal self-government by encouraging tribes to adopt constitutions[39] and to form federally chartered corporations.[40] The Act also legislated a hiring preference for Indians in the BIA, established a revolving loan fund for tribal development, allowed the Secretary of the Interior to accept additional tribal lands in trust, and included other provisions directed toward improving the lot of Indians.[41]

Tribes were given two years in which to accept or reject the IRA. One hundred eighty-one tribes accepted it, motivated perhaps by the Act's objective of eliminating the Department of the Interior's absolute discretionary power over the tribes. Many tribes, however, viewed the IRA's prescribed method for establishing tribal governments as perpetuating the paternalistic assimilation policy. Seventy-seven tribes therefore rejected the IRA.[42]

TRIBAL SELF-GOVERNMENT

The most significant contribution of the IRA was to promote the exercise of self-governing powers. Whether or not they rejected the provisions of the Act, tribes were influenced by it to formalize their political authority in new ways. On some reservations, traditional leaders were excluded from this process deliberately or unintentionally, and they and their followers have been critical of the legislation ever since. In spite of these failings, the Act was an important milestone in providing a framework for the exercise of political authority by tribes.

THE TERMINATION ERA (1945-1961)

Following in the footsteps of the Emancipation Proclamation of 94 years ago, I see the following words emblazoned in the letters of fire above the heads of the Indians—"THESE PEOPLE SHALL BE FREE."
— Sen. Arthur V. Watkins (1953)[43]

Termination represented a ... revolutionary forced change in the traditional Menominee way of life.... Congress expected immediate Menominee assimilation of non-Indian culture, values, and life styles. The truth is that we Menominees have never wanted such changes imposed upon us, any more than white people would want an Indian way of life imposed upon them.... The immediate effect of termination on our tribe was the loss of most of our 100-year-old treaty rights, protections, and services.... We want Federal protection, not Federal domination. The Menominee Restoration Act will be the dawn of a new partnership with the Government—self-determination without termination.

— Ada Deer (1973)[44]

THE INDIAN CLAIMS COMMISSION ACT

Before 1946, Indian tribes lacked a forum in which to sue the federal government for actions or lack of action that tribes considered detrimental to their welfare. Their only recourse was to request from Congress special authority to seek money damages in the Court of Claims. Over the course of a century, more than 140 separate acts containing such authority were passed by Congress, and many others were considered.

Finally, in 1946, Congress created a tribunal to provide Indian tribes an opportunity to obtain damages for the loss of tribal lands.[45] Known as the Indian Claims Commission, this special court was authorized to hear and decide causes of action originating prior to its passage. Tribes were given five years, or until 1951, to file their claims; even ancient land takings could be compensated, and certain claims not previously recognized were to be allowed. (For text of statute, *see* Part Three.)

This claims process has resulted in substantial recoveries to some tribes but its restrictions have been criticized in several respects.[46] The United States was allowed so-called "gratuitous offsets," in the amount of past services provided to tribes, against claims awarded to tribes. No interest was allowed on claims based on takings of aboriginal title or executive order lands. Although the tribes were permitted to select their own lawyers, approval by the Secretary of the Interior was required. Claims usually were then divided into three separate, and time-consuming, stages: determination of title ownership, valuation of the United States' liability, and determination and deduction of offsets to the United States' liability. The monetary awards were distributed to individual tribal members, rather than to tribes, so that an opportunity to strengthen tribal institutions was lost.

Most importantly, if a claim was successful, only money damages were available because the Claims Commission Act did not provide for the recovery of land.

The 1946 Act applies only to claims against the United States and does not cover claims against non-federal entities based on violations of the Nonintercourse Act. Thus, for example, the land claims of eastern tribes—which are often against states, counties, and private entities—are not included. Tribes are free to seek a return of land in the appropriate forum.

In 1978, cases not completed by the Indian Claims Commission were transferred to the Court of Claims (which in 1992 became the United

States Court of Federal Claims). Of the 617 dockets originally filed, some still had not been resolved as of 2004.

THE TERMINATION ACTS

House Concurrent Resolution 108 (HCR 108), adopted in 1953, expressed Congress' desire to bring to an end its special relationship with Indian tribes. (For text of HCR 108, *see* Part Three.) That document called for terminating such relationships as rapidly as possible. In line with that policy, the following groups were terminated from their federal relationship (virtually all have since been restored to federal status):

- Alabama and Coushatta Tribes of Texas;
- Catawba Indian Tribe of South Carolina;
- Klamath, Modoc, and Yahooskin Band of Snake Indians of Oregon;
- Ponca Tribe of Nebraska;
- Mixed Blood Ute Indians of Uintah and Ouray of Utah;
- 40 California Indian Rancherias;
- Western Oregon Indians, including Confederated Tribes of Siletz Indians, Confederated Tribes of the Grand Ronde Community, and Cow Creek Band of Umpqua Tribe of Indians;
- Menominee Tribe of Wisconsin (for text of Menominee Termination and Restoration Acts, *see* Part Three);
- Ottawa Tribe of Oklahoma;
- Peoria Tribe of Oklahoma;
- Wyandotte Tribe of Oklahoma; and
- Southern Paiutes of Utah.

These groups were singled out for what has become known as the termination experiment. Termination fundamentally altered the special federal-tribal relationship by making the following changes:

1. Tribal landownership was altered fundamentally by sale to third parties (although with compensation to tribal members); by transfer to private trusts; or by transfer to new tribal corporations under state law.[47]

2. All special federal programs to tribes were discontinued.

3. Generally all special federal programs (for example, health and education services) to individual Indians were discontinued.

4. State legislative jurisdiction was imposed.

5. State judicial authority was imposed, one exception being the area of hunting and fishing rights, which were found not to be terminated in the cases of several tribes.[48]

6. Exemptions from state taxing authority were ended.

7. Tribal sovereignty, as a practical matter, was ended.

Congress has repudiated HCR 108's termination policy and replaced it with a policy of self-determination. Further, Congress has restored to federal status most of the terminated tribes.[49] In addition, many of the above-mentioned 40 California rancherias no longer are considered to be terminated.

PUBLIC LAW 280

Many tribes saw their sovereignty greatly diminished during the termination era even though they were not actually terminated. The most important piece of legislation in this regard is Public Law 280, passed in 1953, which was the first general federal legislation extending state jurisdiction to Indian Country. (*See discussion in* Chapter 2 *at* pp. 41-42.) In certain named states, Public Law 280 provided for state jurisdiction on specified reservations. Public Law 280 also allowed states unilaterally to assume jurisdiction over other reservations.[50]

OTHER PROGRAMS OF THE TERMINATION ERA

Other assimilationist policies instituted or expanded during the late 1940s and early 1950s included the transfer of many educational responsibilities to the states; the "relocation" program to encourage Indians to leave the reservations and seek employment in various metropolitan centers; and the 1958 BIA revision of the Cohen treatise on federal Indian law (originally prepared by Interior Department Solicitor Felix Cohen in 1942) to make it more compatible with the new assimilationist policies.

THE "SELF-DETERMINATION" ERA (1961-PRESENT)

Whether we can clean out the emotional swamp of white America and recount the Indian-white relations more objectively or whether we must continue to struggle with old beliefs and shibboleths when we could be doing more important work remains to be seen.

— Vine Deloria, Jr. (1987)[51]

Still, no matter where my path leads me, I must always remember where the journey started. It was in San Francisco—at Alcatraz, and at the American Indian Center, and in my own home, where, starting about the time of the Alcatraz takeover, native people often came to sip coffee, make plans, and build indestructible dreams. The occupation of Alcatraz excited me like nothing before. It helped to center me and caused me to focus on my own rich and valuable Cherokee heritage.

— Wilma Mankiller (2000)[52]

The abuses of the termination era led to the reforms of the self-determination era, just as the IRA was a reaction to the negative impact of the allotment era. The self-determination period has been characterized by expanded recognition and application of the powers of tribal self-government, and by the general exclusion of reservations from state authority. The reform movement has been driven by a dramatic increase in tribal initiatives in court, in the Congress, and on the reservations. The progress has not been uniform—Indians have suffered their share of reversals, especially with regard to Supreme Court decisions since the early 1990s—but without question Indian tribes and individuals have benefitted from more favorable legislation and judicial decisions during the self-determination era than in any other period in the history of the United States.

LEGISLATIVE ACTS

A watershed between the termination and self-determination eras was the Indian Civil Rights Act of 1968 (ICRA),[53] which extended most of the protections of the Bill of Rights to tribal members in dealings with their tribal governments. Such action was taken because the U.S. Constitution itself does not limit tribal self-government by imposing the Bill of Rights on Indian tribes. (*See discussion in* Chapter 2 *at* pp. 46-47.) The ICRA also included important provisions allowing states that had assumed jurisdiction under Public Law 280 to "retrocede"—or transfer back—jurisdiction to the tribes and the federal government.

In 1971, Congress passed the Alaska Native Claims Settlement Act (ANCSA).[54] The land claims of Alaska Natives—based on aboriginal title to much of the state—had never been resolved. The complex Act extinguished aboriginal claims and called for the transfer of 44 million acres of land to new Alaska Native-owned and -controlled state-chartered corporations. ANCSA also provided for a total cash payment of approximately $1 billion dollars to Alaska Natives.[55] (*See discussion in* this chapter *at* pp. 24-25.)

Another major statute of this era is the Indian Self-Determination and Education Assistance Act of 1975[56]—often referred to as "638" since it was passed as Public Law 93-638. (For text of statute, *see* Part Three.) Through grants and contracts, the Act encourages tribes to assume administrative responsibility for federally funded programs that were designed for their benefit and that previously were administered by employees of the Bureau of Indian Affairs (BIA) and the United States Indian Health Service (IHS).

Amendments to the Act in 1988, 1991, and again in 1994 have moved toward creating a "compacting" system whereby tribes would eventually manage virtually all BIA and IHS programs.[57] This system is somewhat akin to block grants, which would enable tribes to determine for themselves what services they need and the best ways to implement them.[58] Education and health programs generally were expanded during this period.[59] A significant piece of legislation was the Indian Health Care Improvement Act.[60] Among other things, the Act consolidated Indian Health Service programs, authorized funding that would improve IHS programs, and created programs to educate health professionals for work in Indian Country.

In 1978, Congress enacted two significant pieces of legislation, one dealing with child welfare, the other with religious freedom. The Indian Child Welfare Act (ICWA)[61] treats the long-standing problem of large numbers of Indian children being transferred from their natural parents to non-Indian parents through state adoption and guardianship proceedings. (*See discussion in* Chapter 2 *at* pp. 47-48.) In general, the Act (1) requires that many adoption and guardianship cases take place in tribal courts; and (2) establishes, for those cases that are heard in state courts, a strict set of statutory preferences for Indian guardians over non-Indian guardians. The American Indian Religious Freedom Act (AIRFA), passed in the same year, explicitly recognizes the importance of traditional Indian religious practices and directs all federal agencies to insure that their policies will not abridge the free exercise of Indian religions.[62] (*See discussion in* Chapter 3 *at* pp. 59-60.) While the ICWA remains a powerful means of protecting Indian families, AIRFA's mandate was weakened by the Supreme Court in *Lyng v. Northwest Indian Cemetery Protective Association* (1988).[63] (For text of opinion, *see* Part Four.)

Two significant pieces of legislation that speak to the highly controversial issues of Indian gaming and the repatriation of tribal cultural property were passed by Congress in 1988 and in 1990. In 1988 the Indian Gaming Regulatory Act (IGRA) was passed.[64] The Act clarified that tribes may establish gaming enterprises on their reservations as long as they follow the procedural requirements of IGRA. In most cases, this means negotiating compacts with the states to determine the types of games that will be permitted in tribal casinos. (*See discussion in* Chapter 4 *at* p. 77.)[65] The Native American Graves Protection and Repatriation Act (NAGPRA) was passed in 1990 to rectify the centuries-old practice of storing Indian remains and cultural property in museums and universities under the guise of scientific necessity.[66] The Act directs all federal agencies and museums to return culturally identifiable remains and sacred objects to the appropriate tribes, as well as providing procedures for future excavations. (*See discussion in* Chapter 3 *at* p. 61.)

In addition to the major legislation discussed above, Congress passed various other laws in the 1990s that have operated to increase tribal self-determination. For example in 1991, the Indian Land Consolidation Act was passed as an attempt to remedy the fragmented nature of Indian land ownership.[67] Likewise, the 1990 Law Enforcement Reform Act sought to place heightened responsibility on the BIA and Department of Justice regarding crimes in Indian Country.[68] In addition, tribes increasingly have been treated as states for purposes of regulating some of the most important federal environmental statutes on their reservations.[69] These statutes include the Clean Air Act, the Clean Water Act, Safe Drinking Water Act, Federal Insecticide, Fungicide, and Rodenticide Act, and Superfund laws. (*See discussion in* Chapter 4 *at* p. 69.)

Another legislative development during the modern era has been the appropriation by Congress of increased funds for Indian affairs. At the same time, many fundamental Indian programs remain underfunded. With additional federal funding, as well as tribal revenues from economic development, tribes more ably can combat the high rates of unemployment and the inadequate social services that are still common on many reservations.

EXECUTIVE ACTION

Administrative policy began to shift in the mid-1960s. In 1966, Interior Secretary Stewart Udall told BIA administrators and congressional aides at a meeting in Santa Fe that self-determination for Indians would be the theme of the remainder of his administration. The subject also was covered in President Johnson's congressional message in 1968. Self-determination became firmly installed by President Nixon's historic message to Congress in 1970.[70] Indian preference has resulted in a steadily growing number of Indian BIA employees. Most leadership positions in the BIA now are held by Indians. The Bureau increasingly sees itself as owing its primary allegiance to Indian tribes and individuals. In 1977 the Department of the Interior established a new position—the Assistant Secretary for Indian Affairs. In the 1980s, the Reagan and Bush administrations expressed their support for tribal self-determination and for a government-to-government relationship.[71] In the 1990s the Clinton administration, in conformance with its commitment to self-determination, pushed for increased funding for Indian programs and sought to enhance direct tribal administration of BIA and IHS services.[72]

JUDICIAL ACTION

The decade of the 1970s was an extraordinarily active one for Indian litigation. During that decade, the Supreme Court heard some 33 Indian law cases—more, for example, than in such fields as antitrust, international, environmental, or consumer law. The trend continued in the 1980s and 1990s. In general, the opinions were highly favorable toward the tribes during the 1960s, 1970s, and 1980s. Beginning in the 1990s and continuing through the early 2000s, Supreme Court opinions generally took a turn against the tribes. Many of the cases that have limited tribal powers concern the extent to which tribes may exercise jurisdiction over non-Indians.

Leading cases limiting tribal powers include:

Oliphant v. Suquamish Indian Tribe, 435 U.S. 191 (1978) (Indian tribes cannot exercise criminal jurisdiction over non-Indians; for text of opinion, *see* Part Four);

Montana v. United States, 450 U.S. 544 (1981) (Crow Tribe, on facts of case, cannot regulate hunting and fishing by non-Indians on fee land within reservation boundaries; tribes may exercise civil jurisdiction over non-Indians when an important tribal interest is at stake);

Brendale v. Confederated Tribes & Bands of Yakima Indian Nation, 492 U.S. 408 (1989) (Yakama Nation cannot zone opened areas of the reservation over which they no longer maintain exclusive use and possession);

Strate v. A-1 Contractors, 520 U.S. 438 (1997) (Three Affiliated Tribes of the Fort Berthold Reservation cannot exercise judicial jurisdiction over a personal injury tort action against defendants who are not tribal members, for an automobile accident that occurred on a state right-of-way running through the reservation; for text of opinion, *see* Part Four);

Alaska v. Native Village of Venetie, 522 U.S. 520 (1998) (Native Village of Venetie cannot impose a business activities tax against non-Indian construction firm because the Alaska Native Claims Settlement Act extinguished Indian Country in Alaska; for text of opinion, *see* Part Four);

Atkinson Trading Co. v. Shirley, 532 U.S. 645 (2001) (Navajo Nation cannot impose hotel occupancy tax on hotel located on fee land within reservation boundaries because the tribe lacked sufficient interests to justify exercise of jurisdiction over non-Indians; for text of opinion, *see* Part Four);

Nevada v. Hicks, 533 U.S. 353 (2001) (Fallon Paiute-Shoshone Tribe of Nevada lacks court jurisdiction over civil rights suit brought by tribal member against state game warden for improper search because the game warden's actions did not impair tribal self-government; for text of opinion, *see* Part Four).

Cases establishing important principles in favor of Indians include:

McClanahan v. Arizona State Tax Commission, 411 U.S. 164

(1973) (state tax laws preempted by federal action and do not apply to Indians in Indian Country; for text of opinion, *see* Part Four);

Bryan v. Itasca County, 426 U.S. 373 (1976) (Public Law 280 does not confer authority upon states to tax Indians or Indian property on reservations);

Santa Clara Pueblo v. Martinez, 436 U.S. 49 (1978) (Indian Civil Rights Act of 1968 does not grant jurisdiction to federal courts for a civil action by a tribal member against the tribe; such cases must proceed in tribal forums, including tribal courts; for text of opinion, *see* Part Four);

Washington v. Washington State Commercial Passenger Fishing Vessel Association, 443 U.S. 658 (1979) (treaty providing for "right of taking fish . . . in common with all citizens of the Territory" broadly construed in favor of Indians to mean that treaty tribes reserved the opportunity to harvest 50 percent of the fish that would pass their usual and accustomed off-reservation fishing places; for text of opinion, *see* Part Four);

Merrion v. Jicarilla Apache Tribe, 455 U.S. 130 (1982) (upholding a tribal severance tax on mineral companies and expounding at length on inherent tribal sovereignty; for text of opinion, *see* Part Four);

County of Oneida v. Oneida Indian Nation, 470 U.S. 226 (1985) (upholding tribe's federal common law right to sue to enforce aboriginal land rights despite passage of 175 years since claim first arose; for text of opinion, *see* Part Four);

California v. Cabazon Band of Mission Indians, 480 U.S. 202 (1987) (state cannot regulate gambling operations in Indian Country; for text of opinion, *see* Part Four); (*see discussion in* Chapter 2 *at* p. 42);

Kiowa Tribe v. Manufacturing Technologies, Inc., 523 U.S. 751 (1998) (Kiowa Tribe entitled to sovereign immunity from suit regarding default on a promissory note, as Congress had not authorized the suit and the tribe never waived its immunity);

Minnesota v. Mille Lacs Band of Chippewa Indians, 526 U.S. 172 (1999) (off-reservation hunting and fishing rights not extinguished by statehood, overruling *Ward v. Race Horse*; for text of opinion, *see* Part Four);

United States v. Lara, 124 S. Ct. 1628 (2004) (upholding the power of Congress to override the Supreme Court's decision in *Duro v. Reina* and affirm tribal inherent sovereign authority to exercise criminal jurisdiction over members of other tribes; for text of opinion, *see* Part Four).

TRIBAL ACTION

Tribal councils have chosen to exercise their authority to a much greater degree in modern times. Examples include tribal ordinances dealing with issues such as zoning, air and water pollution, watershed management, hunting and fishing regulation, child welfare, and taxation. Tribes also have implemented the compacting and contracting provisions of the various self-determination acts.

The number of tribal courts has risen markedly since the 1970s and the courts have become increasingly professional. The Supreme Court expressly recognized this when it held that challengers to a tribal court's jurisdiction must exhaust tribal court remedies before proceeding to federal district court.[73] However, the ruling in the *Oliphant* case that tribes lack criminal jurisdiction over non-Indians continues to be an emotional issue for tribal governments. Although the rulings in *Strate* and *Atkinson* place limits on tribal civil jurisdiction, tribes can sometimes exercise their jurisdictional authority in civil contexts to counteract the loss of criminal jurisdiction.[74]

A generalized development, almost revolutionary in nature, is the simple fact that tribes have become far more sophisticated in wielding political power. Increased appropriations and more precise definitions of tribal authority—and for some tribes, revenues from economic development, including gaming—have given tribes the capacities to affect their destinies to an extent unknown since the coming of the Europeans. Tribal lobbying in Congress and even in state legislatures has become much more effective. Several national Indian organizations have become important voices in the formulation of policy. Tribes are by no means winning all of the legislative battles, but the tribes know the rules for fighting those battles and almost always exercise sufficient clout to make their presence felt.

THE EVOLUTION OF FEDERAL POLICY
IN REGARD TO SPECIAL GROUPS

OKLAHOMA TRIBES

Considerable federal legislation has focused solely on Indian tribes in Oklahoma. Despite this separate treatment, the Oklahoma tribes' political and governmental status is similar in many aspects to the status of other tribes throughout the country.[75]

Before 1890, the area now known as Oklahoma was included within the Indian Territory. Tribes in this territory possessed all the governmental powers of Indian tribes in general. In 1890, under the Oklahoma Organic Act, Congress created two territories in what today is the State of Oklahoma. First, a formally organized Territory of Oklahoma was created in western Oklahoma to provide for a non-Indian government. Tribal land then was allotted and tribal influence began to decline.

The second region created by Congress in 1890 was a reduced Indian Territory, comprising what is now eastern Oklahoma. Tribes in that region suffered relatively little land loss as a result of the Organic Act itself, but the federal government began to pursue the allotment process vigorously. The extension of federal laws and jurisdiction to the Indian Territory resulted in a loss of tribal governmental powers. The Five Tribes Act of 1906 provided for allotment. The Act also limited tribal legislative sessions to 30 days annually and required executive approval of all tribal legislative acts and contracts. The year following the Five Tribes Act, the admission of the Indian Territory and the Oklahoma Territory as the State of Oklahoma was proclaimed.

Oklahoma was exempted from many of the important provisions of the Indian Reorganization Act. But two years later, in 1936, Congress passed the Oklahoma Indian Welfare Act (OIWA), which extends most IRA provisions to the Oklahoma tribes. The Act also provides for the formation of local Indian cooperatives for credit administration, production marketing, consumer protection, and land management. In practice, very little use has been made of OIWA beyond the provisions for formulation of constitutions. Nevertheless, Oklahoma tribes recently have been very active in reestablishing tribal regulatory powers, creating social service agencies, forming tribal courts, and asserting tribal prerogatives such as hunting and fishing rights.[76]

ALASKA NATIVES

Alaska Natives experienced relatively little contact with non-Indians following the cession of Alaska by Russia to the United States in 1867 (under which Alaska's "uncivilized" tribes were made subject to the laws and regulations of the United States). Subsequent legislation, most notably the sweeping Alaska Native Claims Settlement Act (ANCSA) of 1971,[77] recognizes the United States' obligations to protect Native allotments and to provide federal services to Alaska Natives in a manner comparable to that provided to Indians in the lower 48 states. The distinctions between Alaska Natives as governments and as landowners, however, have remained clouded. The result has been a variety of conflicts, most notably over subsistence rights, the exercise of sovereignty, and the management of the corporations established by ANCSA.[78]

The originally enacted IRA did not apply fully to Alaska Natives, but was amended in 1936 to include them. Amendments to the IRA permitted the Secretary of the Interior to designate public lands actually occupied by Natives as reservations or as additions to reservations. Natives were permitted to organize as tribes under the IRA if they maintained a common bond of occupation or association, or resided in a well-defined community. Numerous lands were withdrawn and councils created, but litigation ensued calling into question the permanency of the reserves and the nature of Native claims to land. Federal and state policy encouraging the incorporation of Alaska Native communities under state law began in 1963. Many Native communities that chose to incorporate also included IRA provisions in their city charters. Today, about 127 predominantly Native communities are organized under Alaska's state municipal incorporation statute. Thus the IRA tribes and state entities exist side by side.

ANCSA extinguished all Native claims to land or water areas in Alaska. In return, the Act called for Alaska Natives to receive 44 million acres of land—an area larger than the State of Washington. The United States also agreed to transfer about $1 billion into a separate Alaska Native Fund. ANCSA also provided that the lands, patented in fee simple, be transferred to 12 regional corporations and over 200 local village corporations. Native corporations are profit-making entities chartered under state law to perform proprietary functions. Currently, the land is exempt from state and local real property taxes if it has not been developed by third parties.

Subsistence hunting and fishing rights also were extinguished by ANCSA. Presently, Native subsistence rights are recognized to various extents by the Alaska National Interest Lands Conservation Act of 1980 (ANILCA),[79] by state law, and by specific federal laws such as the Marine Mammal Protection Act.[80] The ANILCA subsistence provisions, which have been vigorously contested by the State of Alaska, provide especially significant protections for Alaska Natives.

In 1998, Alaska Natives were dealt a blow by the U.S. Supreme Court in its decision in *Alaska v. Native Village of Venetie Tribal Government* (1998).[81] (For text of opinion, *see* Part Four.) There, the Supreme Court held that the Native lands at issue in ANCSA were not "Indian Country" under the relevant federal statute, 18 U.S.C. § 1151(b). (For text of statute, *see* Part Three.) As a result, although some issues remain unresolved, the tribes of Alaska have a limited geographic area over which to exercise their powers of tribal self-government. Native leaders, however, continue to press for greater sovereignty through legislation, litigation, and negotiation.

HAWAIIAN NATIVES

The Hawaiian Islands were isolated from outside contact for centuries before 1778, when Captain James Cook arrived. High chiefs each controlled a district of an island or an entire island. Other chiefs controlled specific lands, and commoners worked the land for the benefit of the chiefs. Lands typically were divided into parcels enclosed by boundaries that radiated from a point on a mountaintop to the sea so as to enclose a drainage area. The parcel was known as an *ahupua'a*, which usually included farmland, water, and access to the sea. Land was considered to be held for the common benefit. If commoners believed that they were not being treated fairly, they could move to another *ahupua'a* as they were not tied to the land.

The land tenure system came under pressure as foreigners sought land for themselves. This led to the most significant development concerning land. The "Great *Mahele*" in 1848 effected a division of the lands so that clear title could be determined and transferred, but very little land ever reached individual commoners. The *mahele* ultimately resulted in large amounts of some of the best Hawaiian land passing to foreigners.

By 1890 foreigners, mostly Americans, owned over a million acres in Hawaii. They controlled another three-quarters of a million acres under leases procured at bargain rates from the government and the king. The overthrow of the Hawaiian monarchy in 1893 wrested all remaining government and Crown lands from Hawaiian control and put them into the hands of a provisional government and eventually of the United States government.

Upon annexation by the United States, Crown lands and government lands that had been seized by the Provisional Government passed to the United States. Thus, an estimated 1.75 million acres in which Native Hawaiians were to have an interest following the *mahele* became United States property. Congress in turn entrusted management of the lands to a territorial legislature established by the Organic Act of 1900, which set up a government for the Territory of Hawaii.

Early in the 20th century, Congress was made aware of deteriorating social and economic conditions among Native Hawaiians. Recognizing that the situation was related to loss of the Hawaiian land base and the associated culture, Congress took limited measures to remedy the Natives' plight. The result was passage of the Hawaiian Homes Commission Act of 1921,[82] allowing Native homesteads on specific lands.

Under the Hawaiian Homes Commission Act, Congress designated some 200,000 acres of public lands as available for Native homesteads. The Act generally has failed to provide agricultural or residential lands to large numbers of people or to achieve its lofty goal of "rehabilitating" Native Hawaiians. The lands set aside were some of the poorest, largely unsuitable for farming and lacking in necessary irrigation water. Many of the ostensibly available lands actually have been used for ordinary government purposes. The agency in charge of carrying out the Act has not administered it well, sparking intense criticism.

The "Great *Mahele*" and the Hawaiian Homes Commission Act were remarkably similar in purpose and effect to the General Allotment Act. Both actions submerged good intentions in the ambitions of others who coveted the lands. Both were poorly carried out, leaving their purported beneficiaries with parcels of unarable land or no land at all.

Today Native Hawaiians are severely disadvantaged. Statistics on health, education, crime, and employment show that Hawaii's Native people are worse off than any other ethnic group in the state. Hawaiians are experiencing unprecedented population growth while their economic condition worsens. The ancient, land-centered Hawaiian culture has been strained but has survived. Hawaiian Natives, among the most neglected of aboriginal peoples under federal authority, have raised a number of issues, such as their inclusion within federal service programs available to Native

Americans, land rights, subsistence hunting and fishing, access to beaches and other traditional sites, and governmental status.[83]

There is some evidence that the federal government is beginning to take these claims seriously. In 1993, Congress passed a joint resolution acknowledging the 100th anniversary of the overthrow of the Kingdom of Hawaii. The resolution acknowledges that the overthrow occurred "with the participation of agents and citizens of the United States," and offered "an apology to Native Hawaiians on behalf of the United States."[84] The resolution did not, however, modify existing law in any way.[85]

Greater attention to Native Hawaiian claims is being witnessed at the state level. In 1978, the Hawaii Legislature passed an act creating a "Hawaii sovereignty elections council" to "determine the will of Native Hawaiian people for self-governance of their own choosing." In 1996, the council mailed out ballots to all "Hawaiians" (defined as persons descended from pre-1778 inhabitants of the islands) asking whether they wished to elect a delegation to propose a Native Hawaiian government. Seventy-three percent of the Native Hawaiians voted in favor of the approach.[86] The Supreme Court then struck down, in *Rice v. Cayetano* (2000),[87] the election process as violating the Fifteenth Amendment because it prohibited a group of citizens (non-Natives) from voting in a state election. The intense interest in sovereignty among Native Hawaiians continues, however, and as of 2004 Congress was seriously considering legislation to recognize Native Hawaiian sovereignty.

WHAT LEGISLATIVE AND JUDICIAL MODEL
FOR THE FUTURE?

The claim of some Indians, especially "professional" Indians, that the taking of their land and other historical happenings created a debt on the part of the non-Indians to Indian descendants in perpetuity is obviously not in consonance with self-sufficiency.... There is no obligation to subsidize any group in perpetuity.... [T]his would be a death warrant to the integrity and dignity of any such group. The purposelessness and degradation of the human potential one finds in some reservation situations tends to confirm that, without a worthy objective posing a continuing challenge to the best in an individual, people disintegrate. This seems to be just as true of Indians as anybody else.

— Theodore W. Taylor (1972)[88]

The years since 1871 demonstrated the folly of legislatively determining how Indians should live. Their histories show a remarkable talent for determining such matters for themselves. Return the right of decision to the tribes—restore their power to hold the dominant society at arm's length, and to bargain again in peace and friendship. Only by possessing such power can the tribes make useful choices within the social environment encompassing them.

— D'Arcy McNickle (1949)[89]

Federal Indian policy, by its nature, will undergo examination continually. These models, or variations of them, are likely to be proposed during future debates:

1. **Assimilation of Indian Tribes.** Over time, Indian tribes gradually should be required to relinquish their special status as they become economically self-sufficient. Indian reservations either should be abandoned or should become subject to state law.

2. **The Model of the Alaska Native Claims Settlement Act.** Congress should make a major commitment of land and capital to Indians, who would organize corporations under state law. There would be a very limited federal role and Indians would have the opportunity to compete in the corporate world.

3. **Indian Tribes as Permanent, Separate Governments in the Federal System.** Tribes should be accorded permanent recognition as governments, not because of their poverty or their cultural distinctiveness, but because of their right under federal law to exist as domestic sovereigns. An appropriate level of economic and social support should be accorded to tribes as bargained-for results of the treaty-making process.

CHAPTER 2

Governmental Authority in Indian Country: Tribal Sovereignty and the United States Constitution

Indian tribes are part of the constitutional structure of government. Tribal authority was not created by the Constitution—tribal sovereignty predated the formation of the United States and continued after it—but tribes were acknowledged by the Constitution in the reaffirmation of previously negotiated treaties (most of which were with Indian tribes), the two references to "Indians not taxed," and the Indian Commerce Clause. Relations were then cemented through the treaties and treaty substitutes.

To be sure, although a truly substantial portion of early federal business involved Indian affairs, the Founding Fathers almost certainly assumed that tribes would simply die out under the combined weight of capitalism, Christianity, and military power. But the Framers of the Constitution, who were so seldom wrong on structure, were wrong about Indian tribes. The tribes did not die out, and the modern presidency, Congress, and Supreme Court continue squarely to acknowledge this third source of sovereignty in the United States....

— Charles F. Wilkinson (1987)[1]

THE CENTRAL CONCEPTS

INDIAN TRIBE

Although the term "Indian tribe" can be used in both an ethnological and a legal-political sense, our analysis will focus on the definition of an Indian tribe as a political and legal entity. Historically, the federal government has determined that it will recognize particular groups of Indians as Indian tribes pursuant to its authority under the Indian Commerce Clause of the United States Constitution. (*See discussion in* Chapter 3 *at* p. 52.) Thus reservations variously have been set aside for ethnologically defined tribes, for bands or other subgroups of tribes, and for confederations of several tribes or bands. (*See discussion in* Chapter 1 *at* pp. 8-9.) All such Indian groups are considered as tribes for legal purposes. As discussed in Chapter 3 under "Federal Recognition of the Trust Relationship," Indian groups not recognized under federal law may seek recognition through litigation,[2] through the administrative procedures established by the BIA,[3] or through congressional statute.[4]

INDIAN

An Indian is a person with some amount of Indian blood who is recognized as an Indian by the person's tribe or community. Tribal membership requirements can be established by usage, written law, treaty, or intertribal agreement.[5] Today, membership typically is defined by a tribal constitution, and then manifested in a tribal roll; varying degrees of blood quantum are required by different tribes. While membership in a federally recognized tribe is the general criteria used by the BIA for participation in most federal programs,[6] a blood standard also is used as an alternative for determining eligibility for some programs.[7] In recent years Congress has not allowed the BIA to rely solely on a blood standard for federal program eligibility.[8]

INDIAN COUNTRY

A third foundational issue involving tribal sovereignty is the definition of the territorial boundaries of Indian tribal governments. While the general public is familiar with the term "Indian reservation," the relevant legal term is "Indian Country" for purposes of identifying geographical limits of tribal governmental power, or jurisdiction. Indian Country is defined specifically by federal statute in 18 U.S.C. § 1151. (For text of statute, *see* Part Three.) The most important provision is that Indian Country includes all land, regardless of ownership, within the exterior boundaries of federally recognized Indian reservations.

Section 1151 is a federal criminal statute, but the courts have concluded that the statute's definition also applies to questions of federal civil jurisdiction and to tribal jurisdiction.[9] The federal statutory definition can be applied easily in most cases since the great majority of Indian lands are designated clearly as either reservations or allotments. The Indian pueblos of New Mexico do not have their land held in trust, but the courts have found that pueblo lands are Indian Country.[10] On the other hand, the Supreme Court has sharply limited the reach of Indian Country for Alaska Native villages after the passage of the Alaska Native Claims Settlement Act (ANCSA) in 1971.[11] In some instances complex litigation has been required to determine the exterior boundaries of reservations; the question usually arises in regard to whether Congress intended to alter reservation boundaries when large blocks of lands were declared to be surplus lands during the allotment era. If such intent is found to exist, the lands are said to have been "disestablished" from the reservation, and thus no longer within Indian Country.[12]

THE DOCTRINE OF TRIBAL SOVEREIGNTY

> *Perhaps the most basic principle of all Indian law, supported by a host of decisions ... is the principle that* **those powers lawfully vested in an Indian tribe are not, in general, delegated powers granted by express acts of Congress, but rather inherent powers of a limited sovereignty which has never been extinguished.** *Each tribe begins its relationship with the federal government as a sovereign power, recognized as such in treaty and legislation. [Emphasis in original.]*
> — Felix S. Cohen (1942)[13]

Indian governmental powers, with some exceptions, are not delegated powers granted by express acts of Congress, but are inherent powers of a limited sovereignty that have never been extinguished.[14] This doctrine first was articulated in this country by Chief Justice John Marshall in *Worcester v. Georgia* (1832). (For text of *Worcester* opinion, *see* Part Four.)

In modern times the Supreme Court has found that tribal governments are "unique aggregations possessing attributes of sovereignty over
both their members and their territory."[15] Powers not limited by federal
statute, by treaty, by restraints implicit in the protectorate relationship, or
by inconsistency with their status remain with tribal governments or
reservation communities.[16] The Supreme Court has found implied dives-
titures of tribal powers where the tribes' independent freedom to
determine their external relations is necessarily inconsistent with their
dependent status. For example, by 1831 *Johnson v. M'Intosh* (1823) and
Cherokee Nation v. Georgia (1831) had established that Indian tribes
impliedly had been divested of the power to alienate their lands and the
power to make treaties with foreign nations. (For text of *M'Intosh* and
Cherokee opinions, *see* Part Four.) In 1978, the Supreme Court held in
Oliphant v. Suquamish Indian Tribe[17] that criminal jurisdiction over non-
Indians also was subject to the implied divestiture doctrine. (For text of
Oliphant opinion, *see* Part Four.) Therefore, tribes today possess no
criminal jurisdiction over non-Indians. But, as discussed more fully
below, depending upon the circumstances tribes may retain the inherent
sovereign power to exercise civil jurisdiction over non-Indians.[18] In
Merrion v. Jicarilla Apache Tribe (1982) (for text of opinion, *see* Part Four),
the Supreme Court said this:

> To state that Indian sovereignty is different than that of Federal,
> State, or local Governments, does not justify ignoring the prin-
> ciples announced by this Court for determining whether a
> sovereign has waived its taxing authority in cases involving city,
> state, and federal taxes imposed under similar circumstances.
> Each of these governments has different attributes of sovereignty,
> which also may derive from different sources. These differences,
> however, do not alter the principles for determining whether any
> of these governments has waived a sovereign power through
> contract, and we perceive no principled reason for holding that
> the different attributes of Indian sovereignty require different
> treatment in this regard.[19]

FUNDAMENTAL POWERS OF INDIAN TRIBES

As mentioned above, most tribal governments possess inherent powers of self-government and may exercise them to the extent they have not been extinguished. Therefore, powers of tribes cannot be described completely by reference to specific delegations from Congress. The following discussion will identify fundamental categories of tribal governmental power that have been recognized under federal law.

POWER TO ESTABLISH A FORM OF GOVERNMENT

The power to establish a form of government is a basic element of sovereignty. Federal law recognizes that Indian tribes may adopt whatever form of government best suits their own practical, cultural, or religious needs.[20] Tribes are not required to adopt governments patterned after the United States government. Since Indian tribes are not limited by the United States Constitution, they are not subject to such principles as the separation of powers or the Establishment of Religion Clause.[21]

The constitutions adopted by the majority of tribes following passage of the Indian Reorganization Act (IRA) were based on sample governing documents developed by the Bureau of Indian Affairs. It has been held consistently that the exercise of these powers pursuant to IRA constitutions is founded not on delegated authority, but on a tribe's inherent power of sovereignty.[22] Other tribes have organized their formal governments pursuant to their inherent sovereignty, outside the IRA framework, and the courts have upheld the validity of such governments, whether or not a written constitution has been developed.[23]

POWER TO DETERMINE MEMBERSHIP

Also fundamental is the right of tribes to determine tribal membership. Membership determines, among other things, the right to vote in tribal elections, to hold tribal office, to receive tribal resource rights such as grazing and residence privileges on tribal lands, and to participate in distribution of per capita payments when they occur. In *Santa Clara Pueblo v. Martinez* (1978), the Supreme Court found that the 1968 Indian Civil Rights Act did not require tribes to follow Anglo-American concepts of equal protection and due process in determining their membership, even when the denial of membership rights meant the denial of federal health and education benefits.[24] (*See discussion in* this chapter *at* pp. 46-47; for text of *Martinez* opinion, *see* Part Four.) Eligibility for federal benefits and assistance provided to Indians because of their status as Indians often is based on tribal membership. Depending on the statute at issue, however, this determination may involve a minimum quantum of Indian blood higher than the tribal membership provision.[25] (*See discussion in* this chapter *at* p. 30.)

POLICE POWER

The comprehensive authority of Indian tribes to legislate or otherwise adopt substantive civil and criminal laws—directly analagous to the "police power" of the states—follows from their status as sovereign political entities. This authority includes, but is not limited to, the power to regulate the conduct of individuals within the tribal government's jurisdiction, the power to determine domestic rights and relations, the power to dispose of non-trust property and to establish rules for inheritance, the power to regulate commercial and business relations, the power to raise revenues for the operation of the government through taxation, and the power to administer justice through law enforcement and judicial branches.

Tribal authority, as noted above, has been limited from time to time by actions of the Congress and by actions of the states exercising federally delegated powers. Tribal authority also can be limited by tribal action. Many tribal constitutions expressly limit tribal legislatures or courts.[26]

Although federal statutes control most aspects of trust or restricted Indian property inheritances, tribal laws prescribing the manner of descent and distribution of such property have been recognized.[27] As an attribute of property control, tribes may regulate land use by zoning Indian lands and also non-Indian-owned lands in reservation areas populated mostly by Indians.[28] Tribal authority to levy taxes has been recognized in a variety of circumstances, including license and use fees,[29] property taxes,[30] sales taxes,[31] and mineral extraction or severance taxes.[32]

POWER TO ADMINISTER JUSTICE

The maintenance of law and order on the reservations is another element of tribal government that has been upheld firmly by the courts.[33] Tribal criminal jurisdiction has been limited statutorily in terms of sentencing power (the Indian Civil Rights Act, discussed below, limits fines to $5,000 and imprisonment to one year) and has been denied as applied to non-Indians since the Supreme Court's 1978 decision in *Oliphant v. Suquamish Indian Tribe*.[34] (For text of *Oliphant* opinion, *see* Part Four.) In 1990, the Supreme Court in *Duro v. Reina* ruled that tribes also lack criminal jurisdiction over non-member Indians (for example, Navajo Nation courts could not hear criminal charges against non-Navajo Indians, as well as non-Indians). Congress, however, overrode the Supreme Court's decision and legislatively provided in 1991 that tribes possess criminal jurisdiction over non-member Indians. In 2004, the Supreme Court in *United States v. Lara* ruled that Congress did have broad authority to override the Court's own decision in *Duro*.[35] (For text of *Lara* opinion, *see* Part Four.) In any event, tribes possess broad authority to administer civil and criminal justice in Indian Country, especially when Indians are involved or when tribes have consensual relationships with non-Indians.

Most tribal court systems have borrowed quite extensively from Anglo-American court systems. Many have developed extensive rules of procedure and evidence. On the other hand, Indian tribal courts also rely on tribal traditions and often look to informal methods of dispute resolution. These courts—in some tribes referred to as peacemaker courts—have grown in popularity among Indian tribes. Many tribes see a return to traditional justice as a viable way of asserting their inherent sovereignty while reinforcing and practicing cultural values. Some tribal courts have asserted jurisdiction to review actions of tribal governing bodies.[36] A small number of reservation courts still operate as "Courts of Indian Offenses," which are administrative courts established by the Secretary of the Interior rather than by the tribe.

Many tribes have created law enforcement departments. Tribal governments employ police officers with contracted federal funds under the Indian Self-Determination Act of 1975 and with funds appropriated by the tribe.

POWER TO EXCLUDE PERSONS FROM THE RESERVATION

The power of Indian tribes to exclude persons from their territory, which is provided for specifically in a number of Indian treaties, has been recognized as an inherent attribute of sovereignty.[37] This exclusionary power has been treated as a distinct right of sovereignty and given prominent recognition as a fundamental means by which Indian tribes can protect their territory against trespassers.[38] The power to exclude persons is not unlimited, however, and non-members who hold valid federal patents to fee lands within the reservation cannot be denied access to their property.[39] Roads constructed on the reservation with federal funds are required by federal regulation to be kept open to the public. Also, tribes may be required to give access to federal officials legally providing services to the tribe or its members.[40]

POWER TO CHARTER BUSINESS ORGANIZATIONS

The power to charter business organizations is yet another aspect of sovereign power. Indian tribes possess the authority to establish, through charter or otherwise, business organizations for the purpose of managing tribal assets.[41] Tribally chartered enterprises hold the same status as the tribe itself for purposes of federal income tax exemptions and sovereign immunity from suit.[42] A tribe can waive such immunity to the extent of the non-trust assets placed in the tribal corporation. Tribes, like states, also can charter private corporations under tribal law and regulate their activities.

The tribally-issued corporate charters discussed here should be distinguished from the power of the Secretary of the Interior, under 25 U.S.C. § 477 of the IRA, to issue federal corporate charters to IRA tribes for the purpose of conducting business (for text of statute, *see* Part Three). Tribes may waive sovereign immunity as to the assets of such IRA corporations but tribal assets not held by the corporation remain protected by immunity.[43]

SOVEREIGN IMMUNITY

Indian tribes, like other sovereigns, cannot be sued without an "unequivocally expressed" waiver of sovereign immunity. *Kiowa Tribe of Oklahoma v. Manufacturing Technologies, Inc.* (1998).[44] Suing a tribe requires either congressional authorization of the suit, or a tribal waiver of sovereign immunity.[45] Tribal sovereign immunity does not extend to tribal officials acting outside of their official capacity.[46]

TRIBAL CIVIL JURISDICTION OVER NON-INDIANS IN INDIAN COUNTRY

The power of the United States to try and criminally punish is an important manifestation of the power to restrict personal liberty. By submitting to the overriding sovereignty of the United States, Indian tribes therefore necessarily gave up their power to try non-Indian citizens of the United States except in a manner acceptable to Congress.
— Justice William Rehnquist (1978)[47]

Indian sovereignty is not conditioned on the assent of a nonmember, to the contrary, the nonmember's presence and conduct on Indian lands is conditioned by the limitations the Tribe may choose to impose.
— Justice Thurgood Marshall (1982)[48]

The Rehnquist Court has shown that it does not view tribal sovereignty either in a historical context—as part of the arrangements a superior power made with indigenous sovereigns to secure peace and access to most of the land on the continent—or as an instrument to achieve current Indian policy goals of economic and political independence set by Congress.... If the Court, or at least an intellectual leader among the Justices, can assume the hard work of understanding Indian law, its historical roots, and its importance as a distinct field, then cases involving tribal sovereignty and existence could be considered apart from attitudes that shape the Court's work in most other fields.
— David H. Getches (2001)[49]

The exercise of tribal jurisdiction over non-Indians has been one of the most emotional issues in Indian affairs during the modern era. In 1978 the Supreme Court held in *Oliphant v. Suquamish Indian Tribe* that tribes could not exercise criminal jurisdiction over non-Indians, unless authorized to do so by Congress. The controversy continues in a slightly different form today as tribes increasingly exercise modern governmental authority in civil contexts such as taxation and land use control. Federal courts give deference to tribal forums when it comes to ruling on the issue of tribal authority: the determination as to whether tribal jurisdiction exists is normally a matter to be decided first by the tribal courts, with federal courts having authority to act in a review capacity.[50]

In modern times, the Supreme Court, in *Montana v. United States* (1981), initially developed principles allowing for broad tribal civil jurisdiction, both as to tribal regulation and court jurisdiction, over non-Indians within reservation boundaries when important tribal interests were involved.[51] However, in three later cases—*Strate v. A-1 Contractors* (1997),[52] *Atkinson Trading Co. v. Shirley* (2001),[53] and *Nevada v. Hicks* (2001)[54]—the Court departed from the existing approach and sharply limited tribal jurisdiction over non-Indians, especially when non-Indian land within Indian Country is involved. (For text of opinions, *see* Part Four.) In the upcoming years, we will learn whether the Court will continue on this path or whether it will return to previously established principles and provide for more expansive tribal jurisdiction over non-Indians. It also may be that Congress will step in and, exercising its broad authority over Indian affairs, affirm a more expansive tribal authority over non-Indians within Indian Country. The following discussion summarizes the law as it now stands.

Tribal jurisdiction over non-Indians is broadest on tribal lands. A tribal cigarette tax for sales to non-Indians on tribal lands has been upheld by the Supreme Court.[55] A much more difficult situation arose in *Merrion v. Jicarilla Apache Tribe* (1982),[56] where the tribe levied a substantial tax on mineral extraction from tribal lands (for text of *Merrion* opinion, *see* Part Four). In *Merrion*, the tribe exacted the tax from companies even though they already were paying royalties under mineral leases. Comparing the tribe to states and cities, the Supreme Court upheld the tax, reasoning that such sovereigns can receive contract payments as landowners and can subsequently levy taxes in their governmental capacities. In further recognition of tribal self-government powers, the Supreme Court determined in *Kerr-McGee Corp. v. Navajo Tribe* (1985)[57] that non-IRA tribal governments may tax on-reservation business activities without first obtaining secretarial approval. The Court in *Kerr-McGee* indicated that this reasoning applies to IRA governments if such approval is not required under the tribe's constitution. (For text of *Kerr-McGee* opinion, *see* Part Four.)

Tribal authority to regulate non-Indians is less extensive when non-Indian land in Indian Country is involved. The measuring stick for tribal regulation under these circumstances was first articulated by the Supreme Court in *Montana v. United States* (1981): whether (1) non-Indians have "consensual relationships" such as commercial dealings with a tribe or its members; or (2) "the conduct of non-Indians on fee lands within its reservation … threatens or has some direct effect on the political integrity, the economic security, or the health or welfare of the tribe."[58] In applying this test, the Supreme Court held that the Crow Tribe could not regulate fishing over a riverbed not owned by the tribe. The Court seemed to emphasize that the Crow Tribe lacked a significant tribal interest because it was not historically a fishing tribe. Other opinions, such as *National Farmers Union Ins. Co. v. Crow Tribe of Indians* (1985) and *Iowa Mutual Ins. Co. v. LaPlante* (1987), continued to suggest broad tribal authority over non-Indians.

In 2001, the Court handed down two opinions that epitomized its trend toward limiting assertions of tribal powers over non-Indians. In *Atkinson Trading Co. v. Shirley* (2001), the Court struck down a hotel occupancy tax levied by the Navajo Nation on a hotel complex within the boundaries of the reservation. The tribal interests seemed to be strong since the tribe provided many services to the area, but Chief Justice Rehnquist's opinion concluded that the tribal interests in question did not meet the *Montana* test: "The generalized availability of tribal services [is] patently insufficient to sustain the Tribe's civil authority over nonmembers on non-Indian fee land."[59] In *Nevada v. Hicks* (2001), the Court went even further. The Court there, in an opinion by Justice Scalia, ruled that a tribal court lacked jurisdiction in a civil case against a state official who allegedly violated federal law in executing a search warrant against a tribal member residing on tribal land within the reservation. The *Hicks* case presented a narrow question, but the Court used sweeping language with respect to state jurisdiction saying, among other things, that "ordinarily, it is now clear, an Indian reservation is considered part of the territory of the state."[60] Justice O'Connor and two other Justices called the majority opinion "perplexing," saying that such "reasoning does not reflect a faithful application of *Montana* and its progeny."[61] The language of the majority opinion, which was not necessary to decide the case, departed from the central thrust of the Court's traditional approach toward Indian affairs and it remains to be seen how the *Hicks* approach will be used in the future.

CONFLICTS BETWEEN TRIBAL AND STATE JURISDICTION

Our Father the president promised ... he would draw a line and blaze the trees as a boundary between us and [the white man] so that if any of your people should intrude upon us ... he would put them on their own side. It is my wish to ... never leave that promise behind.
> — Cherokee Head Chief Path Killer (1818)[62]

Except for some desegregation cases, the district court [in the Pacific Northwest Indian fishing cases] has faced the most concerted official and private efforts to frustrate a decree of a federal court witnessed in this century.
> — Washington v. Passenger Fishing Vessel Association (1979)[63]

It is, of course, ... true that manifold problems exist between tribes and states, but they are not intractable. In fact, these problems often grow and foster in the recesses of inattention and cultural and political ignorance. There are exciting and creative ways to move tribal-state relations forward. Yet there is also the concommitant need for mutual goodwill, the timely deployment of resources, and a leadership and citizenry who possess a vision committed to an ethical and flourishing future for all.
> — Frank Pommersheim (1995)[64]

STATE JURISDICTION GENERALLY

The general principle that state law does not apply to Indian affairs in Indian Country without congressional consent has been recognized consistently since it first was formulated by the Supreme Court in *Worcester v. Georgia* (1832). (For text of opinion, *see* Part Four.) In this context, state law includes legislative enactments, court jurisdiction, and state or local executive authority. Most state regulatory laws (such as health, zoning, and environmental provisions) do not apply to Indian persons and Indian property in Indian Country. This exemption from state jurisdiction often is in force even where one of the parties to a transaction is a non-Indian.[65] On the other hand, state law normally applies to Indians outside of Indian Country.[66]

In modern times, as evidenced in *McClanahan v. Arizona State Tax Commission* (1973), the Court has characterized Congress' broad power under the Indian Commerce Clause as the constitutional authority to preempt, or oust, state law in favor of tribal self-government.[67] (For text of *McClanahan* opinion, *see* Part Four.) In most fields of law, the preemption doctrine presumes the validity of state law absent an express federal law to the contrary. The normal principles of preemption law, which give deference to state authority, do not apply in Indian law because of the existence of tribal sovereignty and the tradition of comprehensive federal regulation. Therefore, unless Congress manifests a clear intent to allow state regulation of a particular Indian activity, state regulation is preempted.

As noted above, it is unclear whether Justice Scalia's general statement, in *Nevada v. Hicks* (2001), that Indian Country is "part of the state" will affect this traditional approach. (*See discussion in* this chapter *at* p. 39.)

STATE JURISDICTION UNDER PUBLIC LAW 280

Sixteen states acquired, in varying degrees, partial jurisdiction over Indian Country within their borders in accordance with a federal statute commonly referred to as Public Law 280 (for text of statute, *see* Part Three). Originally enacted by Congress in 1953, Public Law 280 delegated to six states jurisdiction over most crimes and many civil matters. (The states included California; Nebraska; Minnesota, except for the Red Lake Reservation; Oregon, except for the Warm Springs Reservation; and Wisconsin, except for the Menominee Reservation. Alaska was included in 1959 at the time of its statehood.)

Public Law 280 also gave any other state the option of amending its own laws to assert such jurisdiction. Ten states acted to exercise this option in varying degrees. Arizona accepted jurisdiction over air and water pollution; Idaho over seven specific subject areas; and Montana over criminal offenses on the Flathead Reservation. Florida assumed full Public Law 280 jurisdiction; North Dakota only if the tribes consented (none did); Iowa over the Sac & Fox Reservation; and Nevada with a provision that tribes could retrocede (most did). South Dakota asserted jurisdiction only if the federal government paid the costs, a procedure later declared invalid by the state supreme court. Utah's acceptance was conditioned on tribal consent (none did). Washington assumed full Public Law 280 jurisdiction over non-Indians on reservations and over Indians on non-trust lands; further, state jurisdiction was extended to Indians on trust lands in eight subject areas (including domestic relations and adoptions) if the tribe in question consented.

In a major victory for tribes, Congress amended Public Law 280 in 1968 to require that no state could obtain jurisdiction in the future under Public Law 280 unless the tribe consented by referendum vote of tribal members. No tribes have consented since then. The 1968 amendments also permit states to retrocede (that is, to return) criminal or civil jurisdiction acquired under Public Law 280.[68]

Public Law 280 specifically excepted from state jurisdiction the regulation and taxation of trust property and the hunting and fishing rights of Indians. In 1976 the Supreme Court concluded that state Public Law 280 civil jurisdiction did not include taxation of Indian-owned personal (non-trust) property, but rather was limited to adjudication of individual civil cases.[69] The Court found that Public Law 280 did not transfer regulatory power to the states. Thus, for example, Public Law 280 does not allow state land use, zoning, and building codes to operate in Indian Country.[70]

If, however, the general law being extended to Indian Country is "prohibitory," as opposed to "regulatory," it is valid under Public Law 280's grant of criminal jurisdiction. For example, a state criminal law forbidding the sale of all fireworks would apply in Indian Country. In *California v. Cabazon Band of Mission Indians* (1987) (for text of opinion, *see* Part Four), the Supreme Court formulated a "state public policy" test for determining whether a state law prohibits or regulates an activity occurring in Indian Country.[71] If the "conduct at issue" generally is permitted by state law, it is not in violation of the "State's public policy," and laws impacting this conduct merely are regulatory. Because California state law permitted some forms of gambling, its laws controlling bingo operations were deemed regulatory, having no force in Indian Country.

Public Law 280 does not expressly extinguish tribal jurisdiction. Tribal courts, therefore, have concurrent jurisdiction with states in areas covered by Public Law 280.[72]

CRIMINAL JURISDICTION OF COURTS

A complex system of federal statutes allocates criminal jurisdiction among tribal, federal, and state courts for crimes occurring in Indian Country. The following is a very general summary.

In Public Law 280 states, all criminal defendants go to state court. If Public Law 280 does not apply, then Indian criminal defendants go to federal courts for most major crimes, to tribal courts for minor and some major crimes, but not to state courts. Non-Indian criminal defendants go to federal or state courts depending on a number of factors but, under the *Oliphant* decision, cannot go to tribal court. The highly technical area of criminal jurisdiction in Indian Country is treated in detail elsewhere.[73]

CIVIL JURISDICTION OF COURTS

Leaving aside those reservations subject to Public Law 280, civil cases often can be brought in tribal courts for incidents occurring in Indian Country. Cases arising in Indian Country are within the exclusive jurisdiction of tribal courts when only Indians are involved.[74] If non-Indians seek to sue Indians for events occurring in Indian Country, tribal courts have exclusive jurisdiction. The Supreme Court has held, however, that suits by non-Indians against non-Indians arising on state highways and rights-of-way within reservations are outside of tribal court jurisdiction.[75] Generally, the determination as to whether a tribe has jurisdiction over a non-Indian is made by the tribal court, although federal courts can review tribal court rulings as to the existence of tribal jurisdiction.[76] As noted, tribal courts retain concurrent jurisdiction with the states even when Public Law 280 applies.

State courts can hear cases involving Indians arising from events occurring outside of Indian Country. When an Indian defendant resides on the reservation, however, state courts may have to follow tribal law to obtain personal jurisdiction. Until the 2001 ruling in *Nevada v. Hicks*,[77] the cases had held that state authority to serve process or execute judgment against an Indian defendant residing on the reservation can be effected validly only through tribal courts in most situations.[78] These issues will not be settled fully until additional decisions have clarified the extent to which state powers may have been expanded by the reasoning in *Hicks*.

These limitations on state court jurisdiction are controversial. Many argue that they unfairly impede the satisfaction of legitimate claims by allowing Indians to hide behind "friendly" tribal courts. Indians and their supporters argue that court jurisdiction is an essential aspect of tribal sovereignty, that Indian tribes have resolved internal disputes since time immemorial, and that they can do so in a fair and efficient manner in modern times. In any event, these legal principles place many demands on tribal courts, since often they are the only forum available.

STATE AND TRIBAL TAXATION

Taxation, that indispensable element of any government, surely has everything to do with the Navajo Nation's political integrity. A sovereign nation that cannot raise revenues to conduct governmental operations cannot function.

— Chief Justice Robert Yazzie,
Navajo Nation Supreme Court (1997)[79]

The steady increase of economic activity in Indian Country has given states added incentive to enforce their tax laws there. Recognizing that the power to tax is the power to destroy,[80] however, the courts uniformly have struck down state taxes that affect Indian land, tribes, or individuals in Indian Country. The Supreme Court has prohibited both state income taxes[81] and state personal property taxes[82] as applied to reservation Indians, including those residing on Public Law 280 reservations.[83] State taxes on tribal mineral lease royalties also will be struck down absent a clear expression of congressional consent.[84] Most state tax laws apply to Indians outside of Indian Country.[85]

In a series of cases, states have sought to impose taxes on non-Indians doing business with Indian tribes or individuals on reservations. The opinions to date have been highly protective of tribal interests, invalidating the taxes if there is any significant impact on tribal activities. Important factors in the cases are whether tribal natural resources are involved and whether there is a comprehensive federal regulatory scheme that is implicitly inconsistent with the exercise of state authority. The major cases are: *Washington v. Confederated Colville Tribes*, 447 U.S. 134 (1980), allowing the tribe to collect state cigarette taxes on sales to non-Indians (no tribal natural resources were involved and the Court feared that a contrary result would allow the tribe to "market" an exemption from state taxation); *White Mountain Apache Tribe v. Bracker*, 448 U.S. 136 (1980), striking down a state tax on motor vehicles owned by a non-Indian timber operator doing business on the reservation with the tribe (the Court emphasized federal timber regulations and the existence of a tribal natural resource) (for text of *White Mountain* opinion, *see* Part Four); *Central Machinery Co. v. Arizona State Tax Comm'n*, 448 U.S. 160 (1980), striking down a state tax on the sale by a non-Indian of farm machinery to a tribal farming enterprise (the Court emphasized the longtime federal regulation of traders under the traders statutes); *Ramah Navajo School Board v. Bureau of Revenue*, 458 U.S. 832 (1982), striking down a state tax on a non-Indian contractor building a tribal school (the Court emphasized federal Indian education statutes and the economic burdens on the tribe, which had agreed to reimburse the contractor for taxes); and *Montana v. Blackfeet Tribe of Indians*, 471 U.S. 759 (1985), striking down a state tax on tribal royalty interests under oil and gas leases issued to non-Indian lessees (the Court required a clear congressional consent to taxation). As discussed by the Supreme Court in *Rice v. Rehner* (1983), state taxes seem to apply in the special case of liquor sales, which expressly are covered by federal law.[86]

Tribes now have well-established authority under the *Merrion* and *Kerr-McGee* cases to tax non-Indians doing business with tribes on tribal lands. Under *Atkinson Trading Co. v. Shirley* (2001),[87] tribal taxing authority over non-Indians doing business on non-Indian fee land is very limited unless there is some consensual agreement between the business and the tribe. As noted in Chapter 3, non-IRA tribes, and many IRA tribes, need not obtain secretarial approval to tax non-Indian business activities in Indian Country. (*See discussion in* Chapter 3 *at* pp. 61-62.) Whether tribal taxation of non-Indian businesses excludes state taxes on the same activity is an important question that affects a tribe's ability to generate revenues. Non-Indian businesses subject to both tribal and state taxation could be driven off the reservation if the combination of taxes is too high. In the 1980 *Colville* case, the Court allowed a state, as well as a tribal, tax on the sale of cigarettes to non-Indians, but the state tax apparently was allowed because no tribal natural resources were involved—there was no "value generated" on the reservation.[88]

FEDERAL INCOME TAXATION

The Internal Revenue Code does not make tribes taxable entities, so tribal income is not subject to federal taxation; like state and local governments, tribal governments are exempted. The situation is different for individual Indians, who have no general exemption from federal income taxation. Congress, however, has provided certain tax exemptions for individual Indians in treaties or statutes. In *Squire v. Capoeman* (1956),[89] the Supreme Court held that income "derived directly" from allotments and similar trust land is not subject to federal income taxation. In *Squire*, the Court concluded that the purposes of the General Allotment Act would be undercut if the subsequently enacted federal income tax were imposed on capital gains from the sale of timber cut on a trust allotment. While some allotment laws have express exemptions from taxation, the Court in *Squire* found that the General Allotment Act created an implied exemption from federal taxation.

Two rules of construction collided in *Squire*. On the one hand in tax law, exemptions rarely are implied; clear expressions in the statutes generally are required before exemptions will be granted. On the other hand in Indian law, federal statutes must be construed liberally in favor of Indians.[90] While this latter principle of federal Indian law prevailed in *Squire*, the "derived directly" test has not led to many federal tax exemptions for individual Indians.

The examples of individual Indian incomes that have been held taxable under federal (but not state) income tax laws are numerous. For instance, the income of a tribal member from cattle grazing on leased tribal trust land was held taxable.[91] The income of an Indian subcontractor from logging on reservation lands also has been held taxable.[92] And even though the reindeer in Alaska are held in trust by the federal government pursuant to the Reindeer Industry Act of 1937, the Ninth Circuit Court of Appeals held as taxable the income from the sale of reindeer and reindeer products.[93] In general, the courts have not allowed individual exemptions from federal taxes much beyond the basic income derived directly from an allottee's own allotment.

THE INDIAN CIVIL RIGHTS ACT OF 1968

Most tribal constitutions contain some individual civil rights guarantees. Indian tribes, however, are not limited by the Bill of Rights of the United States' Constitution, which applies only to the states and the United States.[94] In Title I of the Indian Civil Rights Act of 1968 (ICRA), Congress applied much of the language of the Bill of Rights to Indian tribes, including the equal protection and due process clauses.[95] The ICRA originally limited the sentencing power of tribal courts to confinement for six months and/or a $500 fine; these limits were raised in 1986 to allow imprisonment for one year and/or fines of up to $5,000. (For text of statute, *see* Part Three.) The Supreme Court has ruled that the ICRA allows federal court review of tribal court decisions only in criminal cases involving habeas corpus.[96]

The difficult questions raised by the ICRA are exemplified by the leading case, *Santa Clara Pueblo v. Martinez*, handed down in 1978.[97] (For text of opinion, *see* Part Four.) The Santa Clara Pueblo extended membership to children of male members who marry outside the tribe but denied membership to children of female members who marry outside the tribe. In spite of arguments that the Pueblo's membership ordinance amounted to discrimination on the basis of sex, the Supreme Court held the ICRA does not allow federal courts to hear such cases. Rather, tribal institutions must resolve them.

Congress plainly has authority to protect the rights of tribal members who may have grievances against the tribe by allowing federal courts to hear these intratribal disputes. Similarly, non-Indians who come under tribal authority may believe that they should have greater access to federal court than the limited federal jurisdiction now available to review the issue of the existence of tribal jurisdiction.[98] In granting any additional federal oversight of tribal courts and legislatures, however, Congress must intrude further on tribal sovereignty and it has not yet chosen to do so.

THE INDIAN CHILD WELFARE ACT OF 1978

Even before this country was a nation, the ... precedent had been cast to destroy Indian culture and tribal sovereignty by removing Indian children from their families and tribal settings.... Today, the widespread separation of Indian children from their families has often been brought about by social workers who, untrained in Indian cultural values and social norms, make decisions ... [regarding] the family pattern of Indian life.

— Manuel P. Guerrero (1979)[99]

In 1978 Congress passed the Indian Child Welfare Act (ICWA)[100] to rectify an extaordinarily serious problem: an estimated 25–35 percent of all Indian children had been adopted out into non-Indian families, usually due to state court decrees. By any standard, the ICWA is a sweeping and dramatic development in Indian law and policy. (For text of statute, *see* Part Three.) The ICWA is a reform measure intended to combat the widespread separation of Indian children from their parents. It has revitalized child custody procedures by enacting these basic provisions:

1. Indian children in Indian Country are within the exclusive jurisdiction of tribal courts. (Public Law 280 tribes can obtain such jurisdiction by submitting a petition to the BIA subject to the provisions of the ICWA.)

2. If a child custody proceeding begins in state court, the Indian child's tribe must be notified, and the tribe has the right to intervene in the state proceeding.

3. If the tribe or either parent requests a transfer from state court to tribal court, the state court must transfer the case (subject to declination by the tribal court) absent objection by a *parent* (not a party seeking adoption). The state court can refuse transfer to tribal court for good cause, but good cause is defined narrowly.[101]

4. If a case remains in state court, a termination of parental rights can be ordered only if supported by proof beyond a reasonable doubt, and a foster care placement can be ordered only if supported by clear and convincing evidence.

5. If an Indian parent does lose parental rights in a state court proceeding, the court is required first to follow these preferences in any adoptive placement: (a) members of the child's extended family; (b) other members of the child's tribe; (c) other Indian families. Only then can adoption be made to a non-Indian home.

6. Placement of a child for foster care or preadoptive placement has another set of preferences favoring Indians and Indian institutions.[102]

In all, the ICWA is perhaps the leading example of modern legislation that protects Indian culture, limits state jurisdiction, and respects tribal institutions by recognizing their authority over sensitive, important matters.

INTERGOVERNMENTAL RELATIONS BETWEEN INDIAN TRIBES AND STATES

A major positive development in intergovernmental relations has been increased cooperation between tribes and local, state, and federal governments in order to clarify the complex jurisdictional relationships among the various sovereigns.

INTERGOVERNMENTAL AGREEMENTS

Negotiated agreements between Indian tribes and states or their political subdivisions are recognized as worthy objectives by political leaders of both governments for the purpose of addressing practical needs and difficulties.[103] Congress authorized tribal-state agreements regarding the care and custody of Indian children in the Indian Child Welfare Act of 1978. Such agreements also were mandated regarding the implementation of certain kinds of Indian gaming in the Indian Gaming Regulatory Act of 1988. Where the agreement involves cross-deputization or detention of prisoners, one government simply makes the officers of the other government their agents. Thus, for example, although tribes lack criminal jurisdiction over non-Indians, a tribal police officer who is cross-deputized under state and federal law could arrest a non-Indian who committed a crime within Indian Country and deliver the offender to state or federal officials, as appropriate.

RECIPROCITY

Another significant area of intergovernmental relations between tribes and states involves reciprocity in the recognition of the laws of the other government. The law that is recognized can be substantive (such as a statute) or a court judgment. This issue has been treated as a question of either comity or full faith and credit. Comity, which is the less formal process by which the courts of one sovereign recognize the law of another, frequently has been the basis on which state courts have recognized tribal laws and court judgments.[104] In addition, it is possible that state courts are required by federal statute to give full faith and credit to tribal laws.[105] Ultimately, all of the involved governments will benefit from the stability created by the certainty that their laws will be recognized by the other government.

CONCLUSION

During the modern era, tribes have achieved an historic objective by obtaining clear judicial and legislative recognition that Indian tribes are sovereigns. Although tribes differ from states, Indian governments have a vast reservoir of reserved powers tracing to their inherent sovereignty, just as states have broad reserved rights under the Tenth Amendment of the Constitution. After more than 200 years of jurisprudence, it is at last settled that there are three separate sources of sovereignty—federal, state, and tribal—within the federal constitutional system.

The interlocking relationships between tribal, state and local governments can be exceedingly complex. It is increasingly apparent that, in the future, the resolution of intergovernmental disputes may be achieved best through negotiation, rather than litigation. Such direct government-to-government relationships may, over time, result in a continuing process of tailoring jurisdictional relationships to meet the practical, local needs of the affected sovereigns.

CHAPTER 3

Tribes and the Federal Trust Relationship

INTRODUCTION

[T]he enduring teaching of the Cherokee cases is their perception of the underlying purposes of the trust relationship.... Congress intends specific adherence to the trust responsibility unless it has expressly provided otherwise. Such a formulation preserves the role of Congress as the ultimate umpire of the purposes of the trust while requiring strict executive compliance with the terms of the trust.

— Reid P. Chambers (1975)[1]

"Domestic dependent nations" are permitted an existence in the United States so long as they are weak.

— Mary Shepardson (1963)[2]

> [T]he Government is something more than a mere contracting party.
> Under a humane and self imposed policy which has found expression in
> many acts of Congress and numerous decisions of this Court, it has charged
> itself with moral obligations of the highest responsibility and trust.
>
> — Justice Frank Murphy (1942)[3]

Pervasive Influence of the Trust

The trust relationship between the United States and American
Indian tribes has many unique features that influence most aspects of
Indian law. Although this relationship may have begun as a force to
control tribes, even to subjugate them, it now provides federal protection
for Indian resources and federal aid of various kinds in development of
these resources.

The Trust Duty and Congressional "Plenary Power"

Congress has special authority over Indian affairs under the Indian
Commerce Clause of the Constitution (art. I, § 8, cl. 3), which allows the
national legislature "[t]o regulate commerce with foreign nations, and
among the several states, and *with the Indian Tribes*" (emphasis supplied).
Today, following the Supreme Court's 1973 decision in *McClanahan v.
Arizona State Tax Commission,*[4] the Indian Commerce Clause, along with
the power to make treaties, is seen as the principal basis for broad federal
power over Indians. (For text of *McClanahan* opinion, *see* Part Four.) The
concept of a special federal power over Indian affairs is a basic notion in
Indian law and policy.

Congressional power over Indians is often described as "plenary," the
literal meaning of which is "absolute" or "total." The phrase "plenary
power," however, is misleading; congressional power is broad but not
unlimited. Further, exercises of authority from Congress by administrative officials are limited sharply in many respects, often by statutes and
various applications of the trust duty. And—while federal authority often
has been exercised to the detriment of Indians, as with allotment and
termination—in the modern era we have seen a great many examples
where congressional power has been used to benefit Indians. The broad
federal power under the Indian Commerce Clause can be appreciated
only by an understanding of the rigorous standards of conduct that often
are imposed by the trust doctrine.

ORIGINS OF THE TRUST RELATIONSHIP

The federal government's trust duty is rooted in the land cessions made by the native nations. As expressed in treaties and elsewhere, the land cessions were conditioned upon an understanding that the federal government would safeguard the autonomy of the native nations by protecting their smaller, retained territories from the intrusions of the majority society and its ambitious entrepreneurs.

— Mary Christina Wood (1994)[5]

EARLY RECOGNITION OF THE TRUST

The concept of the federal Indian trust responsibility was evident in the Trade and Intercourse Acts and other late 18th and early 19th century federal laws protecting Indian land transactions and regulating trade with the tribes. The trust first was announced in Chief Justice Marshall's decision in *Cherokee Nation v. Georgia* (1831). (For text of opinion, *see* Part Four.) Suit was filed by the tribe in the United States Supreme Court to enjoin the State of Georgia from enforcing state laws on lands guaranteed to the tribe by treaties. The Court found that the tribe was neither a state nor a foreign nation under the Constitution and therefore was not entitled to bring the suit initially in the Supreme Court. Chief Justice Marshall, however, concluded that Indian tribes "may, more correctly, perhaps, be denominated domestic dependent nations ... in a state of pupilage" and that "their relation to the United States resembles that of a ward to his guardian."

The Supreme Court's subsequent decision in *Worcester v. Georgia* (1832) reaffirmed the status of Indian tribes as self-governing entities. (For text of opinion, *see* Part Four.) Chief Justice Marshall construed the treaties and the Indian Trade and Intercourse Acts as protecting the tribes' status as distinct political communities possessing self-government authority within their boundaries. Thus, Georgia state law could not be applied on Cherokee lands because, as a matter of federal law, the United States had recognized tribal self-governing powers by entering into a treaty with the Cherokees. In spite of its governmental status, however, the Cherokee Nation was placed expressly by the treaties "under the protection of the United States."[6]

Perhaps the most important aspect of the trust relationship is the protection of Indian landownership. Beginning in 1790, the Trade and

Intercourse Acts prohibited the sale of Indian land without federal consent. Indians, although not citizens at that time, held their lands and other property as trust beneficiaries of the United States.[7] This arrangement, in theory at least, protected Indian landownership and allowed the federal government rather than the states to control the opening of Indian lands for non-Indian settlement. The trust relationship, therefore, enhanced federal power, but it also created federal duties relating to Indian lands and other natural resources.

LATER DEVELOPMENTS

The courts consistently have upheld exercises of congressional power over Indian affairs, often relying upon the trust relationship. For example, in *United States v. Kagama* (1886),[8] the Supreme Court affirmed Congress' power to enact the Major Crimes Act.[9] Congress' "plenary" power even includes the power to terminate the trust relationship unilaterally without Indian consent and over Indian objections.[10] Statutes providing for the allotment of tribal lands to tribal members also have been sustained as constitutional by the courts, even where such dilution of tribal property specifically was prohibited by treaty.[11]

Under the special federal-tribal relationship, Indian tribes receive some benefits not available to other citizens. For example, in the 1974 *Morton v. Mancari* decision, the Supreme Court upheld a BIA Indian hiring preference because, like special health and education benefits flowing from the trust relationship, the preference is not based on race; rather, federal programs dealing with Indians derive from the government-to-government relationship between the United States and Indian tribes.[12] The same reasoning applies to off-reservation Indian hunting and fishing rights; they trace to treaties with specific tribal governments and are not rights generally held by members of a race.[13]

FEDERAL RECOGNITION OF THE TRUST RELATIONSHIP

The rights, duties and obligations that make up the trust relationship generally exist only between the United States and those Indian tribes "recognized" by the United States. Once federal recognition is found to exist, it results in the establishment of a government-to-government relationship with the tribe and makes the tribe a "beneficiary" of the trust relationship with the federal government.

An Indian group is a federally recognized tribe if: (1) Congress or the executive created a reservation for the group either by treaty, by statutorily expressed agreement, or by executive order or other valid administrative action; or (2) the United States has some continuing political relationship with the group, such as providing services through the BIA. Accordingly, for example, Indian groups situated on federally maintained reservations are considered tribes under virtually every statute that refers to Indian tribes.[14]

Court decisions of the mid-1970s suggest that even a general act of Congress such as the Trade and Intercourse Act of 1790 (prohibiting the sale of tribal lands without the consent of Congress) serves to establish a partial trust relationship between *all tribes* and the federal government.[15] Determination of tribal existence, therefore, becomes critical.

In 1978, in order to resolve doubts about the status of those tribes lacking federally recognized reservations, the Department of Interior issued regulations entitled "Procedures for Establishing that an American Indian Group Exists as an Indian Tribe," now published at 25 C.F.R. 83. The regulations establish both a procedure to obtain federal acknowledgment and a substantive standard for determining whether a group is in fact an Indian tribe. The regulations can be reduced to four essential requirements: (1) a common identification ancestrally and racially as a group of Native Americans; (2) the maintenance of a community distinct from other populations in the area; (3) the continued historical maintenance of tribal political influence or other governmental authority over members of the group; and (4) the status of not being part of a presently recognized tribe. In these respects, the regulations reflect the basic judicial definitions of the term "Indian tribe." (*See discussion in* Chapter 2 *at* p. 30.) The BIA maintains a current list of federally recognized tribes—which includes more than 500 tribes.

MODERN CONSEQUENCES OF THE TRUST RESPONSIBILITY

[T]he United States Government acts as a legal trustee for the land and water rights of American Indians [and has] a legal obligation to advance the interests of the beneficiaries of the trust without reservation and with the highest degree of diligence and skill.

— President Richard M. Nixon (1970)[16]

Power of Congress

Congressional power over Indians remains broad, but it is not absolute and is subject to both procedural and constitutional limitations. The Supreme Court has held that the trust relationship does not authorize Congress to lessen any of the rights of property protected by the Fifth Amendment without just compensation.[17] Cases around the turn of the 20th century suggested that acts of Congress constitute "political questions" not subject to judicial review in the courts. The leading opinion is *Lone Wolf v. Hitchcock* (1903).[18] (For text of opinion, *see* Part Four.) Later decisions, such as *Delaware Tribal Business Committee v. Weeks* (1977) and *United States v. Sioux Nation* (1980), have found, however, that acts of Congress and executive officials are subject to judicial review under ordinary principles of constitutional and administrative law.[19] Later cases also have considered the trust obligations of the United States as a limiting standard for judging the constitutional validity of an Indian statute. In its 1974 decision in *Morton v. Mancari*, the Supreme Court upheld the constitutionality of a statute granting Indians an employment preference in the Bureau of Indian Affairs, stating: "As long as the special treatment can be tied rationally to the fulfillment of Congress' unique obligations toward the Indian, such legislative judgment will not be disturbed."[20]

Thus, where Congress exercises its specific authority over Indians, the trust obligation appears to require a determination that the protection of the Indians will be served. Otherwise, a statute would not be "tied rationally" to the trust obligation to Indians, as required by the Supreme Court. However, if Congress exercises a constitutional authority distinct from its authority over Indians, such as the power of eminent domain, it can act contrary to the Indians' interest. Additionally, reviewing courts usually will not second-guess a congressional determination that a statute is an appropriate protection of Indian interests.

The trust is relevant in other ways. Courts construe statutes affecting Indians, as well as treaties and executive agreements, as not abrogating prior Indian rights or, in cases of ambiguity, in a manner favorable to the Indians.[21] (*See discussion of canons of construction in* Chapter 1 *at* p. 7.) In addition, although the courts have held that Congress can alter treaty rights unilaterally or act in a fashion adverse to the Indians' interest, the trust requires that Congress set out its intent to do so in "clear," "plain" or "manifest" terms in the statutory language or legislative history.[22]

THE ADMINISTRATION OF INDIAN POLICY AND THE
TRUST RESPONSIBILITY TODAY

Traditionally, most aspects of the trust responsibility were delegated by Congress to the Department of the Interior and the Department of Justice, the latter of which historically has litigated many court cases on behalf of Indian tribes and individuals. As federal programs for Indians have proliferated in modern times, many other federal agencies have become involved in Indian affairs and they, too, must comply with the duties imposed by the special relationship.[23] Now, several other agencies in the Interior Department have become active in Indian policy, including the National Park Service, Bureau of Land Management, U.S. Fish & Wildlife Service (endangered species protection), Bureau of Reclamation (water policy), and U.S. Geological Survey (mineral leasing). In addition to the Department of Justice, federal programs for Indians are administered by the Department of Education, Department of Health and Human Services, National Marine Fisheries Service, Department of Agriculture (including the U.S. Forest Service), Department of Housing and Urban Development, and others. A 1995 Executive Memorandum directed all federal agencies dealing with Indian tribes to articulate their government-to-government policies. As a result, the special relationship reaches far beyond the Bureau of Indian Affairs.

RESPONSIBILITIES OF FEDERAL OFFICIALS

In contrast to the power of Congress, the power of executive officials is constrained more significantly by the trust relationship. Unless the trust relationship has been terminated by Congress, judicial decisions hold executive officials to stringent fiduciary standards in their management of, and dealings with, Indian trust property. Decisions of the Supreme Court reviewing the lawfulness of administrative conduct managing Indian property have held officials of the United States to "obligations of the highest responsibility and trust" and "the most exacting fiduciary standards." Furthermore, executive officials are bound "by every moral and equitable consideration to discharge [the] trust with good faith and fairness."[24] Therefore, executive officials must adhere to the standards of an ordinary fiduciary in dealing with Indian trust property. If they do not, the United States may be sued for money damages, for declaratory relief, or for injunctive relief.

The courts often have used the trusteeship to limit federal administrative power where Indian ownership of land is affected.[25] Other cases have applied trust obligations where trust funds, mineral resources, timber, and water are subject to federal executive management.[26] The Indian trust cases have not always been consistent, as evidenced by two decisions in 2003, when the Supreme Court found strict trust obligations in a statute calling for federal management of a historic fort on the White Mountain Apache Reservation, but then denied recovery to the Navajo Nation when federal officials withheld critical information from the tribe regarding management of tribal mineral resources.[27]

While the actions of the executive in carrying out the federal trust duties are required to adhere to strict fiduciary standards, the United States as trustee has the flexibility to exercise reasonable judgment in choosing between alternative courses of action.[28] The interests of the beneficiary always must be paramount, however, and the fiduciary's duty of loyalty must be observed strictly.[29] In the major *Cobell* litigation during the 1990s and into the 21st century, Indian allottees sued Interior Department officials for mismanagement of Indian money accounts, and the courts have made clear that a high fiduciary duty applies.[30]

The requirement of loyalty is especially important in cases where the United States has a conflict of interest between general public programs and the rights or claims of Indian trust beneficiaries. There are innumerable such conflicts.[31] Indians may claim, for example, lands that are administered as public lands or national forests, waters sought by federal agencies for federally financed water projects, or fishing rights that impinge on federal fish management or energy development projects. As noted, most of these conflicts arise within the Department of the Interior, but the obligations of the trust relationship are not limited to agencies in that department. The case law dictates that, unless Congress clearly authorizes it, federal agencies cannot subordinate Indian interests to other public purposes.[32] One example of a case where Congress did so authorize is the 1983 decision in *Nevada v. United States* (1983),[33] where a federal water project and the Pyramid Lake Indian Reservation had to share water from the Truckee River. In this case the Supreme Court held that the government does not necessarily compromise its responsibility to Indian tribes when Congress has obligated it by statute to represent simultaneously another interest:

These cases, we believe, point the way to the correct resolution of the instant cases. The United States undoubtedly owes a strong fiduciary duty to its Indian wards. [Citations omitted.] It may be that where only a relationship between the Government and the tribe is involved, the law respecting obligations between a trustee and a beneficiary in private litigation will in many, if not all, respects, adequately describe the duty of the United States. But where Congress has imposed upon the United States, in addition to its duty to represent Indian tribes, a duty to obtain water rights for reclamation projects, and has even authorized the inclusion of reservation lands within a project, the analogy of a faithless private fiduciary cannot be controlling for purposes of evaluating the authority of the United States to represent different interests.[34]

DUTY TO REPRESENT INDIAN TRIBES AND INDIVIDUAL INDIANS IN LITIGATION

A federal statute, 25 U.S.C. § 175, requires that: "In all states and territories where there are reservations or allotted Indians, the United States Attorney shall represent them in all suits at law and in equity." The statute does not require federal representation of Indian tribes and individuals in all situations,[35] but the law is a crucial aspect of the trust relationship. Many major court cases have been litigated by the United States concerning allotments and tribal land, water, and hunting and fishing rights. Section 175 has been criticized as extending to Indians important special benefits not received by any other group in the country. One major decision held that the trust responsibility obligates the Department of Justice to represent Indian claims to lands and other resources in court, even though the Justice Department may have doubts about the validity of the claim.[36]

INDIAN RELIGIOUS FREEDOM

THE AMERICAN INDIAN RELIGIOUS FREEDOM ACT (AIRFA)

Federal development of natural resources is often at odds with the protection of, or access to, Indian religious sites. In many instances, the federal government has initiated resource development that has interfered with or destroyed Indian religious sites and practices. AIRFA, passed in

1978, articulates specific policy objectives relating to the preservation of Indian religious sites and practices, but does not create a cause of action or any judicially enforceable individual rights. (For the text of AIRFA, *see* Part Three.) In 1994, AIRFA was amended to prohibit states from penalizing Indians who use peyote in a traditional manner in religious ceremonies.[37]

In 1988, in *Lyng v. Northwest Indian Cemetery Protective Association*,[38] the Supreme Court upheld the Forest Service's right to build a logging road that would be located near a sacred site and would interfere with the ceremonies of religious practitioners. The Court found that, because the federal government's neutral management of its lands did not penalize or coerce Indian religious practitioners, the government should have broad discretion in determining the use of its own land. (For text of *Lyng* opinion, *see* Part Four.)

Importantly, however, the *Lyng* decision found that government officials have authority under AIRFA's policy direction and other laws to "accommodate" Indian religious practices. This discretion has become increasingly important in recent years, as federal land agencies have taken steps to protect Indian religious practices.

On May 24, 1996, President Clinton signed an executive order further bolstering the mandate of the American Indian Religious Freedom Act with respect to sacred sites. The order directed federal agencies to "accommodate access to and ceremonial use of Indian sacred sites by Indian religious practitioners" on federal land. Agencies must "avoid adversely affecting the physical integrity of such sacred sites" through notice to and consultation with tribes. In *Bear Lodge Multiple Use Association v. Babbitt*,[39] a federal district court upheld a National Park Service voluntary ban on climbing for the month of June on Devil's Tower National Monument in Wyoming. The Tower is sacred to several American Indian tribes.

THE FIRST AMENDMENT

The First Amendment of the United States Constitution forbids Congress from making laws "prohibiting the free exercise" of religion. Until recently, this has been interpreted as protecting sincere religious beliefs from infringement by otherwise neutral regulations—unintended effects on the free exercise of religion were allowable only if there was at stake a compelling governmental interest, achievable through the least restrictive means possible.[40] In *Employment Division, Dep't of Human Resources of Oregon v. Smith*,[41] the Court sharply limited the applicability of the compelling governmental interest test, holding instead that the right of free exercise does not relieve an individual from complying with valid and neutral laws of general applicability—here laws against the use of peyote. Congress reacted to the Court's interpretation of the "compelling interest" requirement by enacting the Religious Freedom Restoration Act (RFRA),[42] restoring the "compelling interest" test as set forth in *Sherbert v. Verner*. However, the Supreme Court struck down the RFRA, as applied to the states, in *City of Boerne v. P.F. Flores*,[43] holding that Congress exceeded its remedial powers under the Fourteenth Amendment in enacting RFRA and extending it to the states. Several states, however, subsequently have enacted their own versions of the RFRA.

PROTECTION OF CULTURAL PROPERTY

In the years during the military conflicts between tribes and the American army, it was common practice for Indian remains and cultural property to be confiscated by the military and stored in museums for scientific study. Archaeologists have unearthed remains and artifacts. As a result, countless human remains and sacred objects were locked in museum archives instead of being returned to their ancestors. In 1990, Congress passed the Native American Graves Protection and Repatriation Act (NAGPRA).[44] The Act requires all federal agencies and museums to make inventories of their human remains, funerary objects, and sacred objects, and return them to the rightful tribes. NAGPRA also prohibits remains and objects from being treated as archeological resources, and prohibits sites from being excavated without tribal consent. Penalties are imposed for unauthorized excavation, removal, damage or destruction of Indian burial sites.[45] (For text of NAGPRA, *see* Part Three.)

INTERIOR DEPARTMENT REVIEW AND APPROVAL OF TRIBAL ACTIONS

As another aspect of the trust relationship, the Interior Department reviews or approves certain tribal land and resources decisions. For example, as required by federal law, the Department approves tribal resource leases and grants of rights-of-way over both tribal trust lands and allotted lands.[46] In recent years there has been a great deal of controversy concerning the Secretary's administration of mineral leases on reservations (*see discussion in* Chapter 4 *at* pp. 73-74) and concerning the Secretary's approval of water use ordinances, timber sales, land use ordinances, and mineral tax ordinances. (*See* Chapter 4.)

Another area of dispute involves general secretarial review of tribal ordinances—an issue that arises for many tribes with IRA constitutions that include a clause requiring such secretarial review. As explained by the Supreme Court in *Kerr-McGee Corp. v. Navajo Tribe of Indians* (1985),[47] such provisions are not mandated by the IRA. In the interest of self-determination, the Department now encourages tribes to remove (through tribal constitutional amendment) the requirement for the Secretary to review certain kinds of enactments.

CONCLUSION

The trust relationship has proved to be dynamic and ongoing, evolving over time. One question that constantly arises is whether the trust relationship is permanent. Is it a perpetual relationship, or is it one that can or ought to be "terminated?" Is the purpose to protect Indian landownership and self-governing status? Or is it to give the federal government power to assimilate Indians into the larger society, to rehabilitate them as "conquered subjects," or to "civilize" them?

Different eras have provided different answers to these questions. At the turn of the 20th century the trust relationship was seen as short term and transitory. Indian land was to be protected for a brief transition period while Indians were assimilated into the "mainstream." The trust relationship was seen as the basis for congressional power to pass legislation breaking up tribal landholdings into individual allotments.

More recently, the view has broadened. At the turn of the 21st century the trust relationship is seen as a doctrine that helps support progressive federal legislation enacted for the benefit of Indians, such as the modern laws dealing with child welfare, Indian religion, and tribal economic development. The trust also controls contemporary interpretations of time-honored treaties and statutes. The trust relationship seems to have become a permanent doctrine that will function as John Marshall intended—as a benevolent influence in the development of Indian policy and law.

CHAPTER 4

Tribal Resource Rights, Reservation Environments and Economic Development

INTRODUCTION

Touch water in the West and you touch everything.
— John Gunther (1975)[1]

Why do Tribes earn $2 a barrel for oil and as little as 15 cents a ton for coal? How did the mineral wealth for three generations of Native Americans leak away?
— Denver Post (1984)[2]

There has been a lot said about the sacredness of our land which is our body; and the values of our culture which is our soul; but water is the blood of our tribes, and if its life-giving flow is stopped, or it is polluted, all else will die and the many thousands of years of our communal existence will come to an end.
— Frank Tenorio (1978)[3]

Many tribes possess substantial land bases and natural resources, and resource policy is a main area of decision-making for tribal councils. In some cases, the extent of tribal hunting and fishing or water rights may be uncertain, requiring litigation or negotiation with the states. In addition, although the burgeoning activity in economic development holds promise for alleviating poverty in Indian Country, it can raise conflicts with religious values and environmental concerns. Increasingly, tribes are moving toward management of their natural resources through comprehensive, reservation-wide planning.

CONFLICTS BETWEEN DEVELOPMENT AND OTHER TRIBAL VALUES

Unlike the predominant religions of modern America, Native American religion cannot be separated from day-to-day activities. It is a way of life in which geography, language, and nature play central roles. The fact that humans cannot survive without the natural environment is recognized by tribal societies, and tribes, as place-based peoples, feel responsible for protecting the ancestral territories provided them by their Creator. Indian religions focus upon nature's continuous renewal of life, not upon a particular individual or event.[4] Finally, while Native American religion requires or encourages collective tribal participation, it simultaneously recognizes the importance of individual spiritual development.[5]

The decision of whether and how to develop natural resources is a subject of great debate in Indian communities. Indian people hold various and conflicting opinions concerning the effect of resource development on a tribe's social structure and deeply-held traditional, religious and environmental values. There is broad agreement, however, that natural resource development must be approached as a part of a larger plan of social and economic development rather than as an end in itself.

NATURAL RESOURCE DEVELOPMENT AND INDIAN RELIGION

The development of natural resources on Indian-controlled property necessitates a thorough evaluation of the impact such development would have upon traditional values. (*See discussion in* Chapter 3 *at* pp. 59-60.) This is true whether the tribe determines to develop its natural resources or to protect sacred sites from development.

TRUST RESPONSIBILITY

Another consideration is that in the management of Indian natural resources, the United States acts in a fiduciary or trust capacity, particularly where trust resources, treaties, and explicit statutory regulations are involved. (*See* Chapter 3.) A 1983 Supreme Court decision upholding allottees' claims for damages due to BIA mismanagement of their timber lands recognizes the United States' fiduciary obligations regarding Indian natural resources.[6]

WATER RESOURCES

Most Indian lands, like lands in the American West generally, are arid. Nevertheless, the lands can produce substantial crops if they are irrigated. Certainly there is great potential for Indian irrigation projects because virtually all reservations have rivers on them. The positioning of Indian lands on most major river systems, however, has created inevitable and major conflicts with public and private water interests in the water-scarce West. In addition to this longtime concern over water rights, tribes are active in combating water pollution and in managing their water resources through comprehensive planning and enforcement systems.

INDIAN RESERVED WATER RIGHTS

Substantive Law: The Winters Doctrine

Western states (and now most states in the Midwest) always have used the prior appropriation doctrine to allocate water rights. It is based on the notion of "first in time, first in right." Basically, under state law a water user obtains a right senior and superior to all later users if he or she appropriates the water by: (1) diverting water out of a watercourse; and (2) putting it to a beneficial use for such purposes as irrigation (still the major water use in the West), mining, industrial, municipal, or domestic use. Once these conditions are met, the water user has established an appropriation date and a vested property right to the quantity of water divested.

In contrast, Indian water rights are defined by federal rather than state law. The first landmark Supreme Court case on this issue is *Winters v. United States* (1908).[7] (For text of opinion, *see* Part Four.) That case arose from a factual situation where a tribal irrigation project on the Fort

Belknap Reservation began diverting water from the Milk River in 1898. Upstream non-Indian water users had beneficially diverted a substantial portion of the Milk River in the early 1890s, before the tribe's appropriation. The Supreme Court, applying federal law, held that sufficient water impliedly was reserved to fulfill the purposes of the reservation at or before the time the reservation was established—1874. This doctrine of federal reserved rights established a vested right whether or not the resource was actually put to use, and enabled the tribe to expand its water use over time in response to changing reservation needs. In making its decision, the Court construed the agreement establishing the reservation in favor of the tribe, but failed to clarify whether the tribe or the federal government reserved the water.

In *Arizona v. California* (1963)[8] federal reserved rights on the Colorado River were upheld for Indian reservations established by executive order, and for public lands such as national recreation areas and national forests. The amount of water reserved was an amount sufficient to satisfy the future as well as the present needs of the tribe. The test used was the amount of water necessary to irrigate all the "practicably irrigable acreage" on the reservation.

The Court in *Arizona v. California* applied the reserved rights doctrine to federal public lands as well as to Indian reservations. Later cases have limited the extent of reserved water rights for federal, non-Indian reservations of land (such as national forests).[9] Reserved water rights for these reservations are limited to the primary purposes for which the reservation was created, *i.e.*, those purposes actually stated. Water rights necessary for secondary uses must be obtained pursuant to state law. The courts still must determine the extent to which these limitations apply to reserved water rights for Indian reservations. The Supreme Court of Wyoming attempted to do so in *In re General Adjudication of all Rights to Use Water in the Big Horn River System*.[10] There the court held that the tribes of the Wind River Indian Reservation were only entitled to water rights that were reserved for the purpose of "agriculture" as found on the face of their 1868 Treaty. (*See discussion of* canons of construction *in* Chapter 1 *at* p. 7.) The Wyoming Supreme Court found that *Winters* rights do not extend to groundwater, but, in reasoning more likely to be followed, the Arizona Supreme Court held in a 1999 opinion that groundwater rights are reserved to the tribe.[11]

Procedural Issues: The McCarran Amendment

The McCarran Amendment,[12] passed by Congress in 1952, consents to the joinder of the United States as a defendant in federal and state court adjudications of water rights. In *Colorado River Water Conservation District v. United States* (1976), the Supreme Court ruled that, although federal courts continue to have concurrent jurisdiction, the McCarran Amendment provides state courts with jurisdiction to adjudicate Indian water rights held in trust by the United States.[13] In its 1983 decision in *Arizona v. San Carlos Apache Tribe*, the Supreme Court held that the McCarran Amendment allows state adjudication of Indian water rights even in those states that expressly have disclaimed jurisdiction in their constitutions or enabling acts.[14] (For text of *San Carlos* opinion, *see* Part Four; for example of enabling act, *see* Montana Enabling Act in Part Three.)

It should be noted that the McCarran Amendment allows joinder of tribes only in general stream adjudications—comprehensive actions in which all potential water users in a watershed are joined. In addition, the statute confers judicial jurisdiction only; Indian water rights continue to be determined according to federal substantive law.

Indian Reserved Rights: Many Unresolved Questions

Numerous substantive questions remain concerning the scope of Indian reserved water rights and include the following:

1. Who reserved the water—the federal government or the tribes?

2. What priority dates do the tribes possess? In one case, involving a tribe that did not use water for irrigation in pre-treaty times, the court held that for traditional purposes, *e.g.*, hunting and fishing, tribes possess a priority date of time immemorial, while for other purposes, *e.g.*, agriculture, the date each particular reservation was established is the priority date.[15]

3. What quantity of water is reserved? Is "practicably irrigable acreage" the maximum extent of Indian reserved water rights? What does "practicably irrigable" mean? Does it, as a special master has suggested to the Supreme Court, mean "economically feasible" using present technology?[16]

4. Do Indian water rights include future needs, those not foreseeable at the time of the establishment of the reservation (*e.g.*, the development of coal resources)?

5. Do Indian reserved rights include instream flows for fishery purposes? The Ninth Circuit Court of Appeals has upheld such a reservation,[17] but the Supreme Court of Wyoming in *Big Horn* declined to allow instream flows where the Treaty made no mention of fisheries and was limited to agricultural purposes as the reason for creating the reservation.

6. Do, as the Arizona Supreme Court has held, tribal reserved rights include groundwater?

7. Can Indian reserved rights be sold (or leased) to non-Indians? It has been argued that Indian water rights do not exist apart from tribal land and, therefore, cannot be sold separately.[18]

8. Does a non-Indian purchaser of an allotment also purchase the *Winters* rights? The few decided cases in this area agree that a non-Indian purchaser of an allotment succeeds to some water rights, although they disagree on the nature and extent of those rights.[19]

9. To what extent may tribes regulate water uses within their reservations? The Ninth Circuit Court of Appeals has denied state regulatory authority over non-Indian water use on fee land in a situation where the stream was entirely within the boundaries of the reservation.[20] Although the BIA has issued a moratorium on secretarial approval of tribal water codes, many tribes now are processing water codes to regulate water uses within their reservations.[21]

10. Is it in the best interests of tribes to quantify their rights? Legally, *Winters* rights include future needs and are not lost if they are not exercised. Practically, states are awarding new non-Indian rights regularly and tribal rights in part may go by the wayside under the "use it or lose it" philosophy that always has governed western water policy.[22]

The McCarran Amendment leaves many procedural questions unresolved. For example, it remains unclear whether the consent to joinder extends to state administrative proceedings. Also, although it has been established that an Indian water rights adjudication in federal court may be dismissed if a state adjudication is initiated during an "early" stage of the federal proceeding, it is not certain at what stage a federal adjudication becomes developed sufficiently to avoid dismissal in deference to a later initiated state proceeding.

POLLUTION CONTROL

Public alarm over pollution problems provoked a series of sweeping federal statutes beginning in the 1970s and continuing to the present. One major theme in these modern environmental laws has been the congressional delegation of authority to the states so that substantial enforcement authority to achieve federal standards will lie at the local level. Since the 1980s, however, Congress has recognized that tribes are the appropriate local governments in Indian Country. Accordingly, several environmental programs now provide that tribes are treated as states and may administer these major initiatives.

The Clean Water Act[23] established the National Pollutant Discharge Elimination System (NPDES) to regulate discharges of pollutants from "point sources," that is, pipes, canals, and other discrete sources that discharge pollutants. Tribes now are eligible to receive grants for waste water treatment and to plan and operate their own regulatory programs. A challenge was raised when the EPA approved tribal water quality standards under the Clean Water Act. (For text of Clean Water Act, *see* Part Three.) The issue involved water quality standards of the Pueblo of Isleta, which had the effect of regulating effluent discharges by the City of Albuquerque, five miles upstream. The Tenth Circuit Court of Appeals upheld the Pueblo and EPA action, given the language of the statute and inherent tribal sovereignty.[24]

Tribes also are recognized as governments eligible for funding and regulatory authority under the Safe Drinking Water Act,[25] the Federal Insecticide, Fungicide, and Rodenticide Act (FIFRA),[26] the Clean Air Act (CAA), the Resources Conservation and Recovery Act (RCRA),[27] and the Comprehensive Environmental Response, Compensation, and Liability Act (CERCLA or "Superfund"),[28] providing for clean-up activities and the recovery of damages resulting from hazardous wastes. More and more tribes either have been granted regulatory control under these environmental statutes by EPA or are petitioning the agency for regulatory authority. The recognition of tribal sovereignty and the treatment of tribes as states in these high-priority national initiatives is one of the clearest indications of the major responsibilities accorded to Indian governments in the federal system.

TRIBAL WATER MANAGEMENT

Tribal administrative capabilities have become more elaborate in modern times and that development, coupled with a rapidly growing complexity of water and environmental law, has caused tribes to expand their management of water resources. Water management programs include the preliminary determination of the priority that ought to be accorded to water management; the creation of a resource inventory and a legal, economic, and political assessment; the design of a water management system; and the implementation and enforcement of a tribal water policy through a code and an administrative agency. The result ought to be a practical, integrated system that coordinates water quantity and water quality considerations; takes account of the impacts of activities such as timber harvesting, grazing, and farming; sets priorities among water needs for domestic, industrial, wildlife, and religious purposes; and provides for fair administration of the agreed plan.

Tribes have faced obstacles in developing comprehensive water programs. The states—even though they themselves have done little to pursue true comprehensive watershed management—regularly oppose tribal initiatives in the contentious area of water. The extensively-funded federal reclamation program mostly excluded tribes. As a result, although the situation is improving, historically the tribes have lacked the funding either to build water projects or to develop their own management programs. As the American Indian Resources Institute explained in its book on tribal water management, however, there are actually some advantages to be found in such a situation:

> In one sense ... the current lack of water facilities in Indian Country can be viewed as an opportunity. In planning future water projects, tribes can engage in comprehensive, environmentally conscious watershed planning that has seldom been employed by federal or state agencies for water projects in the past. Thus, although Indian tribes and their water managers face a substantial shortage of funding, they have the chance to ensure that future water projects are done right.[29]

TRIBAL FOREST MANAGEMENT

There is a striking potential for managed Indian forests to serve as models of sustainability. Reservations are permanent homelands where Indians live intimately with the environmental and economic conse-quences of forest-management actions.... They have a well recognized commitment to protect the resources that are both their heritage and their legacy.

— Indian Forest Management Assessment Team, John Gordon, Dean of the Yale Forestry School, Chairman (1993)[30]

Non-Indians have a fondness for the written word, for laws, regula-tions, and plans. If it's not on paper, it doesn't count. But that's usually not the Indian way. A coordinated management plan is more than a piece of paper. It's an attitude. To respect and honor the earth, its plants, and creatures, in thought and action. To adapt and change. To use the best that science and technology have to offer and discard the rest. To know that all things are interconnected, yet to have the will and the courage to make tough choices, understanding that the future of their children and grandchildren lies in the balance. That's really what it's all about.

— Gary Morishima (1998)[31]

Traditionally, the Bureau of Indian Affairs managed the millions of acres of forest lands held by some 97 timber-owning tribes. On many reservations, high-yield practices led to severe environmental damage. Now, nearly all of those tribes manage their own lands under the self-determination legislation and the National Indian Forest Resources Management Act of 1990.[32] Although funding levels remain unacceptably low, modern tribes are managing their timber lands on a sustained-yield basis with broad-based tribal participation to assure that wildlife habitat and traditional values are protected fully.[33]

HUNTING AND FISHING RIGHTS

Hunting for subsistence purposes is common among reservation Indians. Deer and elk are migratory animals and cross-jurisdictional conflicts arise as herds move from tribal to public, state and private lands.

A growing number of tribes are stocking and managing big game herds in order to provide improved hunting for tribal members and to attract non-Indians to the reservation for recreation. In the Pacific Northwest and the Great Lakes area, Indian tribes have become embroiled in controversies over salmon, steelhead and lake trout. Most of these fish are sold for commercial purposes by Indian fishers, but the subsistence and ceremonial value is also significant.

ON-RESERVATION RIGHTS

Indians in Indian Country normally can hunt and fish free of state control.[34] Several cases have considered the question of whether non-Indians hunting and fishing on the reservation with tribal licenses are required to purchase state licenses also. This issue is similar to that of dual taxation: if non-Indians are required to pay double license fees (often very substantial for deer and elk), they may not come to the reservation at all, thus crippling tribal recreational programs.

The federal courts generally have struck down the state license fees. In its 1983 decision in *New Mexico v. Mescalero Apache Tribe*, the Supreme Court upheld the exclusive authority of the tribe to regulate non-Indian hunting and fishing on the reservation.[35] (For text of opinion, *see* Part Four.)

OFF-RESERVATION RIGHTS

In the Pacific Northwest, many treaties provide for off-reservation fishing rights: they often guarantee the "right of taking fish, at usual and accustomed grounds and stations … in common with all citizens of the territory." The states have argued that the treaty provisions allow tribes access to their usual and accustomed places, but permit no special rights beyond that. The tribes have believed that "in common with" guarantees them half of the resource and allows tribal fishers to fish under tribal, not state, regulations. A long line of court decisions has accepted the tribal view of expansive off-reservation rights.

In the 1974 "Boldt decision," a federal district court judge in the State of Washington ruled that the tribes possess the right to harvest up to 50 percent of the salmon and steelhead at their off-reservation sites. Sit-ins and demonstrations by vocal non-Indians, including sports and commercial fishermen, followed. On several occasions, the federal courts openly criticized the State of Washington for disobeying the Boldt decision. Finally, the case went to the Supreme Court, which, in *Washington v. Washington State Commercial Passenger Fishing Vessel Association* (1979) (for text of opinion, *see* Part Four), upheld almost all aspects of the Boldt decision.[36] In 1998, a federal court held that the Pacific Northwest treaties provided for the harvesting of shellfish, often on private lands.[37] In the Great Lakes, similar off-reservation fishing rights were upheld.[38] In *Minnesota v. Mille Lacs Band of Chippewa* (1999) (for text of opinion, *see* Part Four),[39] the Supreme Court held that the Mille Lacs Band's off-reservation hunting and fishing rights were not terminated upon Minnesota's statehood.

Tribal involvement in hunting and fishing issues has moved beyond establishing treaty rights to active management of the resources. Tribal wildlife programs have become large and sophisticated, and in many regions of the country are integral components of coordinated federal, tribal and state efforts to protect and enhance wildlife populations.

MINERAL LEASING

Indian reservations contain nearly 5 percent of the proven reserves of U.S. oil and gas, 30 percent of the strippable low-sulfur coal, and 50 to 60 percent of the uranium. Ownership of such large percentages of the country's energy resources makes the decisions of what to do with the resources of great importance to Indians and non-Indians alike.

STATUTES

Generally, federal statutes permit the leasing of tribal and allotted lands for resource development.[40] In 1938 the Omnibus Leasing Act[41] was passed, providing comprehensive legislation governing the leasing of tribal lands for mining purposes and repealing all earlier inconsistent legislation. This Act allows tribal councils to enter into mineral leases for a period not to exceed 10 years subject to secretarial approval. Sales of mineral rights must be by public auction or sealed bid. The Act, however, allows exceptions to this requirement: the Secretary, with tribal council consent, may negotiate a lease without competitive bidding, and tribes organized under the IRA may lease lands in accordance with the provisions of their constitutions or charters.

In 1982, Congress enacted a reform measure, the Indian Mineral Development Act.[42] The Act authorizes tribes to enter into various types of commercial agreements (joint venture, operating, production sharing, service, managerial, lease, or other agreements) for the development and sale of their mineral resources. The Act is meant to further self-determination and to maximize financial return for tribes by allowing them greater flexibility in determining the type of agreements they will enter into for the development of tribal mineral resources.

ENVIRONMENTAL IMPACTS AND REGULATION

The EPA, in a policy statement issued in December 1980, held that federal environmental standards apply to Indian tribes. In *Nance v. Environmental Protection Agency* (9th Cir. 1981),[43] however, the Ninth Circuit Court of Appeals held that states possess no jurisdiction over the reservation environment since the requisite explicit congressional consent for state authority is not contained in the federal environmental laws.[44] (*See* discussion of pollution control in this chapter *at* p. 69.) Under the decision in *Davis v. Morton* (10th Cir. 1972),[45] the National Environmental Policy Act (NEPA) is applicable to major development activities on Indian lands when some federal funding or approval is involved.

TAXATION

The right of tribes to tax non-Indian mineral development on tribal land was upheld by the Supreme Court in *Merrion v. Jicarilla Apache Tribe* (1982) and *Kerr-McGee Corp. v. Navajo Tribe of Indians* (1985).[46] (For text of *Merrion* and *Kerr-McGee* opinions, *see* Part Four.) It also is now clear that state taxes on tribal mineral lease royalties will be struck down absent congressional consent.[47] The Supreme Court decided in *Cotton Petroleum Corp. v. New Mexico* (1989)[48] that New Mexico was not preempted by federal law, nor precluded by the imposition of tribal taxes, from levying state severance taxes against a non-Indian oil and gas company operating on the reservation. The Court reasoned that states have an interest in imposing nondiscriminatory severance taxes on non-Indian lessees where Congress has not explicitly or impliedly preempted the tax. The Court's decision in *Cotton Petroleum* potentially harms economic development in Indian Country, as the possibility of double state and tribal taxation might deter investors from the reservations. The scope of the holding, however, remains to be seen since the *Cotton Petroleum* decision was based on the 1938 Omnibus Leasing Act, rather than the 1982 Indian Mineral Development Act, which is intended to further tribal self-determination.

TRIBAL ECONOMIC DEVELOPMENT

The effect of recent state tax policies has been to place limits on the ability of the tribes to raise their taxes. In setting up their initial tax programs, many tribes started their tax rates low and have kept them low so as not to force an exodus of taxpayers off the reservations. The goal was to stimulate reservation economies. The states, on the other hand, have been steadily raising their tax rates. Now, as tribes find it necessary to raise their taxes, it is the tribes who are portrayed as ... taxing excessively, affecting marginal production, and businesses ... decide to look elsewhere....

This is all the more ironic when you stop and realize that many reservation enterprises are generating tax revenues for the state far in excess of the basic services that come back. At the same time, it is a documented fact that [the tribes are] suffering a drain of economic wealth and depletion of their resources.

— Susan M. Williams (1990)[49]

Tribes are pursuing the increased economic development opportunities on the reservations in various fashions. They can, for example, establish tribal business corporations as business arms of the tribe; allow tribal members and non-Indians to charter private corporations under tribal law, much as is done under state corporate codes; encourage non-Indian businesses, chartered under the law of a state, to do business in Indian Country; and regulate and tax businesses within reservation boundaries. All of these activities have come into play increasingly as the added responsibilities brought by the self-determination era cause the tribes to address high unemployment and poverty levels in Indian Country.[50]

Tribal decisions concerning economic development commonly raise questions of the extent, type, and speed of economic development and may require a determination of whether the tribe or its members will operate reservation business enterprises. The answers to these questions rest on the emphasis individual tribes place on traditional views that advocate subsistence endeavors and resist the exploitation of the land through economic development. (*See discussion in* this chapter *at* p. 64.) The opposing view endorses tribal economic development and sees the intensive use of tribal natural resources as necessary for the tribe's future. Ultimately, the best answer to tribal economic development questions will depend on the dynamics of each tribe and likely will fall somewhere between these two extreme viewpoints.[51]

Development of Indian land must occur in a context considerably different than is the case with other lands in the United States. Because of the federal-tribal trust relationship, and because the title to Indian trust lands and natural resources is held by the United States, such land and resources cannot be sold absent express federal approval. This situation has necessitated the formulation of a leasing scheme that permits tribal economic development of trust lands.[52] One remaining problem that stems from the trust status of tribal lands is that trust lands may not be mortgaged or otherwise used by tribes as collateral to obtain operating capital.

Another legal consideration is tribal sovereign immunity. Absent an effective waiver, a tribal sovereign is immune from suit when functioning within its governmental capacity. Outside business interests, however, are reluctant to deal with businesses when, for example, no remedy for a breached contract exists. Therefore it generally is necessary for tribes who own and operate business enterprises to agree that the tribally-owned businesses may sue and be sued; often such agreements contain conditions, such as that any suits must be brought in tribal court. When the enterprise is owned and operated by a tribal member, a different situation is presented. Here, the tribal member, who has no claim to sovereign immunity, ultimately is liable for the business' dealings.

Tribes are pursuing many different kinds of economic development programs. Employment programs, designed to increase on-reservation jobs and improve job skills of individual Indians, have been created federally and tribally.[53] Similarly, several federal programs encourage tribal economic development by providing funds to Indian enterprises and financial incentives to outside business interests.[54] The effectiveness of the latter programs, however, has been hindered by improper implementation, including inadequate technical assistance and business counseling.[55] In some cases, the Tribal Tax Status Act of 1982 may provide tribes a favored tax status, including the right to issue bonds for "essential governmental functions" similar but not identical to economic development bonds that can be issued by states for quasi-public or purely private business ventures.[56] As a general matter, some businesses may find investment in Indian Country to be attractive because state tax laws may be inapplicable.

TRIBAL GAMING

Indian gaming is an important and developing source of income for tribes that desperately need enhanced funding to bolster inadequate social services on the reservations. In 1987, the Supreme Court opened the door for tribes to establish high stakes casinos free from state regulation in *California v. Cabazon Band of Mission Indians* (1987). (For text of the opinion *see* Part Four.) As a response to *Cabazon*, Congress passed the Indian Gaming Regulatory Act in 1988 (IGRA). (For text of the statute *see* Part Three.) Although IGRA somewhat limits the scope of the *Cabazon* opinion, the Act sets forth explicit procedural requirements for the implementation of Indian gaming. IGRA also establishes a National Indian Gaming Commission to regulate gaming under the Act. IGRA sets forth three classes of tribal gaming and requires that tribes negotiate compacts with the states if they wish to implement Class III gaming (this includes high stakes games, such as blackjack, baccarat, and slot machines).[57]

Although IGRA requires that states compact with the tribes in good faith, the Supreme Court decision in *Seminole Tribe of Florida v. Florida* (1996),[58] held that "notwithstanding Congress' clear intent in the IGRA to abrogate the states' sovereign immunity, the Indian Commerce Clause does not grant the power to do so." Thus, the Eleventh Amendment protects the states from being sued in order to compel them to adhere to IGRA's good-faith negotiating requirement. There is, however, the potential for a stalemate because the tribes are protected by their own sovereign immunity from suits by the states.

While tribal gaming enterprises have been lucrative for some tribes (Indian gaming generated more than $12 billion in total revenues in 2002, approximately 10 percent of the Nation's total gambling revenue) and bolstered many tribal economies, the perception that all Indians have become instantly wealthy is simply not true. Most gaming enterprises provide only modest returns—revenues that are used primarily to support essential tribal government services and needs. The majority of the reservations are too remote to support successful gaming operations. The erroneous perceptions surrounding Indian gaming also have opened up the tribes to attacks from certain political quarters. For example, in 1997 former U.S. Senator Slade Gorton of Washington proposed the implementation of "needs-based" analysis for tribes to receive federal funding.[59] Likewise, in 1998 Senator Gorton introduced legislation that would have stripped tribes of their sovereign immunity.[60]

CONCLUSION

I wish we were managing thirty years before Judge Boldt issued his ruling in '74 [upholding tribal rights to manage fisheries]. I wish we had co-management then. We might have been able to use the treaties and our professionals back when we really needed it.

But we do have that decision and it gives us a chance. We're the advocates for the salmon, the animals, the birds, the water. We're the advocates for the food chain. We're an advocate for all of society. Tell them about our life. Put out the story of our lives, and how we live with the land, and how they're our neighbors. And how you have to respect your neighbors and work with your neighbors.

So what you do is, you do what you can in your lifetime. Then that'll go on to another lifetime. Then another lifetime. Then another.

— Billy Frank, Jr. (2000)[61]

Since the mid-19th century, economic development and natural resource management in Indian Country has been very limited—and what little activity existed was directed mostly by the Bureau of Indian Affairs. In modern times tribes have asserted self-determination. There is a keen awareness in Indian Country that tribal governments must control the development of reservation economies. The extent to which tribes can utilize their land and other natural resources, and the potential of economic enterprises such as gaming and tourism, to achieve steady economic growth while preserving reservation environments and traditions will be a central determinant in the kind of societies that will exist in Indian Country in the decades to come.

REFERENCE NOTES

CHAPTER 1

1. *The Spanish Origin of Indian Rights in the Law of the United States*, 31 GEO. L.J. 1, 17 (1942).

2. *See, e.g.*, FELIX S. COHEN'S HANDBOOK OF FEDERAL INDIAN LAW 50-58 (1982). The French may have had a somewhat different view than the English, Spanish, and Dutch. *Id.* at 54 n.38. The leading authority on federal Indian law and policy is, F. Prucha, THE GREAT FATHER: THE UNITED STATES GOVERNMENT AND THE AMERICAN INDIAN (1984) (two volumes). Father Prucha's history also has been released in an abridged one-volume version.

3. *Worcester v. Georgia*, 31 U.S. (6 Pet.) 515, 551 (1832).

4. H.R. Exec. Doc. No. 102, 22d Cong., 1st Sess. 3 (1832).

5. *Quoted in* M. BEAL, "I WILL FIGHT NO MORE FOREVER": CHIEF JOSEPH AND THE NEZ PERCE WAR (1963).

6. 21 U.S. (8 Wheat.) 543 (1823).

7. 30 U.S. (5 Pet.) 1 (1831).

8. 31 U.S. (6 Pet.) 515 (1832).

9. *See* F. Prucha, AMERICAN INDIAN POLICY IN THE FORMATIVE YEARS (1962).

10. 25 U.S.C. § 177. *See County of Oneida v. Oneida Indian Nation*, 470 U.S. 226 (1985); Clinton and Hotopp, *Judicial Enforcement of the Federal Restraints on Alienation of the Indian Land*, 31 MAINE L. REV. 17 (1979).

11. 21 U.S. (8 Wheat.) 543 (1823).

12. *Tee-Hit-Ton Indians v. United States*, 348 U.S. 272 (1955).

13. *See, e.g., United States v. Creek Nation*, 295 U.S. 103 (1935).

14. Treaty of Dancing Rabbit Creek with the Choctaw Nation, Sept. 27, 1830, 7 Stat. 333, letter from Andrew Jackson in Journal of Proceedings connected with the Negotiation of a Treaty (Aug. 23, 1830).

15. *Cherokee Nation v. Georgia*, 30 U.S. (5 Pet.) 1 (1831).

16. *Williams v. Lee*, 358 U.S. 217 (1959). *See discussion in* Chapter 2, pp. 37-39, "Tribal Civil Jurisdiction over Non-Indians in Indian Country."

17. *United States v. Winans*, 198 U.S. 371 (1905).

18. *See, e.g., Antoine v. Washington*, 420 U.S. 194 (1975).

19. *See, e.g., Arizona v. California*, 373 U.S. 546 (1963).

20. *See, e.g., United States v. Dion*, 476 U.S. 734 (1986); *Squire v. Capoeman*, 351 U.S. 1 (1956).

21. *Lone Wolf v. Hitchcock*, 187 U.S. 553 (1903).

22. *See* FELIX S. COHEN'S HANDBOOK OF FEDERAL INDIAN LAW 62-70 (1982).

23. *See* G. Foreman, INDIAN REMOVAL (1932).

24. *United States v. John*, 437 U.S. 634 (1978).

25. 25 U.S.C. § 71.

26. *See generally Antoine v. Washington*, 420 U.S. 194 (1975).

27. *United States v. Kagama*, 118 U.S. 375, 383 (1886).

28. 18 U.S.C. § 1151.

29. *Quoted in* D.S. Otis, The Dawes Act and the Allotment of Indian Lands 9 (F. Prucha ed., 1973).

30. *Quoted in* S.L. Tyler, A History of Indian Policy 104 (1973).

31. *See generally* D.S. Otis, The Dawes Act and the Allotment of Indian Lands (F. Prucha ed., 1973).

32. *See generally* A. Debo, And Still the Waters Run (1972).

33. 18 U.S.C. § 1153.

34. 18 U.S.C. § 1401(b).

35. "The Indian New Deal, 1928-1945" *in* Indian Self-Rule 14 (Institute of the American West, 1983).

36. The Indian in America 254 (1975).

37. *See generally* Institute for Government Research, The Problem of Indian Administration (L. Meriam ed., 1928) (commonly referred to as the Meriam Report).

38. 25 U.S.C. §§ 461-479.

39. 25 U.S.C. § 476 (Section 16).

40. 25 U.S.C. § 477 (Section 17).

41. *See generally* Comment, *Tribal Self-Government and the Indian Reorganization Act of 1934*, 70 Mich. L. Rev. 955 (1972). On John Collier, the primary mover behind the IRA, *see* K.R. Philip, John Collier's Crusade for Indian Reform (1977).

42. *See* S.L. Tyler, A History of Indian Policy 95-124 (1973).

43. *Quoted in* D. Getches and C. Wilkinson, Cases and Materials on Federal Indian Law 130 (1986).

44. *Hearings on H.R. 7421, Before the Subcomm. on Indian Affairs*, 93d Cong., 1st Sess. 32-36 (1973).

45. 25 U.S.C. §§ 70-70v.

46. *See* Danforth, *Repaying Historical Debts: The Indian Claims Commission*, 49 N.D.L. Rev. 359 (1973).

47. *See generally* Wilkinson and Biggs, *The Evolution of the Termination Policy*, 5 Am. Ind. L. Rev. 139 (1977).

48. *See, e.g., Menominee Tribe of Indians v. United States*, 391 U.S. 404 (1968).

49. *See, e.g.*, the Menominee Restoration Act of 1973, 25 U.S.C. §§ 903-903f.

50. *See* Goldberg, *Public Law 280, The Limits of State Jurisdiction Over Reservation Indians*, 22 UCLA L. Rev. 535 (1975).

51. V. Deloria, Jr., "Revision and Reversion" *in* The American Indian and the Problem of History (Calvin Martin, ed., 1987).

52. W. Mankiller, Mankiller: A Chief and Her People 192-193 (2000).

53. 25 U.S.C. §§ 1301-1303 (also codified in scattered sections of 18 U.S.C. and 28 U.S.C.).

54. 43 U.S.C. §§ 1601-1628.

55. *See generally* Lazarus and West, *The Alaska Native Claims Settlement Act: A Flawed Victory*, 40 Law and Contemp. Prob. 132 (1976).

56. 25 U.S.C. §§ 450a-450n.

57. 25 U.S.C. §§ 450b, 450c, 450e, 450f, 450j-*l*, 450k to 450m-*l*, 450n.

58. D. Getches, C. Wilkinson and R. Williams, Jr., Cases and Materials on Federal Indian Law 231 (4th ed., 1998).

59. *See, e.g.*, Rosenfelt, *Toward a More Coherent Policy for Funding Indian Education*, 40 Law and Contemp. Prob. 190 (1976).

60. Pub. L. No. 94-437, 90 Stat. 1400 (codified at 25 U.S.C. §§ 1601-1603, 1611-1615, 1621, 1631-1633, 1651-1658, 1661, 1671-1675, 42 U.S.C. §§ 1395f, 1395n, 1395qq, 1396j).

61. 25 U.S.C. §§ 1901-1963.

62. *See* 42 U.S.C. § 1996.

63. 485 U.S. 439 (1988).

64   25 U.S.C. §§ 2701-2721.

65. D. Getches, C. Wilkinson and R. Williams, Jr., Cases and Materials on Federal Indian Law 232 (4th ed., 1998).

66. 25 U.S.C. §§ 3001-3013.

67. 25 U.S.C. §§ 2201-2211.

68. 25 U.S.C. §§ 2802-2809.

69. D. Getches, C. Wilkinson and R. Williams, Jr., Cases and Materials on Federal Indian Law 231 (4th ed., 1998).

70. *See* D. Getches, C. Wilkinson and R. Williams, Jr., Cases and Materials on Federal Indian Law 226-228 (4th ed., 1998).

71. President Reagan's Statement on American Indian Policy, 19 Weekly Comp. Pres. Doc. 98-102 (Jan. 24, 1983).

72. "Proposed Budget for FY 1996 to Indian Programs" (Press Release: Executive Office of the President, 1995).

73. *National Farmers Union Ins. Co. v. Crow Tribe of Indians*, 471 U.S. 845 (1985); *Iowa Mutual Insurance Co. v. LaPlante*, 480 U.S. 9 (1987).

74. *Babbitt Ford, Inc. v. Navajo Indian Tribe*, 710 F.2d 587 (9th Cir. 1983), *cert. denied*, 466 U.S. 926 (1984) (tribal court civil jurisdiction extends to repossession action brought by non-Indians against tribal members).

75. *See generally* Felix S. Cohen's Handbook of Federal Indian Law 770-75 (1982); David S. Case, Alaska Natives and American Laws (2d ed., 2001).

76. *See, e.g.*, *Cheyenne-Arapaho Tribes v. Oklahoma*, 618 F.2d 665 (10th Cir. 1980).

77. 43 U.S.C. §§ 1601-1628.

78. *See generally* Felix S. Cohen's Handbook of Federal Indian Law 739-70 (1982); on Hawaiian Natives, *see generally* Native Hawaiian Rights Handbook (1991) (MacKenzie ed.).

79. 16 U.S.C. §§ 3101-3133.

80. *See* FELIX S. COHEN'S HANDBOOK OF FEDERAL INDIAN LAW 758-61 (1982).

81. 522 U.S. 520 (1998).

82. 42 Stat. 108, ch. 42.

83. *See generally* D. Getches, C. Wilkinson and R. Williams, Jr., CASES AND MATERIALS ON FEDERAL INDIAN LAW 952-956 (4th ed., 1998). For an example of a case in which a group of Hawaiian Natives sought federal recognition, *see Price v. Hawaii*, 764 F.2d 623 (9th Cir. 1985), *cert. denied sub nom. Hou Hawaiians v. Hawaii*, 474 U.S. 1055 (1986).

84. Pub. L. 103-150, 107 Stat. 1510 (1993).

85. D. Getches, C. Wilkinson and R. Williams, Jr., CASES AND MATERIALS ON FEDERAL INDIAN LAW 951 (4th ed., 1998).

86. *Id.*

87. 528 U.S. 495 (2000).

88. THE STATES AND THEIR INDIAN CITIZENS 125, 130 (1972).

89. THEY CAME HERE FIRST 285 (1949).

CHAPTER 2

1. AMERICAN INDIANS, TIME, AND THE LAW 103-04 (1987).

2. *See Joint Tribal Council of Passamaquoddy Tribe v. Morton*, 528 F.2d 370 (1st Cir. 1975).

3. 25 C.F.R. 83.

4. Pascua Yaqui Recognition Act, September 18, 1978, Pub. L. No. 95-375, 95 Stat. 712 (codified at 25 U.S.C.A. §§ 1300f to 1300f-2).

5. *Delaware Indians v. Cherokee Nation*, 193 U.S. 127 (1904).

6. *See Zarr v. Barlow*, 800 F.2d 1484, 1485, n.1 (9th Cir. 1986).

7. *Zarr v. Barlow*, 800 F.2d 1484 (9th Cir. 1986); *see also* 25 C.F.R. § 20.1(n) (1986).

8. *See Zarr v. Barlow*, 800 F.2d at 1489-93.

9. *DeCoteau v. District County Court*, 420 U.S. 425, 427 n.2 (1975). *See also Moe v. Confederated Salish and Kootenai Tribes*, 425 U.S. 463, 478-79 (1976).

10. *United States v. Chavez*, 290 U.S. 357 (1933).

11. *See Alaska v. Native Village of Venetie Tribal Government*, 522 U.S. 520 (1998).

12. *See, e.g., Solem v. Bartlett*, 465 U.S. 463 (1984) (portion of Cheyenne River Sioux Reservation not disestablished); *DeCoteau v. District County Court*, 420 U.S. 425 (1975) (Lake Traverse Sioux Reservation disestablished).

13. F. Cohen, HANDBOOK OF FEDERAL INDIAN LAW 122 (1942).

14. *See, e.g., United States v. Winans*, 198 U.S. 371 (1905).

15. *United States v. Wheeler*, 435 U.S. 313 (1978).

16. FELIX S. COHEN'S HANDBOOK OF FEDERAL INDIAN LAW 232-35 (1982).

17. 435 U.S. 191 (1978).

18. *Montana v. United States*, 450 U.S. 544 (1981); *Atkinson Trading Co. v. Shirley*, 532 U.S. 645 (2001). *See discussion in* this chapter, pp. 37-39, "Tribal Civil Jurisdiction over Non-Indians in Indian Country."

19. 455 U.S. 130, 148 (1982).

20. *See Santa Clara Pueblo v. Martinez*, 436 U.S. 49, 62-63 (1978); *see also Pueblo of Santa Rosa v. Fall*, 273 U.S. 315 (1927).

21. *See Talton v. Mayes*, 163 U.S. 376 (1896); *United States v. Wheeler*, 435 U.S. 313 (1978).

22. 55 INTERIOR DEPARTMENT 14 (1934); *see also Washington v. Confederated Tribes of the Colville Indian Reservation*, 447 U.S. 134, 152-54 (1980).

23. *Kerr-McGee Corp. v. Navajo Tribe of Indians*, 471 U.S. 195 (1985).

24. 436 U.S. 49 (1978).

25. *See generally* Funke, *Educational Assistance and Employment Preference: Who is an Indian?*, 4 AM. IND. L. REV. 1, 29-30 (1976).

26. *See* American Indian Lawyer Training Program, Inc., INDIAN TRIBES AS GOVERNMENTS (1975).

27. *See Jones v. Meehan*, 175 U.S. 1 (1899).

28. *Brendale v. Confederated Tribes and Bands of Yakima Indian Nation*, 492 U.S. 408 (1989).

29. *Barta v. Oglala Sioux Tribe*, 259 F.2d 553 (8th Cir. 1958).

30. *Morris v. Hitchcock*, 194 U.S. 384 (1904).

31. *Washington v. Confederated Tribes of the Colville Indian Reservation*, 447 U.S. 134 (1980).

32. *Kerr-McGee Corp. v. Navajo Tribe of Indians*, 471 U.S. 195 (1985); *Merrion v. Jicarilla Apache Tribe*, 455 U.S. 130 (1982).

33. *See, e.g., Ex Parte Crow Dog*, 109 U.S. 556 (1883); *United States v. Wheeler*, 435 U.S. 313 (1978).

34. 435 U.S. 191 (1978).

35. The case denying jurisdiction over non-member Indians is *Duro v. Reina*, 495 U.S. 676 (1990). The congressional override was codified as an amendment to the Indian Civil Rights Act. *See* 25 U.S.C. §§ 1301(2), 1301(4). The case upholding the congressional override is *United States v. Lara*, 124 S. Ct. 1628 (2004).

36. *See* American Indian Lawyer Training Program, Inc., INDIAN SELF-DETERMINATION AND THE ROLE OF TRIBAL COURTS (1975); American Indian Lawyer Training Program, Inc., JUSTICE IN INDIAN COUNTRY (1980).

37. *Hardin v. White Mountain Apache Tribe*, 779 F.2d 476 (9th Cir. 1985). *See* Article 5 of Treaty with Wiandots, Jan. 21, 1785, 7 Stat. 16. *See also Worcester v. Georgia*, 31 U.S. (6 Pet.) 515 (1832).

38. *See, e.g.*, 55 INTERIOR DEPARTMENT 14, 48-50 (1934).

39. *United States v. Montana*, 604 F.2d 1162, 1167-69 (9th Cir. 1979), *rev'd on other grounds*, 450 U.S. 544 (1981).

40. *United States v. White Mountain Apache Tribe*, 784 F.2d 917 (9th Cir. 1986).

41. Memo. Sol. Int., Mar. 6, 1937, *reprinted in* 1 Opinions of the Solicitor of the Department of Interior Relating to Indian Affairs 1917-1974 at 758.

42. *See Morgan v. Colorado River Indian Tribe*, 103 Ariz. 425, 443 P.2d 421 (1968); Felix S. Cohen's Handbook of Federal Indian Law 390 n.11, 438-39 (1982).

43. *See, e.g., Atkinson v. Haldane*, 569 P.2d 151 (Alaska 1977).

44. 523 U.S. 751 (1998).

45. 523 U.S. 751 (1998).

46. *Puyallup Tribe v. Department of Game*, 391 U.S. 392 (1968).

47. *Oliphant v. Suquamish Indian Tribe*, 435 U.S. 191 (1978).

48. *Merrion v. Jicarilla Apache Tribe*, 455 U.S. 130 (1982).

49. Getches, *Beyond Indian Law: The Rehnquist Court's Pursuit of States' Rights, Color-Blind Justice and Mainstream Values*, 86 Minn. L. Rev. 260, 360-61 (2001).

50. *National Farmers Union Ins. Co. v. Crow Tribe of Indians*, 471 U.S. 845 (1985).

51. 450 U.S. 544 (1981).

52. 520 U.S. 438 (1997).

53. 532 U.S. 645 (2001).

54. 533 U.S. 353 (2001).

55. *Washington v. Confederated Tribes of the Colville Indian Reservation*, 447 U.S. 134 (1980).

56. 455 U.S. 130 (1982).

57. 471 U.S. 195 (1985).

58. 450 U.S. 544 (1981).

59. 532 U.S. 645 (2001).

60. 533 U.S. 353 (2001).

61. *Nevada v. Hicks*, 533 U.S. 353 (2001).

62. Treaty with the Cherokee Nation, February 27, 1819, 7 Stat. 195, Letter from Head Chief Path Killer in connection with Negotiation of Treaty (June 12, 1818).

63. *Washington v. Passenger Fishing Vessel Association*, 443 U.S. 658, 696 (1979) (Quoting from *Puget Sound Gillnetters Ass'n v. United States District Court*, 573 F.2d 1123, 1126 (9th Cir. 1978).

64. F. Pommersheim, Braid of Feathers: American Indian Law and Contemporary Tribal Life 161 (1995).

65. *Williams v. Lee*, 358 U.S. 217 (1959). *But see Oliphant v. Suquamish Indian Tribe*, 435 U.S. 191 (1978) (criminal jurisdiction over non-Indians).

66. *Mescalero Apache Tribe v. Jones*, 411 U.S. 145 (1973).

67. 411 U.S. 164 (1973). The basic authority of Congress to preempt state law is discussed in Felix S. Cohen's Handbook of Federal Indian Law 270-79 (1982).

68. 25 U.S.C. §§ 1321-1323. For the details of Public Law 280, *see* Felix S. Cohen's Handbook of Federal Indian Law 361-72 (1982).

69. *Bryan v. Itasca County*, 426 U.S. 373 (1976).

70. *See, e.g., Santa Rosa Band v. Kings County*, 532 F.2d 655 (9th Cir. 1975), *cert. denied*, 429 U.S. 1038 (1978).

71. 480 U.S. 202 (1987).

72. *See Walker v. Rushing*, 898 F.2d 672 (8th Cir. 1990); Felix S. Cohen's Handbook of Federal Indian Law 344, 367 (1982).

73. *See generally* Felix S. Cohen's Handbook of Federal Indian Law 335-41 (1982); D. Getches, C. Wilkinson and R. Williams, Jr., Cases and Materials on Federal Indian Law 531-543 (4th ed. 1998); American Indian Lawyer Training Program, Inc., An Introduction to Criminal Jurisdiction in Indian Country (1981).

74. *Fisher v. District Court*, 424 U.S. 382 (1976); *see, e.g., Williams v. Lee*, 358 U.S. 217 (1959) (contract case); *Kennerly v. District Court*, 400 U.S. 423 (1971) (contract case); *Schantz v. White Lightening*, 231 N.W.2d 812 (N.D. 1975) (automobile accident).

75. *Strate v. A-1 Contractors*, 520 U.S. 438 (1997).

76. *National Farmers Union Ins. Co. v. Crow Tribe of Indians*, 471 U.S. 845 (1985); *Iowa Mutual Insurance Co. v. LaPlante*, 480 U.S. 9 (1987).

77. 533 U.S. 353 (2001).

78. *See generally Francisco v. State*, 113 Ariz. 427, 556 P.2d 1 (1976); Felix S. Cohen's Handbook of Federal Indian Law 357-61 (1982). *But see Little Horn State Bank v. Stops*, 170 Mont. 510, 555 P.2d 211 (1976), *cert. denied*, 431 U.S. 924 (1977).

79. *In the Matter of Atkinson Trading Company, Inc.*, 24 Indian L. Rep. 6191 (Navajo Nation Sup. Ct. 1997).

80. *See McCulloch v. Maryland*, 17 U.S. (4 Wheat.) 316, 431 (1819).

81. *McClanahan v. Arizona State Tax Commission*, 411 U.S. 164 (1973).

82. *Moe v. Confederated Salish and Kootenai Tribes*, 425 U.S. 463 (1976).

83. *Bryan v. Itasca County*, 426 U.S. 373 (1976).

84. *Montana v. Blackfeet Tribe of Indians*, 471 U.S. 759 (1985).

85. *Mescalero Apache Tribe v. Jones*, 411 U.S. 145 (1973).

86. 463 U.S. 713 (1983).

87. 532 U.S. 645 (2001).

88. *Washington v. Confederated Tribes of the Colville Indian Reservation*, 447 U.S. 134 (1980).

89. 351 U.S. 1 (1956).

90. *See also Chickasaw Nation v. United States*, 534 U.S. 84 (2001).

91. *Holt v. Commissioner*, 364 F.2d 38 (8th Cir. 1966), *cert. denied*, 386 U.S. 931 (1967).

92. *Fry v. United States*, 557 F.2d 646 (9th Cir. 1977), *cert. denied*, 434 U.S. 1011 (1978).

93. *Karmun v. Commissioner*, 749 F.2d 567 (9th Cir. 1984), *cert. denied*, 474 U.S. 819 (1985). The Alaskan Natives subsequently went to Congress and gained an explicit exemption from federal taxes for reindeer-related income. *See* Tax Reform Act of 1986, Pub. L. No. 99-514, § 1709, 100 Stat. 2085, 2783 (1986).

94. *Talton v. Mayes*, 163 U.S. 376 (1896).

95. 25 U.S.C. §§ 1301-1326.

96. *Santa Clara Pueblo v. Martinez*, 436 U.S. 49 (1978).

97. 436 U.S. 49 (1978).

98. *National Farmers Union Ins. Co. v. Crow Tribe of Indians*, 471 U.S. 845 (1985).

99. *Indian Child Welfare Act of 1978*, 7 Am. Ind. L. Rev. 51 (1979).

100. 25 U.S.C. §§ 1901-1963.

101. *In the Matter of the Appeal in Pima County Juvenile Action No. S-903*, 130 Ariz. 202, 635 P.2d 187 (Ct. App. 1981), *cert. denied*, 455 U.S. 1007 (1982).

102. 25 U.S.C. § 1915(b).

103. *See Hearings Before the Senate Select Committee on Indian Affairs on S. 2502, The Tribal Compact Act*, 95th Cong., 2d Sess. 15-16 (1978).

104. *See, e.g., Smith v. Confederated Tribes of Warm Springs*, 783 F.2d 1409, 1412 (9th Cir.), *cert. denied*, 479 U.S. 964 (1986). *In re Marriage of Red Fox*, 23 Or. App. 393, 542 P.2d 918 (1975); *Begay v. Miller*, 70 Ariz. 380, 222 P.2d 624 (1950).

105. *See generally* Ragsdale, *Problems in the Application of Full Faith and Credit for Indian Tribes*, 7 N.M. L. Rev. 133 (1977); *compare Jim v. CIT Financial Services Corp.*, 87 N.M. 362, 533 P.2d 751 (1975) *with Brown v. Babbitt Ford Inc.*, 117 Ariz. 192, 571 P.2d 689 (1977).

Chapter 3

1. *Judicial Enforcement of the Federal Trust Responsibility to Indians*, 27 Stan. L. Rev. 1213 (1975).

2. *Navajo Ways in Government*, 65 Amer. Anthro. Assoc. 1, 113 (1963).

3. *Seminole Nation v. United States*, 316 U.S. 286, 296 (1942).

4. 441 U.S. 164, 172 n.7 (1973).

5. Wood, *Indian Land and the Promise of Native Sovereignty: The Trust Doctrine Revisited*, 1994 Utah L. Rev. 1471, 1567.

6. *See Cherokee Nation v. Georgia*, 30 U.S. (5 Pet.) 1, 17-18 (1831); *Worcester v. Georgia*, 31 U.S. (6 Pet.) 515 (1832); *United States v. Douglas*, 190 F. 482 (8th Cir. 1911).

7. *See also Johnson v. M'Intosh*, 21 U.S. (8 Wheat.) 543 (1823).

8. 118 U.S. 375 (1886).

9. 18 U.S.C. § 1153 (federal criminal statute punishing murder and other serious felonies committed by Indians against Indians).

10. *Affiliated Ute Citizens v. United States*, 406 U.S. 128 (1972).

11. *Lone Wolf v. Hitchcock*, 187 U.S. 553, 564-66 (1903).

12. 417 U.S. 535 (1974).

13. *See Antoine v. Washington*, 420 U.S. 194 (1975).

14. *See* Felix S. Cohen's Handbook of Federal Indian Law 3-19 (1982).

15. *Joint Tribal Council of Passamaquoddy v. Morton*, 388 F. Supp. 649 (D. Maine 1975), *aff'd*, 528 F.2d 370 (1st Cir. 1975). *See also Narragansett Tribe of Indians v. Southern Rhode Island Land Development Corp.*, 418 F. Supp. 798 (D.R.I. 1976).

16. *Quoted in* Chambers, *Judicial Enforcement of the Federal Trust Responsibility to Indians*, 27 STAN. L. REV. 1213, 1215 n.12 (1975).

17. *See Choate v. Trapp*, 224 U.S. 665, 678 (1912).

18. 187 U.S. 553, 565 (1903). *See also, e.g., Sioux Indians v. United States*, 277 U.S. 424, 437 (1928).

19. *Delaware Tribal Business Committee v. Weeks*, 430 U.S. 73 (1977); *United States v. Sioux Nation*, 448 U.S. 371 (1980).

20. 417 U.S. 535, 555 (1974).

21. *See, e.g., Bryan v. Itasca County*, 426 U.S. 373, 392 (1976); *Northern Cheyenne Tribe v. Hollowbreast*, 425 U.S. 649, 655, n.7 (1976); *Antoine v. Washington*, 420 U.S. 194 (1975); *United States v. Santa Fe Pac. Ry.*, 314 U.S. 339, 354 (1941).

22. *See, e.g., United States v. Dion*, 476 U.S. 734 (1986); *Rosebud Sioux Tribe v. Kneip*, 430 U.S. 584 (1977). *But see DeCoteau v. District County Court*, 420 U.S. 425 (1975).

23. *See, e.g., White v. Califano*, 581 F.2d 697 (8th Cir. 1978); *Eric v. H.U.D.*, 464 F. Supp. 44 (D. Alaska 1978).

24. *Seminole Nation v. United States*, 316 U.S. 286, 296, 297 (1942); *United States v. Payne*, 264 U.S. 446, 448 (1924).

25. *See Lane v. Pueblo of Santa Rosa*, 249 U.S. 110 (1919); *Cramer v. United States*, 261 U.S. 219 (1923); *United States v. Creek Nation*, 295 U.S. 103 (1935).

26. *See, e.g., Menominee Tribe v. United States*, 101 Ct. Cl. 10 (1944) (duty to make trust property productive); *Navajo Tribe v. United States*, 364 F. 2d 320 (Ct. Cl. 1966) (duty to manage mineral resources properly); *United States v. Mitchell*, 463 U.S. 206 (1983) (duty to manage forest resources properly on allotted lands).

27. *See United States v. White Mountain Apache Tribe*, 537 U.S. 465 (2003); *United States v. Navajo Nation*, 537 U.S. 488 (2003).

28. *See United States v. Mason*, 412 U.S. 391 (1973).

29. *But see Nevada v. United States*, 463 U.S. 110 (1983) (Pyramid Lake case).

30. *See Cobell v. Norton*, 240 F.3d 1081 (D.C. Cir. 2001).

31. *See* Chambers, *Judicial Enforcement of the Federal Trust Responsibility to Indians*, 27 STAN. L. REV. 1213, 1246 (1975).

32. *See, e.g., United States v. Winnebago Tribe*, 542 F.2d 1002 (8th Cir. 1976); *United States v. Southern Pacific Trans. Co.*, 543 F.2d 676 (9th Cir. 1976). *But see Seneca Nation of Indians v. United States*, 338 F.2d 55 (2d Cir. 1964), *cert. denied*, 380 U.S. 952 (1965); *Seneca Nation of Indians v. Brucher*, 262 F.2d 27 (D.C. Cir. 1958), *cert. denied*, 360 U.S. 909 (1959).

33. *Nevada v. United States*, 463 U.S. 110 (1983).

34. *Id.* at 143.

35. *Rincon Band of Mission Indians v. Escondido Mutual Water Co.*, 459 F.2d 1082 (9th Cir. 1972).

36. *Joint Tribal Council of Passamaquoddy v. Morton*, 388 F. Supp. 649, 655-66 (D. Maine), *aff'd*, 528 F.2d 370 (1st Cir. 1975).

37. 42 U.S.C. § 1996(a) (1994).

38. 485 U.S. 439 (1988).

39. 2 F. Supp. 2d 1448 (D. Wyo. 1998), *aff'd on other grounds*, 175 F.3d 814 (10th Cir. 1999).

40. *See Sherbert v. Verner*, 374 U.S. 398 (1963).

41. 494 U.S. 872 (1990).

42. 42 U.S.C. § 2000bb (1993).

43. 521 U.S. 507 (1997).

44. 25 U.S.C. §§ 3001-3013 (1990).

45. *See generally* D. Getches, C. Wilkinson, and R. Williams, Jr., CASES AND MATERIALS ON FEDERAL INDIAN LAW 789 (4th ed., 1998).

46. *See generally* FELIX S. COHEN'S HANDBOOK OF FEDERAL INDIAN LAW 528-44 (1982).

47. 471 U.S. 195 (1985).

CHAPTER 4

1. INSIDE U.S.A. (1975).

2. "The New Indian Wars," *Denver Post* (1984) (special reprint).

3. *Quoted in* American Indian Lawyer Training Program, Inc., INDIAN WATER POLICY IN A CHANGING ENVIRONMENT 2 (1982).

4. *See generally* Suagee, *American Indian Religious Freedom and Cultural Resources Management: Protecting Mother Earth's Caretakers*, 10 AM. INDIAN L. REV. 1 (1982).

5. Barsh, *The Illusion of Religious Freedom for Indigenous Americans*, 65 OR. L. REV. 363 (1986).

6. *United States v. Mitchell*, 463 U.S. 206 (1983). *But see United States v. Mitchell*, 445 U.S. 535 (1980).

7. 207 U.S. 564 (1908).

8. 373 U.S. 546 (1963).

9. *See United States v. New Mexico*, 438 U.S. 696 (1978).

10. 753 P.2d 76, *aff'd sub nom. Wyoming v. United States*, 492 U.S. 406 (1988).

11. *See In re General Stream Adjudication of All Rights to Use Water in the Gila River System and Source*, 195 Ariz. 411, 989 P.2d 739 (1999).

12. 43 U.S.C. § 666.

13. 424 U.S. 800 (1976) (*Akin* case).

14. 463 U.S. 545 (1983).

15. *See United States v. Adair*, 723 F.2d 1394 (9th Cir. 1983).

16. Special Master's Report, *Arizona v. California*, Feb. 22, 1982.

17. *See, e.g., Colville Confederated Tribes v. Walton*, 752 F.2d 397 (9th Cir. 1985), *cert. denied*, 475 U.S. 1010 (1986).

18. *See* Palma, *Transferability of Indian Water Rights*, 20 Nat. Res. J. 91 (1980); *see also,* Getches, *Colorado River Governance: Sharing Federal Authority as an Incentive to Create a New Institution*, 68 Colo. L. Rev. 573, 609-623 (1997).

19. Getches, *Water Rights on Indian Allotments*, 26 S.D. L. Rev. 405 (1981).

20. *Colville Confederated Tribes v. Walton*, 647 F.2d 42 (9th Cir.), *cert. denied*, 454 U.S. 1092 (1981). *But see United States v. Anderson*, 736 F.2d 1358 (9th Cir. 1984) (absent infringement or a consensual agreement between the parties, state may regulate use of excess waters by non-Indians on fee land); *Holly v. Confederated Tribes and Bands of the Yakima Indian Nation*, 655 F. Supp. 557 (E.D. Wash. 1985) (tribe does not have inherent power to regulate or administer non-Indian excess waters flowing through reservation), *aff'd sub nom. Holly v. Totus*, 812 F.2d 714 (9th Cir. 1987).

21. *See generally*, Williams, *Indian Winters Water Rights Administration: Averting a New War*, 11 Public Land L. Rev. 536 (1990).

22. *See generally*, L. Burton, American Indian Water Rights and the Limits of Law (1991); D. McCool, Command of the Waters (1994).

23. 33 U.S.C. §§ 1251-1376, as amended by Water Quality Act of 1987, 101 Stat. 7. The provisions relating to Indian tribes are in section 507, 101 Stat. 78.

24. *City of Albuquerque v. Browner*, 97 F.3d 415 (10th Cir. 1996), *cert. denied*, 522 U.S. 965 (1997).

25. 42 U.S.C. §§ 300j-11. EPA authority to delegate regulatory power to tribes was upheld in *Phillips Petroleum Co. v. United States Environmental Protection Agency*, 803 F.2d 545 (10th Cir. 1986).

26. 7 U.S.C. § 136(u).

27. 42 U.S.C. §§ 6901-6987. *See Washington Dep't of Ecology v. Environmental Protection Agency*, 752 F.2d 1465 (9th Cir. 1985).

28. 42 U.S.C. §§ 9601-9657.

29. American Indian Resources Institute, Tribal Water Management Handbook 8 (1987). *See also* Shupe, *Water in Indian Country: From Paper Rights to a Managed Resource*, 57 U. Colo. L. Rev. 561 (1986).

30. Indian Forest Management Assessment Team, *An Assessment of Indian Forests and Forest Management in the United States* (1993).

31. Morishima, Promises to Keep: Paradigms and Problems with Coordinated Resource Management in Indian Country, Evergreen, p. 22, 25 (1998).

32. 25 U.S.C. §§ 3101-3111.

33. *See generally* Journal of Forestry, Vol. 95, No. 11 (Nov. 1997), a full issue devoted to forestry on tribal lands.

34. *See, e.g., Menominee Tribe v. United States*, 391 U.S. 404 (1968).

35. 462 U.S. 324 (1983), *aff'g Mescalero Apache Tribe v. New Mexico*, 630 F.2d 724 (10th Cir. 1980), 677 F.2d 55 (10th Cir. 1982).

36. 443 U.S. 658, *modified in*, 444 U.S. 816 (1979).

37. *See United States v. Washington*, 157 F.3d 630 (9th Cir. 1998).

38. *See, e.g., United States v. Michigan*, 653 F.2d 277 (6th Cir. 1981).

39. 526 U.S. 172 (1999).

40. *See, e.g.*, 25 U.S.C. § 415.

41. Act of May 11, 1938, ch. 198, 52 Stat. 347 (codified as amended at 25 U.S.C. §§ 396a-396g).

42. Pub. L. No. 97-382 (formerly known as S. 1894) (codified as amended at 25 U.S.C. §§ 2101-2108).

43. 645 F.2d 701 (9th Cir. 1981).

44. *See generally* Felix S. Cohen's Handbook of Federal Indian Law 283-86 (1982).

45. 469 F.2d 593 (10th Cir. 1972).

46. *Merrion v. Jicarilla Apache Tribe*, 455 U.S. 130 (1982); *Kerr-McGee Corp. v. Navajo Tribe of Indians*, 471 U.S. 195 (1985).

47. *See Montana v. Blackfeet Tribe of Indians*, 471 U.S. 759 (1985).

48. 490 U.S. 163 (1989).

49. S. Williams, "A Vision for Indian Country" *in* Toward A National Indian Legislative Agenda for the 1990s 126, 129, American Indian Resources Institute (1992).

50. *See* Department of the Interior, *Report of the Task Force on Indian Economic Development* 6 (1986).

51. Haberfeld, Posner, Lee, Dewan, Adamson & Taylor, A Self-Help Manual for Tribal Economic Development 1-1–1-4 (1982) (prepared for the Indian Law Support Center of the Native American Rights Fund).

52. *See* 25 U.S.C. § 415 (a).

53. *See* Felix S. Cohen's Handbook of Federal Indian Law 724-28 (1982).

54. *See, e.g.*, 42 U.S.C. §§ 3121-3246(g) (Public Works and Economic Development Act of 1965); 25 U.S.C. §§ 1451-1543 (Indian Financing Act of 1974); 15 U.S.C. § 633 (Small Business Investment Act of 1958).

55. *See* Felix S. Cohen's Handbook of Federal Indian Law 723-24 (1982).

56. Tribal Tax Status Act, Pub. L. No. 97-473, 96 Stat. 2607 (codified as amended at 26 U.S.C. § 7871 and scattered sections of 26 U.S.C. *See generally* Williams, *Small Steps on the Long Road to Indian Self-Sufficiency: The Indian Tribal Governmental Tax Status Act of 1982*, 22 Harv. J. on Legis. 335 (1985).

57. *See generally* Tourism and Gaming on American Indian Lands (Lew & Van Otten eds., 1998); D. Getches, C. Wilkinson and R. Williams, Jr., Cases and Materials on Federal Indian Law 739-753 (4th ed., 1998).

58. 517 U.S. 44 (1996).

59. Scott Sonner, *In Funding Some Tribes are More Equal Than Others*, Seattle Times (Sept. 2, 1997).

60. American Indian Equal Justice Act, S. 1691 (introduced Feb. 27, 1998).

61. *Quoted in* C. Wilkinson, Messages from Frank's Landing: A Story of Salmon, Treaties, and the Indian Way 103-104 (2000).

PART TWO

The History of Treaty Negotiations Between the United States and Indian Tribes; Selected Treaty and Executive Order

INTRODUCTION

Part Two provides a brief narrative history of treaty negotiations between the United States and Indian tribes. Following the historical narrative, an example of a treaty and an executive order are provided. Before Congress ended Indian treaty making in 1871, over 380 treaties were negotiated with the tribes. Moreover, 99 executive order reservations were created, totaling over 20 million acres.

The treaty and executive order included here were chosen because both have been involved in some of the more significant developments in Indian law and policy. The Treaty of Point Elliott provided the Supreme Court with the foundation to establish the reserved rights doctrine—that tribal rights were not granted to tribes by the United States; rather, tribes, as prior and continuing sovereigns, retained or reserved their rights. The Executive Order Establishing the Walker River Reservation was the basis for an early decision that executive order tribes have reserved water rights similar to those rights retained by tribes on reservations established by treaties and statutes.

Historical discussions of judicial interpretations of the Treaty of Point Elliott and the Walker River Executive Order are followed by reproductions of the actual text of each document.

THE HISTORY OF TREATY NEGOTIATIONS BETWEEN THE UNITED STATES AND INDIAN TRIBES

AGREEMENTS BETWEEN SUBSTANTIAL EQUALS (1776-1816)

The relationship between the United States and Indian tribes was premised in large part upon a rich and well-established body of law and policy that had been developed by the European nations in which the sovereignty and property rights of aboriginal people were given legal recognition.[1] By the time of the American Revolution, Indian tribes were accorded a secure place in international law as sovereign nations with legally protected property rights.

In the years immediately following the outbreak of the Revolutionary War, the United States government considered Indian tribes to have generally the same sovereign status and property rights as foreign nations.[2] Prior to the conclusion of the War of 1812, Indian tribes negotiated treaties from a position of relative strength because they had the option of allying with either the British or the United States. The new American nation, struggling for its survival, needed Indian support or at least Indian promises of non-hostility. Congress was determined to encourage a stable relationship between the tribes and the United States and to avoid hostilities.[3]

The earliest treaties reflected these political realities by their "language of equality."[4] For example, President Washington recommended that the 1784 Ft. Harmer Treaty with the Six Nations be submitted for formal ratification in the same manner as treaties with European nations.[5] In several instances these early treaties expressly provided for tribal jurisdiction over civil and criminal matters.[6]

Some treaties in the late 1700s, however, included provisions for "protection" by the United States.[7] Several tribes made known their dissatisfaction with the use of the "conquered province" concept as a basis for treaty negotiations.[8] Nevertheless, Indian lands insulated United States' territory from European garrisons and colonies to the west and south, so the protection of Indian lands was a centerpiece of the policy by which peace on the frontiers was preserved.[9]

During the late eighteenth century, the United States used treaties to promote an increasingly lucrative trade with the Indians. Similarly, the Indian Trade and Intercourse Acts of 1790, 1793, 1796, and 1802, embodied congressional efforts to deal statutorily with Indian trade. A system of factories was established to facilitate trade with the Indians and to provide the Indians opportunities to produce products for United States' markets.[10]

Land cessions, which were fundamental to Indian treaties since pre-Revolutionary days, were given increased emphasis from 1800 to 1817 as the United States began to expand westward. Large tracts of land were ceded to the federal government in exchange for the provision to the tribes of yearly annuities and various goods and services. Government implementation of these obligations, where it existed at all, developed by statute into a general program of services to Indians. The general program simplified the administration of the specific provisions of the various treaties, and was probably consistent with the Indians' desires.[11]

The extent of the United States' land purchases in the later stages of this period created dissatisfaction among Indian leaders such as Tecumseh, Chief of the Shawnee, and his brother, the Prophet. The United States refused to agree to rescission of the 1809 land cessions in spite of Tecumseh's threat of Indian alliance with Britain. Various tribes, including some factions of the Creeks, then went to war against the United States in 1813 and 1814, while the War of 1812 was fought elsewhere. Andrew Jackson led American military operations in the Upper Creek area. He waged a relentless campaign, destroying whole towns in the process of subduing the hostile tribes.[12] Jackson demanded the surrender of 23,000,000 acres of Creek land, much of which belonged to friendly Indians, as an indemnity for United States' war expenses. An agreement effecting this transfer was signed under protest on August 9, 1814.[13]

Viewed in retrospect, Jackson's campaign was one of the clearest signals that federal policy would no longer be directed toward military alliances with the tribes. Rather, the goal of federal policy would be to open Indian land for settlement by non-Indians.

INDIAN REMOVAL (1816-1846)

The close of the War of 1812 marked the end of British influence in the New World. The tribes thus lost an important bargaining advantage—the specter of Indian alliance with England. Beginning in 1816, the United States turned its attention more directly toward Indians and embarked on an intensive effort to convince tribes to exchange their traditional homelands for new residences in vacant lands to the west. But, after twelve years and various contradictory treaties on the subject, a large part of the Cherokee Nation refused to agree to such a land exchange and removal.[14]

With the election of Andrew Jackson to the presidency in 1828 expansionist desires for forceful removal of Indians were largely satisfied. Jackson's first message to Congress urged voluntary removal. Less than six months later, the Indian Removal Act was passed. Proposed amendments guaranteeing protection to the Indians from the states and respect for treaty rights until removal were rejected.[15]

In 1829 and 1830, the State of Georgia passed laws imposing state jurisdiction on Cherokee territory. The Supreme Court then was called upon to decide two landmark cases in which the petitioners challenged Georgia's laws as violations of the Cherokee treaties, other federal laws, and the Constitution.[16] Both cases placed the Supreme Court in an exceptionally difficult political position[17] and both have been instrumental in shaping Indian law.

The Supreme Court refused to hear the merits of the first case, *Cherokee Nation v. Georgia.*[18] The Court found that it had no original jurisdiction because the Cherokee Nation was not a "foreign state" within the meaning of article III, section 2 of the Constitution. This was a serious blow to the concept of Indian tribes as sovereign entities. Nevertheless, Chief Justice Marshall announced the existence of a special federal trust obligation to Indians and affirmed the validity of the Cherokee treaties in dictum: "The acts of our government plainly recognise the Cherokee Nation as a state, and the courts are bound by those acts."[19]

During the following year, the Court decided in *Worcester v. Georgia*[20] that the same state laws challenged in *Cherokee Nation* were void because they were incompatible with treaties, the Constitution, and the laws "giving effect to the treaties."[21] The mandate of the Court in *Worcester v. Georgia* was, however, never enforced by federal officials, and state interference with the Cherokee Nation continued. Finally, the Cherokee leaders acceded to federal and state pressure for removal and exchange of lands.[22] The infamous Treaty of New Echota was signed in 1835.[23] So despite the Cherokee Nation's legal victories, the eventual outcome of the Cherokee-Georgia conflict was that most members of the tribe were forced to make the deadly march westward on the "Trail of Tears."[24]

The migration program was in effect during the middle fifty years of the nineteenth century, but it was most emphasized from 1828 to 1840. Strict observance of treaty obligations was disregarded by the United States during this period. Federal policy focused on the rapid removal of tribes to more "convenient" locations, often in the newly established "Indian territory."[25]

WESTERN LAND ACQUISITION (1846-1871)

The expanding nation's ambitions often superseded its ideals during this period. Reliable accounts substantiate repeated abuses of the treaty process. United States' negotiators often resorted to overt pressure in the form of threats and bribery. Federal officials sometimes selected friendly Indians as tribal negotiators and gave them power over their tribes, disregarding the tribes' own methods of making decisions and choosing leaders. Some treaties signed by these unauthorized leaders purported to bind tribes who did not even participate in the negotiations.[26]

Interpretative problems arising from differences of language and culture also posed serious obstacles for the Indians at treaty negotiations. Federal negotiators capitalized on the language barrier, using tactics that included dishonest translation. Breaches of completed treaties by the United States were common. One treaty was respected for only twelve days before the government negotiator violated it.[27]

These tactics, especially the manner in which the United States capitalized on the language differences, have been important in the development of Indian treaty law. Today courts continue to construe treaties in favor of the Indians, largely because "the party with the presumptively superior negotiating skills and superior knowledge of the language in which the treaty is recorded, has a responsibility to avoid taking advantage of the other side."[28]

THE PEACE TREATIES (1860-1871)

Dissatisfaction and bitterness were common Indian reactions to unfavorable results of treaty negotiations and to the aggressive policy of westward expansion into Indian lands. During and after the Civil War, various Indian wars broke out in the Great Plains and Rocky Mountain regions. The Sioux uprising of 1862 in Minnesota, for example, was followed by "bloody vengeance" and the passage of two congressional acts of 1863, abrogating earlier treaties and providing for removal of various Sioux bands from Minnesota and Dakota. Nevertheless, hostilities continued over an increasing area, and what had been an uprising became the Sioux War of 1866-67."[29]

In 1867, the Indian Peace Commission was appointed "to arrange for peace" with the belligerent tribes throughout the West. Various treaties were signed, including the 1868 Fort Laramie Treaty with the Sioux, where Red Cloud and other Sioux leaders successfully negotiated for the closing of the Powder River Road, a main route of access to the West. This treaty also called for the provision of various goods and services to the Indians. Importantly, although it guaranteed a different land base, the Fort Laramie Treaty substantially reaffirmed earlier treaties that had been breached. Bargained for by the tribes as consideration for "peace," this reaffirmation was an intrinsic part of the peace negotiation.[30]

These treaties serve as reminders that, although the United States was in most respects militarily superior to the tribes, many tribes posed formidable barriers to westward expansion. The Supreme Court, therefore, has said that "a treaty, including one between the United States and an Indian tribe, is essentially a contract between two sovereign nations."[31]

AN END TO TREATY MAKING (1871)

Jealousy between the House of Representatives and the Senate over the latter's exclusive power to ratify Indian treaties led to the passage of 25 U.S.C. § 71, which terminated Indian treaty making *per se* in 1871. Existing Indian treaties, however, remained in force. The practice of negotiating "agreements" replaced treaty making. These agreements differed from treaties only in that the agreements negotiated in the field were ratified by both houses of Congress, rather than by the Senate alone.[32] Similarly, executive orders were executed in order to accomplish much the same results as treaties. The 1871 Act ending treaty making, therefore, had surprisingly little legal impact. It left intact the sovereignty of tribes,[33] and the objectives of treaties were achieved by other means.

CONCLUSION

From the earliest days of the Republic, Congress and the courts have recognized the special nature of promises made in Indian treaties. Indian treaty law developed a rigorous moral content and Indian treaties were elevated to a high station in our legal system—a higher station, even, than international treaties because treaties with foreign nations do not involve relations between a trustee and a beneficiary. Although the cases have not always favored Indians,[34] the results have most often reflected the notions that Indian treaties represent "the word of the Nation"[35] and that "[g]reat nations, like great men, should keep their word."[36] Professor Monroe E. Price has summarized well the moral content of Indian treaties saying,

"[An Indian treaty] is a bulwark against State encroachment. It is a monument to past guilt, and efforts to change the law include in themselves, evidences of continued uneasiness."[37]

REFERENCE NOTES

1. *See generally* FELIX S. COHEN'S HANDBOOK OF FEDERAL INDIAN LAW Ch. 2b(1)(1) (1982 ed.) (hereinafter cited as Cohen); Cohen, *The Spanish Origin of Indian Rights in the Law of the United States*, 31 GEO. L.J. 1 (1942); Cohen, *Original Indian Title*, 32 MINN. L. REV. 28 (1947); W. Washburn, RED MAN'S LAND/WHITE MAN'S LAW 3-23 (1971). The Supreme Court has acknowledged adoption by the United States of these legal doctrines of the European nations. *E.g., Johnson v. McIntosh*, 21 U.S. (8 Wheat.) 543 (1823); *Worcester v. Georgia*, 31 U.S (6 Pet.) 515 (1832); *Mitchel v. United States*, 34 U.S. (9 Pet.) 711 (1835).

2. *E.g.*, Washburn, *The Historical Context of American Indian Legal Problems*, 40 LAW & CONTEMP. PROBS. 12, 16 (1976).

3. *E.g., Worcester v. Georgia*, 31 U. S. (6 Pet.) 515, 549 (1832); S. Morison, H. Commager, & W. Leuchtenberg, THE GROWTH OF THE AMERICAN REPUBLIC 362-65 (6th ed. 1969).

4. *Worcester v. Georgia*, 31 U. S. (6 Pet.) 515, 548 (1832).

5. 1 DEBATES AND PROCEEDINGS IN THE CONGRESS OF THE UNITED STATES 40-41 (1789-90).

6. *See, e.g.*, Treaty of Hopewell with the Cherokee Tribe, Nov. 28, 1785, 7 Stat. 18; Treaty with the Choctaw Tribe, Jan. 3, 1786, 7 Stat. 21.

7. Cohen, *supra* note 1, at 60-61.

8. Chambers, *Judicial Enforcement of the Federal Trust Responsibility to Indians*, 27 STAN. L. REV. 1213, 1222, (1975).

9. Cohen, *supra* note 1, at 70-78.

10. *See generally* F. Prucha, AMERICAN INDIAN POLICY IN THE FORMATIVE YEARS: THE INDIAN TRADE AND INTERCOURSE ACTS, 1790-1834 (1962).

11. *Id.*, and Cohen, *supra* note 1, Ch. 13A.

12. G. Foreman, INDIAN REMOVAL 317 (1932); A. Debo, A HISTORY OF THE INDIANS OF THE UNITED STATES 111-13 (1970).

13. 7 Stat. 120.

14. On removal generally, *see* G. Foreman, INDIAN REMOVAL (1932).
15. *E.g.*, R. Satz, AMERICAN INDIAN POLICY IN THE JACKSONIAN ERA 9-31 (1975).
16. *Cherokee Nation v. Georgia*, 30 U.S. (5 Pet.) 1 (1831); *Worcester v. Georgia*, 31 U.S. (6 Pet.) 515 (1832).
17. *See generally* Burke, *The Cherokee Cases: A Study in Law, Politics, and Morality*, 21 STAN. L. REV. 500 (1969).
18. 30 U.S. (5 Pet.) 1 (1831).
19. *Id.* at 15.
20. 31 U.S. (6 Pet.) 515 (1832).
21. *Id.* at 561-62.
22. The pressures on the Cherokee Nation to remove are discussed in many sources, including Satz, *supra* note 15, at 98-100; Debo, *supra* note 12 at 120-25; and Foreman, *supra* note 12, at 238-69.
23. 7 Stat. 478.
24. *See* Chambers, *supra* note 8, at 1223 nn.47, 49. The Choctaw removal is analyzed in *United States v. John*, 437 U.S. 634 (1978).
25. *E.g.*, Debo, *supra* note 12, at 117-49. The Cherokees and the other "Five Civilized Tribes" were by no means the only tribes that were forcibly removed. Scores of other tribes were moved to the Indian Territory, which first included parts of Kansas and Arkansas, as well as all of Oklahoma except the panhandle. *Id.* at 206. The Indian Territory was reduced to what is now Oklahoma, except the panhandle, as non-Indian homesteaders advanced into Kansas and Arkansas. The western half of the Indian Territory was then opened to settlement in the early 1850s and the eastern half (the lands of the Five Civilized Tribes) was opened to the Oklahoma land rush when Oklahoma became a state in 1907. *See generally* A. Debo, AND STILL THE WATERS RUN (1972); Cohen, *supra* note 1, at 770-74. Removals also took place in other parts of the country. *See* D. Brown, BURY MY HEART AT WOUNDED KNEE 13-36 (1970) (description of "The Long Walk" of the Navajos during the 1860s) and S. Beckham, REQUIEM FOR A PEOPLE (1969) (description of the relocation of the coastal Oregon tribes during the 1850s).
26. *E.g.*, S. Morison, H. Commager, P. W. Leuchtenberg, THE GROWTH OF THE AMERICAN REPUBLIC 439-41 (6th ed. 1969); W. Hagan, AMERICAN INDIANS 55-56 (1961); W. Washburn, THE INDIAN IN AMERICA 170-208 (1975); and A. Josephy, Jr., THE NEZ PERCE INDIANS 285-332 (abr. ed. 1971).
27. For discussion of the language difficulties faced by the tribes, *see*, *e.g.*, *Whitefoot v. United States*, 293 F 2d 658, 667 n.15 (Ct. Cl. 1961), *cert. denied,* 369 U.S. 818 (1962); and *Jones v. Meehan*, 175 U.S. 1, 11 (1899). On breach of the treaties by the United States, *see*, *e.g.*, A. de Tocqueville, DEMOCRACY IN AMERICA 309-10 (1966); A Josephy, Jr., *supra* note 26, at 336-38.
28. *Washington v. Passenger Fishing Vessels Ass'n,* 443 U. S. 658, 675-76 (1979).
29. On the 1862 Sioux uprising in Minnesota, *see* T. Blegen, MINNESOTA: A HISTORY OF THE STATE 259-84 (1975). On the Sioux War of 1866-67 and the Peace Commission, *see* F. Prucha, AMERICAN INDIAN POLICY IN CRISIS: CHRISTIAN REFORMERS AND THE INDIAN (1976), and the authorities cited there.

30. *See* Treaty with the Sioux, arts. I & II, April 29, 1868, 15 Stat. 635. The Fort Laramie Treaty is considered one of the most favorable treaties negotiated by any Indian tribe but it was later abrogated in many respects, including the taking of the Black Hills. *See United States v. Sioux Nation*, 448 U.S. 371 (1980) and the historical authorities cited there.

31. *Washington v. Passenger Fishing Vessels Ass'n*, 443 U.S. 658, 675 (1979).

32. *E.g., Antoine v. Washington*, 420 U.S. 194, 201-04 (1975).

33. *E.g.*, Rice, *Indian Rights: 25 U.S.C. § 71: The End of Tribal Sovereignty or a Self-Limitation of Contractual Ability?* 5 AM. IND. L. REV. 239 (1977).

34. *E.g., Seneca Nation of Indians v. United States*, 338 F.2d 55 (2d Cir. 1964), *cert. denied*, 380 U.S. 952 (1965).

35. *United States v. Winans*, 198 U.S. 371, 380 (1905).

36. *F.P.C. v. Tuscarora Indian Nation*, 362 U.S. 99, 142 (1960) (BLACK, J., dissenting).

37. M. Price, LAW AND THE AMERICAN INDIAN 294 (1973).

JUDICIAL INTERPRETATIONS OF
THE TREATY OF POINT ELLIOTT

The Treaty of Point Elliott, which has been involved in several of the most important decisions in Indian law, was signed by a group of tribes and bands residing in western Washington. Successor tribes today include the Lummi, Muckleshoot, Nooksack, Saux-Suiattle, Suquamish, Stillaquamish, Swinomish, Tulalip, and Upper Skagit River Tribes. The treaty is reproduced here at page 105 in its original form to demonstrate the high level of formality and solemnity accorded to Indian treaties.

The Treaty of Point Elliott was one of the "Isaac Stevens" treaties negotiated in 1854 and 1855 between the United States and the tribes of western Washington. The dominant tribal figure at the Point Elliott negotiations was Chief Seattle, the famous Dwamish leader.

Stevens, the first Governor and Superintendent of Indian Affairs of the Washington Territory, has been criticized for many of his methods. His tactics included the arbitrary grouping of Indian families and bands to create political entities for treaty-making purposes, the designation of favored Indians as chiefs to represent those political entities, and the use of coercion in the treaty-making process. Proof of such devious or fraudulent conduct is not a basis upon which Indians can set aside unfavorable treaty provisions once a treaty has gone into effect. *Lone Wolf v. Hitchcock*, 187 U.S. 553 (1903). (For text of opinion, *see* Part Four.)

In the case of the Treaty of Point Elliott, for example, Stevens negotiated with both the saltwater Indians of the lower Dwamish drainage and the inland Indians of the White and Green rivers as a group. There were long-standing hostilities between these bands, and the inland Indians bitterly resented being moved to a reservation on the saltwater portion of the Dwamish River. Because of these divisions, the inland tribes were later moved to the Muckleshoot Indian Reservation pursuant to an executive order signed in 1857. Many other members of the signatory tribes also refused to move to the reservation called for by the treaty, accounting for the many separate "Point Elliott" tribes that exist today.

Article 1 of each of the Isaac Stevens treaties contained land cessions from the tribes. In all, the Stevens treaties resulted in the transfer of some 64 million acres of land in Washington, Idaho, and Montana. The Point Elliott tribes, for instance, ceded a parcel bordered by Puget Sound on the west, the Canadian border on the north, the summit of the Cascade Range on the east, and a line running just above Tacoma on the south. In addition to much of the Puget Sound itself, this area today includes Seattle, Belling-ham and numerous smaller towns and cities.

Although the land actually reserved by tribes in the Pacific Northwest was relatively small, the treaties guaranteed the Indians important rights off the reservation. In Article 4 of the Point Elliott Treaty the signatory tribes retained extensive off-reservation fishing rights: "the right of taking fish, at usual and accustomed grounds and stations … in common with all citizens of the Territory."

For half a century salmon and steelhead runs were plentiful. Eventu-ally, however, fishing by non-Indians, spurred by the booming canning industry, created intense competition for a dwindling resource. Dams on the major rivers choked off the runs and flooded prime spawning grounds. The growth of industry, poor logging practices, and construc-tion of roads and homes altered the run-off patterns and impaired water quality and quantity. *See, e.g.*, A. Netboy, *The Columbia River Salmon and Steelhead Trout* (1980). By the mid-twentieth century the State of Wash-ington had begun to deny fishing to the Indian tribes in order to allow non-Indian commercial and sports fishers to harvest salmon and steel-head. Years of sit-ins, arrests, and violence followed. *See, e.g.,* American Friends Service Committee, *Uncommon Controversy* (1975).

The tribes of the Point Elliott Treaty and the other tribes of western Washington engaged in extensive litigation on a number of fronts to preserve their treaty rights. The famous "Boldt decision," handed down in 1973 by Senior District Court Judge George Boldt, upheld the tribes in virtually all respects and ruled that they are entitled to harvest 50 percent of the resources that they are guaranteed "in common with" non-Indians. *United States v. Washington*, 384 F. Supp. 312 (W.D. Wash. 1973). Later the United States Supreme Court upheld most aspects of Judge Boldt's ruling. *Washington v. Washington State Commercial Passenger Fishing Vessel Ass'n*, 443 U.S. 658 (1979) (For text of opinion, *see* Part Four). In that decision, the Supreme Court pointedly made reference to the Ninth Circuit Court of Appeals' discussion of the recalcitrance of Washington State officials. The Court noted that the Ninth Circuit called the conduct, except for some desegregation cases in the South, "the most concerted official and private efforts to frustrate a decree of a federal court witnessed in this century." 443 U.S. at 696 n.36.

The litigation continues. Enforcement of rights recognized by the Supreme Court is a daily chore for the tribes and their lawyers, who face continuing court hearings over the allocation of individual runs among treaty tribes and non-Indian fishers. In a major victory, the courts held in the 1990s that the treaties also protect tribal harvesting of shellfish, even on private lands. *United States v. Washington*, 157 F.3d 630 (9th Cir. 1998; *cert. denied*, 526 U.S. 1060 (1999)). In addition, the tribes are pursuing major litigation, called *United States v. Washington*, Phase II; if successful, this assertion by the tribes of an "environmental right" would require enhancement actions by the State of Washington in order to provide partial restitution for the various state development activities that have contributed to the decline in the runs of anadromous fish. As of 2004, this litigation has been inconclusive. Getches, Wilkinson, Williams, CASES AND MATERIALS ON FEDERAL INDIAN LAW, pp. 894-896 (4th ed. 1998).

The fishing decisions in the Pacific Northwest stand as vivid monuments to the enduring nature of Indian treaties. Leaving aside the specific treaty rights enforced in those cases, the court opinions make it clear that Indian treaties are not made obsolete by the passage of time. Treaty rights cannot be lost simply because tribes have not exercised those rights due to harassment by state officials or other factors. There are no statutes of limitations against the exercise of those rights. Congress can diminish treaty rights, but the passage of time, standing alone, cannot.

The Treaty of Point Elliott came to the Supreme Court in another modern case, where the results were not so favorable to the tribes. In *Oliphant v. Suquamish Indian Tribe*, 435 U.S. 191 (1978), the Court held that the Suquamish Tribe did not possess criminal jurisdiction over non-Indians. (For text of opinion, *see* Part Four.) Although normally treaties reserve to tribes all attributes of sovereignty except those expressly granted away in the treaties, in *Oliphant* the Court held that tribes also fail to possess those sovereign powers "inconsistent with their status." Such authority, which was surrendered by implication, includes criminal jurisdiction over non-Indians. The Court relied in part upon article 9 of the Treaty of Point Elliott, where the Suquamish "acknowledge their dependence on the Government of the United States."

The decision in *Oliphant* highlights the manner in which post-treaty federal policy can infringe on treaty rights without ever explicitly referring to them. The Suquamish Reservation was allotted pursuant to the General Allotment, or Dawes, Act of 1887. (For text of statute, *see* Part Three.) The tribal land base was broken up and tracts of land were transferred from the tribe to individual tribal members. Later, large amounts of allotted land passed out of Indian hands, often due to sharp dealing or forced tax sales. *See, e.g.*, D. Otis, *The Dawes Act and the Allotment of Indian Lands* (F. Prucha ed. 1973).

Although the *Oliphant* Court technically was construing the Treaty of Point Elliott to determine whether the Suquamish Tribe retained criminal jurisdiction over non-Indians, it is highly probable that the Court also looked to the realities of the situation and was reluctant to allow tribal authority because of the heavy influx of non-Indians into the reservation as a result of allotment. Thus in *Oliphant* the Court expressly noted that almost 3,000 non-Indians live within the reservation boundaries and own 63 percent of land there, while only 50 Suquamish tribal members reside on the reservation.

The allotment scheme has had other indirect impacts on treaty rights. The Treaty of Point Elliott and other treaties reserved the right to govern reservation lands. Nevertheless, a tribe's ability to govern effectively is diminished on those reservations where land is checkerboarded and many disparate kinds of landownership exist. Comprehensive land management and government under such circumstances is difficult at best. *See, e.g.*, Williams, *Too Little Land, Too Many Heirs—The Indian Heirship Land Problem*, 46 WASH. L. REV. 709 (1971).

In addition to the allotment process, the reservations of the Point Elliott tribes have been subjected to state court jurisdiction pursuant to Public Law 280, passed in 1953. The implementation of Public Law 280 in Washington has been complex and controversial but it has been upheld by the Supreme Court. *Washington v. Confederated Bands and Tribes of the Yakima Indian Nation*, 439 U.S. 463 (1979). So the treaty has been indirectly abrogated in yet another way, by allowing court cases covered by Public Law 280 to be adjudicated by the state; this weakens the tribes' inherent right, reserved in the treaty, to administer their own judicial systems.

Thus the historic treaty fishing rights, many powers of self-government, and the trust relationship established at Point Elliott continue in force today, but the allotment process has effectively abrogated some of the powers of those treaty tribes, including the Point Elliott tribes, who were subjected to it. The passage of Public Law 280 implicitly abrogated other treaty rights. Both events are reminders of the vigilance that tribes must constantly exercise, in the face of increasingly sophisticated attacks, in order to preserve the treaty rights that their ancestors established during the negotiating process.

The full text of the treaty follows.

THE TREATY OF POINT ELLIOTT WITH THE DWAMISH, SUQUAMISH AND OTHER ALLIED AND SUBORDINATE TRIBES OF INDIANS IN WASHINGTON

(Signed January 22, 1855; ratified March 8, 1859)

(12 Stat. 927)

Treaty between the United States and the Dwamish, Suquamish, and other allied and subordinate Tribes of Indians in Washington Territory. Concluded at Point Elliott, Washington Territory, January 22, 1855. Ratified by the Senate, March 8, 1859. Proclaimed by the President of the United States, April 11, 1859.

JAMES BUCHANAN,

PRESIDENT OF THE UNITED STATES,

TO ALL AND SINGULAR TO WHOM THESE PRESENTS SHALL COME,

GREETING:

Jan. 22. 1855.

Preamble.

WHEREAS a treaty was made and concluded at Múckl-te-óh or Point Elliott, in the Territory of Washington, the twenty-second day of January, one thousand eight hundred and fifty-five, by Isaac I. Stevens, governor and superintendent of Indian affairs for the said Territory, on the part of the United States, and the hereinafter-named chiefs, headmen, and delegates of the Dwámish, Suquámish, Sk-táhl-mish, Sam-áhmish, Smal- hkahmish, Skope-áhmish, St-káh-mish, Snoquálmoo, Skai-wha-mish, N'Quentl-má-mish, Sk-táh-le-jum, Stoluck-whá-mish, Sno-ho-mish, Skagit, Kik-i-állus, Swin-á-mish, Squin-áh-mish, Sah-ku-méhu, Noo-whá-há, Nook-wa-cháh-mish, Mee-see-qua-guilch, Cho-bah-áh-bish, and other allied and subordinate tribes and bands of Indians occupying certain lands situated in said Territory of Washington, on behalf of said tribes and duly authorized by them; which treaty is in the words and figures following to wit:

Contracting Parties.

Articles of agreement and convention made and concluded at Múckl-te-óh, or Point Elliott, in the Territory of Washington, this twenty-second day of January, eighteen hundred and fifty-five, by Isaac I. Stevens, governor and superintendent of Indian affairs for the said Territory, on the part of the United States, and the hereinafter-named chiefs, headmen, and delegates of the Dwámish, Suquámish, Sk-táhl-mish, Sam-áhmish, Smal-hkahmish, Skope-áhmish, St-káh-mish, Snoquálmoo, Skai-wha-mish, N'Quentl-má-mish, Sk-táh-le-jum, Stoluck-whá-mish, Sno-ho-mish, Skagit, Kik-i-állus, Swin-á-mish, Squin-áh-mish, Sah-ku-méhu, Noo-whá-há, Nook-wa-cháh-mish, Mee-see-qua-guilch, Cho-bah-áh-bish, and other allied and subordinate tribes and bands of Indians occupying certain lands situated in said

Territory of Washington, on behalf of said tribes and duly authorized by them.

ARTICLE I. The said tribes and bands of Indians hereby cede, relinquish and convey to the United States all their right, title, and interest in and to the lands and country occupied by them, bounded and described as follows: Commencing at a point on the eastern side of Admiralty Inlet, known as Point Pully, about midway between Commencement and Elliott Bays; thence east-

wardly, running along the north lines of lands heretofore ceded to the United States by the Nisqually, Puyallup, and other Indians, to the summit of the Cascade range of mountains; thence northwardly, following the summit of said range to the 49th parallel of north latitude; thence west, along said parallel to the middle of the Gulf of Georgia; thence through the middle of said gulf and the main channel through the Canal de Arro to the

Straits of Fuca, and crossing the same through the middle of Admiralty Inlet to Suquamish Head; thence southwesterly, through the peninsula, and following the divide between Hood's Canal and Admiralty Inlet to the portage known as Wilkes' Portage; thence northeastwardly, and following the line of lands heretofore ceded as aforesaid to Point Southworth, on the western side of Admiralty Inlet, and thence round the foot of Vashon's Island eastwardly and southeastwardly to the place of beginning, including all the islands comprised within said boundaries, and all the right, title, and interest of the said tribes and bands to any lands within the territory of the United States.

ARTICLE II. There is, however, reserved for the present use and occupation of the said tribes and bands the following tracts of land, viz: the amount of two sections, or twelve hundred and eighty acres, surrounding the small bight at the head of Port Madison, called by the Indians Noo-sohk-um; the amount of two sections, or twelve hundred and eighty acres, on the north side of Hwhomish Bay and the creek emptying into the same called Kwilt-seh-da, the peninsula at the southeastern end of Perry's Island called Sháis-quihl, and the island called Chah-choo-sen, situated in the Lummi River at the point of separation of the mouths emptying respectively into Bellingham Bay and the Gulf of Georgia. All which tracts shall be set apart, and so far as

necessary surveyed and marked out for their exclusive use; nor shall any white man be permitted to reside upon the same without permission of the said tribes or bands, and of the superintendent or agent, but, if necessary for the public convenience, roads may be run through the said reserves, the Indians being compensated for any damage thereby done them.

Further reservation for school.

ARTICLE III. There is also reserved from out the lands hereby ceded the amount of thirty-six sections, or one township of land, on the northeastern shore of Port Gardner, and north of the mouth of Snohomish River, including Tulalip Bay and the before-mentioned Kwilt-seh-da Creek, for the purpose of establishing thereon an agricultural and industrial school, as hereinafter mentioned and agreed, and with a view of ultimately drawing thereto and settling thereon all the Indians living west of the Cascade Mountains in said Territory. Provided, however, that the President may establish the central agency and general reservation at such other point as he may deem for the benefit of the Indians.

Tribes to settle on reservation within one year.

ARTICLE IV. The said tribes and bands agree to remove to and settle upon the said first above mentioned reservations within one year after the ratification of this treaty, or sooner, if the means are furnished them. In the meantime it shall be lawful for them to reside upon any land not in the actual claim and occupation of citizens of the United States, if with the permission of the owner.

Rights and privileges secured to Indians.

ARTICLE V. The right of taking fish at usual and accustomed grounds and stations is further secured to said Indians in common with all citizens of the Territory, and of erecting temporary houses for the purpose of curing, together with the privilege of hunting and gathering roots and berries on open and unclaimed lands. Provided, however, that they shall not take shell-fish from any beds staked or cultivated by citizens.

Payment by the United States.

How to be applied.

ARTICLE VI. In consideration of the above cession, the United States agree to pay to the said tribes and bands the sum of one hundred and fifty thousand dollars, in the following manner—that is to say: For the first year after the ratification hereof, fifteen thousand dollars; for the next two years, twelve thousand dollars each year; for the next three years, ten thousand dollars each year; for the next four years, seven thousand five hundred dollars each year; for the next five years, six thousand dollars each year; and for the the last five years, four thousand two hundred and fifty dollars each year. All which said sums of money shall be applied to the use and benefit of the said Indians under the direction of the President of the United States, who may from time to time determine at his discretion upon what beneficial objects to expend the same; and the Superintendent of Indian Affairs, or other proper officer, shall each year inform the President of the wishes of said Indians in respect thereto.

Indians may be removed to reservation, etc.

ARTICLE VII. The President may hereafter, when in his opinion the interests of the Territory shall require and the welfare of the said Indians be promoted, remove them from either or all of the special reservations hereinbefore made to the said general reservation, or such other suitable place within said Territory as he may deem fit, on remunerating them for their improvements and the expense of such removal, or may consolidate them with other friendly tribes or bands; and he may further at his discretion cause the whole or any portion of the lands hereby reserved, or of such other land as may be selected in lieu thereof, to be surveyed **Lots may be** into lots, and assign the same to such individuals or families as are **assigned to** willing to avail themselves of the privilege, and will locate on the **individuals.** same as a permanent home on the same terms and subject to the same regulations as are provided in the sixth article of the treaty with the Omahas, so far as the same may be applicable. Any sub-**Vol. x. p. 1044.** stantial improvements heretofore made by any Indian, and which he shall be compelled to abandon in consequence of this treaty, shall be valued under the direction of the President and payment made accordingly therefor.

ARTICLE VIII. The annuities of the aforesaid tribes and bands shall not be taken to pay the debts of individuals.

Tribes to preserve ARTICLE IX. The said tribes and bands acknowledge their depen-
friendly relations. dence on the government of the United States, and promise to be friendly with all citizens thereof, and they pledge themselves to commit no depredations on the property of such citizens. Should any one or more of them violate this pledge, and the fact be **To pay for** satisfactorily proven before the agent, the property taken shall be **depradations.** returned, or in default thereof, or if injured or destroyed, compensation may be made by the government out of their annuities. **Not to make war** Nor will they make war on any other tribe except in self-defence, **except, & etc.** but will submit all matters of difference between them and the other Indians to the government of the United States or its agents for decision, and abide thereby. And if any of the said Indians commit depredations on other Indians within the Territory the same rule shall prevail as that prescribed in this article in cases of depredations against citizens. And the said tribes agree not to **To surrender** shelter or conceal offenders against the laws of the United States, **offenders.** but to deliver them up to the authorities for trial.

Annuities to be ARTICLE X. The above tribes and bands are desirous to exclude **withheld from** from their reservations the use of ardent spirits, and to prevent **those who drink** their people from drinking the same, and therefore it is provided **etc., ardent spirits.** that any Indian belonging to said tribe who is guilty of bringing liquor into said reservations, or who drinks liquor, may have his or her proportion of the annuities withheld from him or her for such time as the President may determine.

Tribes to free all slaves and not to acquire others.

ARTICLE XI. The said tribes and bands agree to free all slaves now held by them and not to purchase others hereafter.

Not to trade out of the United States.

ARTICLE XII. The said tribes and bands further agree not to trade at Vancouver's Island or elsewhere out of the dominions of the United States, nor shall foreign Indians be permitted to reside in their reservations without consent of the superintendent or agent.

$15,000 appropriated for expenses of removal and settlement.

ARTICLE XIII. To enable said Indians to remove to and settle upon their aforesaid reservations, and to clear, fence, and break up a sufficient quantity of land for cultivation, the United States further agree to pay the sum of fifteen thousand dollars to be laid out and expended under the direction of the President and in such manner as he shall approve.

United States to establish school and provide instructors, furnish mechanics, shops, physicians, & c.

ARTICLE XIV. The United States further agree to establish at the general agency for the district of Puget's Sound, within one year from the ratification hereof, and to support for a period of twenty years, an agricultural and industrial school, to be free to children of the said tribes and bands in common with those of the other tribes of said district, and to provide the said school with a suitable instructor or instructors, and also to provide a smithy and carpenter's shop, and furnish them with the necessary tools, and employ a blacksmith, carpenter, and farmer for the like term of twenty years to instruct the Indians in the respective occupations. And the United States finally agree to employ a physician to reside at the said central agency, who shall furnish medicine and advice to their sick, and shall vaccinate them; the expense of said school, shops, persons employed, and medical attendance to be defrayed by the United States, and not deducted from the annuities.

Treaty when to take effect.

ARTICLE XV. This treaty shall be obligatory on the contracting parties as soon as the same shall be ratified by the President and Senate of the United States.

In testimony whereof, the said Isaac I. Stevens, governor and superintendent of Indian affairs, and the undersigned chiefs, headmen, and delegates of the aforesaid tribes and bands of Indians, have hereunto set their hands and seals, at the place and on the day and year hereinbefore written.

ISAAC I. STEVENS, *Governor and Superintendent.*	[L.S.]
SEATTLE, *Chief of the Dwamish and Suquamish tribes.*	his x mark. [L.S.]
PAT-KA-NAM, *Chief of the Snoqualmoo, Snohomish and other tribes.*	his x mark. [L.S.]
CHOW-ITS-HOOT, *Chief of the Lummi and other tribes.*	his x mark. [L.S.]
GOLIAH, *Chief of the Skagits and other allied tribes.*	his x mark. [L.S.]
KWALLATTUM, or General Pierce, *Sub-chief of the Skagit tribe.*	his x mark. [L.S.]
S'HOOTST-HOOT, *Sub-chief of Snohomish.*	his x mark. [L.S.]
SNAH-TALC, or Bonaparte, *Sub-chief of Snohomish.*	his x mark. [L.S.]
SQUUSH-UM, or The Smoke, *Sub-chief of the Snoqualmoo.*	his x mark. [L.S.]
SEE-ALLA-PA-HAN, or The Priest, *Sub-chief of the Sk-tah-le-jum.*	his x mark. [L.S.]
HE-UCH-KA-NAM, or George Bonaparte, *Sub-chief of Snohomish.*	his x mark. [L.S.]
TSE-NAH-TALC, or Joseph Bonaparte, *Sub-chief of Snohomish.*	his x mark. [L.S.]
NS'SKI-OOS, or Jackson, *Sub-chief of Snohomish.*	his x mark. [L.S.]
WATS-KA-LAH-TCHIE, or John Hobtst-hoot, *Sub-chief of Snohomish.*	his x mark. [L.S.]
SMEH-MAI-HU, *Sub-chief of Skai-wha-mish.*	his x mark. [L.S.]
SLAT-EAH-KA-NAM, *Sub-chief of Snoqualmoo.*	his x mark. [L.S.]
ST'HAU-AI, *Sub-chief of Snoqualmoo.*	his x mark. [L.S.]
LUGS-KEN, *Sub-chief of Skai-wha-mish.*	his x mark. [L.S.]
S'HEHT-SOOLT, or Peter, *Sub-chief of Snohomish.*	his x mark. [L.S.]
DO-QUEH-OO-SATL, *Snoqualmoo tribe.*	his x mark. [L.S.]
JOHN KANAM, *Snoqualmoo sub-chief*	his x mark. [L.S.]
KLEMSH-KA-NAM, *Snoqualmoo*	his x mark. [L.S.]
TS'HUAHNTL, *Dwamish sub-chief.*	his x mark. [L.S.]
KWUSS-KA-NAM, or George Snatelum, Sen., *Skagit tribe.*	his x mark. [L.S.]
HEL-MITS, or George Snatelum, *Skagit sub-chief.*	his x mark. [L.S.]
S'KWAI-KWI, *Skagit tribe, sub-chief.*	his x mark. [L.S.]
SEH-LEK-QU, *Sub-chief Lummi tribe.*	his x mark. [L.S.]
S'H'-CHEH-OOS, or General Washington, *Sub-chief of Lummi tribe.*	his x mark. [L.S.]
WHAI-LAN-HU, or Davy Crockett, *Sub-chief of Lummi tribe.*	his x mark. [L.S.]
SHE-AH-DELT-HU, *Sub-chief of Lummi tribe.*	his x mark. [L.S.]
KWULT-SEH, *Sub-chief of Lummi tribe.*	his x mark. [L.S.]
KWULL-ET-HU, *Lummi Tribe*	his x mark. [L.S.]
KLEH-KENT-SOOT, *Skagit tribe.*	his x mark. [L.S.]
SOHN-HEH-OVS, *Skagit tribe.*	his x mark. [L.S.]
S'DEH-AP-KAN, or General Warren, *Skagit tribe.*	his x mark. [L.S.]
CHUL-WHIL-TAN, *Sub-chief of Suquamish tribe.*	his x mark. [L.S.]
SKE-EH-TUM, *Skagit tribe.*	his x mark. [L.S.]
PATCHKANAM, or Dome, *Skagit tribe.*	his x mark. [L.S.]
SATS-KANAM, *Squin-ah-nush tribe.*	his x mark. [L.S.]
SD-ZO-MAHTL, *Kik-ial-lus band.*	his x mark. [L.S.]
DAHTL-DE-MIN, *Sub-chief of Sah-ku-meh-hu.*	his x mark. [L.S.]
SD'ZEK-DU-NUM, *Me-sek-wi-guilse sub-chief.*	his x mark. [L.S.]

Now-A-Chais, *Sub-chief of Dwamish.*   his x mark. [L.S.]
Mis-Lo-Tche, or *Wah-hehl-tchoo, Sub-chief of Suquamish.*   his x mark. [L.S.]
Sloo-Noksh-Tan, or Jim, *Suquamish tribe.*   his x mark. [L.S.]
Moo-Whah-Lad-Hu, or Jack, *Suquamish tribe.*   his x mark. [L.S.]
Too-Leh-Plan, *Suquamish tribe.*   his x mark. [L.S.]
Ha-Seh-Doo-An, or Keo-kuck, *Dwamish tribe.*   his x mark. [L.S.]
Hoovilt-Meh-Tum, *Sub-chief of Suquamish.*   his x mark. [L.S.]
We-Ai-Pah, *Skaiwhamish tribe.*   his x mark. [L.S.]
S'Ah-An-Hu, or Hallam, *Snohomish tribe.*   his x mark. [L.S.]
She-Hope, or General Pierce, *Skagit tribe.*   his x mark. [L.S.]
Hwn-Lah-Lakq, or Thomas Jefferson, *Lummi tribe.*   his x mark. [L.S.]
Cht-Simpt, *Lummi Tribe.*   his x mark. [L.S.]
Tse-Sum-Ten, *Lummi Tribe.*   his x mark. [L.S.]
Klt-Hahl-Ten, *Lummi Tribe.*   his x mark. [L.S.]
Kut-Ta-Kanam, or John, *Lummi Tribe.*   his x mark. [L.S.]
Ch-Lah-Ben, *Noo-qua-cha-mish band.*   his x mark. [L.S.]
Noo-Heh-Oos, *Snoqualmoo tribe.*   his x mark. [L.S.]
Hweh-Uk, *Snoqualmoo tribe.*   his x mark. [L.S.]
Peh-Nus, *Skai-whamish tribe.*   his x mark. [L.S.]
Yim-Ka-Nam, *Snoqualmoo tribe.*   his x mark. [L.S.]
Twooi-As-Kut, *Skaiwhamish tribe.*   his x mark. [L.S.]
Luch-Al-Kanam, *Snoqualmoo tribe.*   his x mark. [L.S.]
S'Hoot-Kanam, *Snoqualmoo tribe.*   his x mark. [L.S.]
Sme-A-Kanam, *Snoqualmoo tribe.*   his x mark. [L.S.]
Sad-Zis-Keh, *Snoqualmoo.*   his x mark. [L.S.]
Heh-Mahl, *Skaiwhamish tribe.*   his x mark. [L.S.]
Charley, *Skagit tribe.*   his x mark. [L.S.]
Sampson, *Skagit tribe.*   his x mark. [L.S.]
John Taylor, *Snohomish tribe.*   his x mark. [L.S.]
Hatch-Kwentum, *Skagit tribe.*   his x mark. [L.S.]
Yo-I-Kum, *Skagit tribe.*   his x mark. [L.S.]
T'Kwa-Ma-Han, *Skagit tribe.*   his x mark. [L.S.]
Sto-Dum-Kan, *Swinamish band.*   his x mark. [L.S.]
Be-Lole, *Swinamish band.*   his x mark. [L.S.]
D'Zo-Lole-Gwam-Hu, *Skagit tribe.*   his x mark. [L.S.]
Steh-Shail, William, *Shaiwhamish band.*   his x mark. [L.S.]
Kel-Kahl-Tsoot, *Swinamish tribe.*   his x mark. [L.S.]
Pat-Sen, *Skagit tribe.*   his x mark. [L.S.]
Pat-Teh-Us, *Noo-wha-ah sub-chief.*   his x mark. [L.S.]
S'hoolk-Ka-Nam, *Lummi sub-chief.*   his x mark. [L.S.]
Ch-Lok-Suts, *Lummi sub-chief.*   his x mark. [L.S.]

Executed in the presence of us —
M.T. Simmons, *Indian Agent*.
C.H. Mason, *Secretary of Washington Territory*.   Orrington Cushman.
Benj. F. Shaw, *Interpreter*.   Ellis Barnes.
Chas. M. Hitchcock.   R.S. Bailey.
H.A. Goldsborough.   S.M. Collins.
George Gibbs.   Lafayetee Balch.
John H. Scranton.   E.S. Fowler.
Henry D. Cock.   J.H. Hail.
S.S. Ford, Jr.   Rob't. Davis.

And whereas, the said treaty having been submitted to the Senate of the United States for its constitutional action thereon, the Senate did, on the eighth day of March, one thousand eight hundred and fifty-nine, advise and consent to the ratification of its articles by a resolution in the words and figures following, to wit:

"IN EXECUTIVE SESSION,
SENATE OF THE UNITED STATES, MARCH 8, 1859"

Resolved, (two-thirds of the senators present concurring.) That the Senate advise and consent to the ratification of treaty between the United States and the chiefs, headmen and delegates of the Dwamish, Suquamish and other allied and subordinate tribes of Indians occupying certain lands situated in Washington Territory, signed the 22nd day of January, 1855.

"Attest: "ASBURY DICKINS, *Secretary*"

Now, therefore, be it known that I, James Buchanan, President of the Untied States of America, do, in pursuance of the advice and consent of the Senate, as expressed in their resolution of the eighth of March, one thousand eight hundred and fifty-nine, accept, ratify, and confirm the said treaty.

In testimony whereof, I have caused the seal of the United States to be hereto affixed, and have signed the same with my hand.

Done at the city of Washington, this eleventh day of April, in the year of our Lord one thousand eight hundred and fifty-nine, and of the independence of the United States the eighty-third.

[SEAL]   JAMES BUCHANAN.

By the President:
Lewis Cass, Secretary of State.

———————————————

HISTORICAL CONTEXT OF THE ESTABLISHMENT OF THE WALKER RIVER RESERVATION

The Great Basin is that region bordered on the west by the Sierra Nevada and on the east by the Wasatch Range in Utah. It extends north to the Columbia River basin and south to the Colorado River drainage. It includes most of Nevada, western Utah, southeastern Oregon, and southern Idaho. The Great Basin, which has no outlet to the sea, is arid desert and high plains country.

In aboriginal times the Great Basin was peopled mainly by tribes and bands of Paiute Indians. When the reservation system was established during the last half of the nineteenth century, the Paiutes were placed on numerous different reservations. Often they were consolidated with other distinct tribes as, for example, at Klamath and Warm Springs. In other cases, mainly in Nevada, reservations were set aside for Paiutes only.

In 1874 a reservation in excess of 300,000 acres was established in west-central Nevada for the Paiute Indians who resided near the Walker River. No treaty was ever executed with the tribe; rather, the land was set aside by an executive order signed by President Grant. In all, some 99 executive order reservations, totaling more than 20 million acres, were established between 1855 and 1919.

Court cases involving the Walker River Tribe show that for most purposes their rights under the 1874 executive order are substantially identical to the rights held by treaty tribes. One leading decision involved water, which is essential to life and development on the Walker River Tribe's arid lands because agriculture cannot succeed without irrigation. The water rights of tribes on reservations created by treaties and agreements had been firmly established in the early case of *Winters v. United States*, 207 U.S. 564 (1908), which held that those tribes possess reserved water rights superior to rights subsequently established under state law. But the question remained whether reserved rights under the *Winters* doctrine apply on executive order reservations. That issue was resolved in favor of executive order tribes in *United States v. Walker River Irrigation Dist.*, 104 F. 2d 334, 336 (9th Cir. 1939), involving the water rights of the Walker River Tribe:

> The trial court thought *Winters v. United States* distinguishable, as being based on an agreement or treaty with the Indians. Here there was no treaty. It said that at the time the Walker River reservation was set apart

the Pahutes [sic] were at war with the whites, hence no agreement between them and the government was possible.

In the *Winters* case, as in this, the basic question for determination was one of intent—whether the waters of the stream were intended to be reserved for the use of the Indians, or whether the lands only were reserved. We see no reason to believe that the intention to reserve need be evidenced by treaty or agreement. A statute or an executive order setting apart the reservation may be equally indicative of the intent. While in the *Winters* case the court emphasized the treaty, there was in fact no express reservation of water to be found in that document. The intention had to be arrived at by taking account of the circumstances, the situation and needs of the Indians and the purpose for which the lands had been reserved.

The Supreme Court affirmed the same principle in *Arizona v. California*, 373 U.S. 546, 596-601 (1963), involving the water rights of executive order tribes along the Colorado River. *See also United States v. Truckee-Carson Irrigation Dist.*, 649 F.2d 1286 (9th Cir. 1981) (water rights of the Pyramid Lake Paiute Tribe of Nevada).

Executive order reservations are Indian Country. Thus tribes such as the Walker River Tribe can exert sovereignty, and be free of state jurisdiction, within the exterior boundaries of the reservation in the same manner as treaty tribes. *See Donnelly v. United States*, 228 U.S. 243 (1913); 18 U.S.C. § 1151(a).

In modern times, the Walker River Tribe engaged in litigation that further clarified its right to a legal status similar to treaty tribes. In 1882 a predecessor to the Southern Pacific Railroad had constructed a railroad across tribal lands. The tribe took the position that the transaction had never been approved by the federal government pursuant to the Nonintercourse Act, 25 U.S.C. § 177, and other federal laws protecting tribal possession. The tribe sued to eject the railroad and to recover trespass damages dating from the time of the construction of the line. The railroad's primary defense was that executive order reservations should be distinguished from other kinds of Indian reservations. The Ninth Circuit Court of Appeals held for the tribe and, in so doing, explained the legal status of executive order reservations. *See United States v. Southern Pacific Transportation Co.*, 543 F.2d 676, 687, 699 (9th Cir. 1976):

[T]he status of executive order reservations can be summarized as follows: the Indians have the exclusive right to possession but title to the lands remains with the United States. Congress has plenary authority to control use, grant adverse interests or extinguish the Indian title. In these respects, executive order reservations do not differ from treaty or statutory reservations. The one difference is that so long as Congress has not recognized compensable interests in the Indians, executive order reservations may be terminated by Congress or the Executive without payment of compensation. In light of this background, we now turn to the specific arguments advanced by Southern Pacific.

....

Although it may appear harsh to condemn an apparently good-faith use as a trespass after 90 years of acquiescence by the owners, we conclude that an even older policy of Indian law compels this result. Southern Pacific does not have and has never had a valid right-of-way across lands within the original 1874 executive order boundaries of the Walker River Reservation except through the lands ceded by the Tribe to the United States in 1906. Southern Pacific has never had a revocable license to operate a railway across the reservation.

As the opinion just quoted explains, Congress is not constitutionally required to pay just compensation when land is taken from executive order reservations by the United States and put to another use. When treaty lands are taken, the United States is obligated under the Fifth Amendment to make full restitution. Congress, however, has partially eliminated that distinction. A 1927 act requires that the boundaries of an executive order reservation can be changed only by an act of Congress, not by executive action (25 U.S.C. § 398d). Further, takings of executive order land before 1946 were made compensable in the Indian Claims Commission, 25 U.S.C. § 70a, and takings of executive order land after 1946 are apparently compensable in the Claims Court, 28 U.S.C. § 1505. Those claims, however, do not involve "recognized" title (such as is created by a treaty) and therefore takings of executive order land do not give rise to the payment of interest in claims against the United States. The award of interest is extremely important in claim cases, especially for older takings, and the prohibition against recovery for interest when land is taken by the United States constitutes a significant difference between the legal status of executive order and treaty lands. *See generally* Felix S. Cohen's Handbook of Federal Indian Law 493-99 (1982 ed.).

The limitations just discussed, however, apply only to takings of land by the United States. As the Walker River suit against the railroad shows, private parties and the states are prohibited from taking executive order lands in precisely the same manner as if treaty lands are involved. The jurisdictional limitations on states are the same for all kinds of reservations. The result is that for most purposes executive order tribes such as the Walker River Tribe stand in the same position as treaty tribes. *See generally* FELIX S. COHEN'S HANDBOOK OF FEDERAL INDIAN LAW 127-28, 493-99 (1982 ed.).

As can be seen from the reproduction of it which follows, the executive order establishing the Walker River Reservation is extremely brief. All of the executive orders were. But the special rules of Indian law apply, and executive order tribes are entitled to invoke the trust relationship, to exercise inherent tribal sovereignty, to exercise reserved resource rights, to receive federal services, and generally to stand in the same position as those tribes who established their relationship with the federal government by treaty.

EXECUTIVE ORDER OF MARCH 19, 1874, ESTABLISHING THE WALKER RIVER RESERVATION

Executive Order

Walker River Reservation.
Department of the Interior,
Office of Indians Affairs,
November 29, 1859.

Sɪʀ: My attention has been called, by a letter of the 25th instant from F. Dodge, Esq., agent for the Indians in Utah Territory, now in this city, to the consideration of the propriety and necessity of reserving from sale and settlement, for Indian use, a tract of land in the northern portion of the valley of the Truckee River, including Pyramid Lake, and a tract in the northeastern part of the valley of Walker's River, including Walker's Lake, as indicated by the red coloring upon the inclosed map, and fully concurring in the suggestion of Agent Dodge respecting this subject, I have to request that you will direct the surveyor general of Utah Territory to respect said reservations upon the plats of survey when the public surveys shall have been extended over that part of the Territory, and in the meantime that the proper local land officers may be instructed to respect the reservations upon the books of the offices when such offices shall have been established.

Very respectfully, your obedient servant,

A.B.Gʀᴇᴇɴᴡᴏᴏᴅ, Commissioner.

Hon. Sᴀᴍᴜᴇʟ A. Sᴍɪᴛʜ,
   Commissioner General Land Office.

Dᴇᴘᴀʀᴛᴍᴇɴᴛ ᴏғ ᴛʜᴇ Iɴᴛᴇʀɪᴏʀ,
Washington, March 18, 1874.

Sɪʀ: I have the honor to present herewith a communication, dated the 17th instant, from the Commissioner of Indian Affairs, together with the accompanying map showing the survey made by Eugene Monroe in December, 1864, of the Walker River Reservation in Nevada, and respectfully recommend that the President issue an order withdrawing from sale or other disposition and setting apart said reservation or tract of country for the use and occupation of the Pah-Ute Indians located thereon.

The form of order necessary in the premises is engrossed on the inclosed map.

Very respectfully, your obedient servant,

C. Dᴇʟᴀɴᴏ, *Secretary.*

THE PRESIDENT.   EXECUTIVE MANSION,
March 19, 1874.

It is hereby ordered that the reservation situated in Walker River, Nevada, as surveyed by Eugene Monroe, December, 1864, and indicated by red lines on the above diagram in accordance with the fifteen courses and distances thereon given, be withdrawn from public sale or other disposition and set apart for the use of the Pah-Ute Indians residing thereon.

U.S. GRANT.

PART THREE

SELECTED FEDERAL STATUTES
(Edited)

INTRODUCTION

Numerous statutes mentioned throughout both Part One and the cases in Part Four have had, and continue to have, a significant impact on Indian tribes as sovereign governments. Many old statutes control major issues in Indian law today. Part Three, therefore, provides the text of many of the most often mentioned and important federal Indian statutes. Where the statutes are long, only the most relevant portions are presented. The statutes are listed in chronological order, with the earliest enactment reprinted first.

THE NONINTERCOURSE ACT OF 1790

25 U.S.C. § 177

§ 177. Purchases or grants of lands from Indians

No purchase, grant, lease, or other conveyance of lands, or of any title or claim thereto, from any Indian nation or tribe of Indians, shall be of any validity in law or equity, unless the same be made by treaty or convention entered into pursuant to the Constitution. Every person who, not being employed under the authority of the United States, attempts to negotiate such treaty or convention, directly or indirectly, or to treat with any such nation or tribe of Indians for the title or purchase of any lands by them held or claimed, is liable to a penalty of $1,000. The agent of any State who may be present at any treaty held with Indians under the authority of the United States, in the presence and with the approbation of the commissioner of the United States appointed to hold the same, may, however, propose to, and adjust with, the Indians the compensation to be made for their claim to lands within such State, which shall be extinguished by treaty.

THE TREATIES STATUTE OF 1871

25 U.S.C. § 71

§ 71. Future treaties with Indian tribes

No Indian nation or tribe within the territory of the United States shall be acknowledged or recognized as an independent nation, tribe, or power with whom the United States may contract by treaty; but no obligation of any treaty lawfully made and ratified with any such Indian nation or tribe prior to March 3, 1871, shall be hereby invalidated or impaired.

THE GENERAL ALLOTMENT (OR DAWES) ACT OF 1887

25 U.S.C. §§ 331-334, 339, 341, 342, 348, 349, 354, 381

§ 331. Allotments on reservations; irrigable and nonirrigable lands

In all cases where any tribe or band of Indians has been or shall be located upon any reservation created for their use by treaty or stipulation, Act of Congress, or executive order, the President shall be authorized to cause the same or any part thereof to be surveyed or resurveyed whenever in his opinion such reservation or any part may be advantageously utilized for agricultural or grazing purposes by such Indians, and to cause allotment to each Indian located thereon to be made in such areas as in his opinion may be for their best interest not to exceed eighty acres of agricultural or one hundred and sixty acres of grazing land to any one Indian. And whenever it shall appear to the President that lands on any Indian reservation subject to allotment by authority of law have been or may be brought within any irrigation project, he may cause allotments of such irrigable lands to be made to the Indians entitled thereto in such areas as may be for their best interest, not to exceed, however, forty acres to any one Indian, and such irrigable land shall be held to be equal in quantity to twice the number of acres of nonirrigable agricultural land and four times the number of acres of nonirrigable grazing land: *Provided*, That the remaining area to which any Indian may be entitled under existing law after he shall have received his proportion of irrigable land on the basis of equalization herein established may be allotted to him from nonirrigable agricultural or grazing lands: *Provided further*, That where a treaty or Act of Congress setting apart such reservation provides for allotments in severalty in quantity greater or less than that herein authorized, the President shall cause allotments on such reservations to be made in quantity as specified in such treaty or Act, subject, however, to the basis of equalization between irrigable and nonirrigable lands established herein, but in such cases allotments may be made in quantity as specified herein, with the consent of the Indians expressed in such manner as the President in his discretion may require.

[*As originally enacted, this section provided for allotments of different quantities of land to various classes of Indians, i.e., one-quarter section to heads of families, one-eighth section to single persons over the age of 18 years, one-eighth section to orphaned children under the age of 18, and one-sixteenth section to all other single persons under the age of 18.*]

MONTANA ENABLING ACT OF 1889
§ 4, 25 Stat. 677 (1889)

[The people inhabiting Montana] agree and declare that they forever disclaim all right and title to ... all lands ... owned or held by individual Indians or Indian tribes ... and said lands shall remain under the absolute jurisdiction and control of the Congress of the United States....

THE INDIAN REORGANIZATION ACT OF 1934
25 U.S.C. §§ 461-479

§ 461. Allotment of land on Indian reservations
On and after June 18, 1934, no land of any Indian reservation, created or set apart by treaty or agreement with the Indians, Act of Congress, Executive order, or otherwise, shall be allotted in severalty to any Indian.

§ 462. Existing periods of trust and restrictions on alienation extended

The existing periods of trust placed upon any Indian lands and any restriction on alienation thereof are hereby extended and continued until otherwise directed by Congress.

§ 463. Restoration of lands to tribal ownership; protection of existing rights; Papago Indian Reservation

The Secretary of the Interior, if he shall find it to be in the public interest, is authorized to restore to tribal ownership the remaining surplus lands of any Indian reservation opened before June 18, 1934, or authorized to be opened, to sale, or any other form of disposal by Presidential proclamation, or by any of the public land laws of the United States: *Provided, however,* That valid rights or claims of any persons to any lands so withdrawn existing on the date of the withdrawal shall not be affected by sections 461, 462, 463, 464, 465, 466 to 470, 471 to 473, 474, 475, 476 to 478, and 479 of this title: ...

.....

§ 476. Organization of Indian tribes; constitution and bylaws; special election

Any Indian tribe, or tribes, residing on the same reservation, shall have the right to organize for its common welfare, and may adopt an appropriate constitution and bylaws, which shall become effective when ratified by a majority vote of the adult members of the tribe, or of the adult Indians residing on such reservation, as the case may be, at a special election authorized and called by the Secretary of the Interior under such rules and regulations as he may prescribe. Such constitution and bylaws when ratified as aforesaid and approved by the Secretary of the Interior shall be revocable by an election open to the same voters and conducted in the same manner as hereinabove provided. Amendments to the constitution and bylaws may be ratified and approved by the Secretary in the same manner as the original constitution and bylaws.

In addition to all powers vested in any Indian tribe or tribal council by existing law, the constitution adopted by said tribe shall also vest in such tribe or its tribal council the following rights and powers: To employ legal counsel, the choice of counsel and fixing of fees to be subject to the approval of the Secretary of the Interior; to prevent the sale, disposition, lease, or encumbrance of tribal lands, interests in lands, or other tribal assets without the consent of the tribe; and to negotiate with the Federal, State, and local Governments. The Secretary of the Interior shall advise such tribe or its tribal council of all appropriation estimates or Federal projects for the benefit of the tribe prior to the submission of such estimates to the Office of Management and Budget and the Congress.

§ 477. Incorporation of Indian tribes; charter; ratification by election

The Secretary of the Interior may, upon petition by at least one-third of the adult Indians, issue a charter of incorporation to such tribe: *Provided,* That such charter shall not become operative until ratified at a special election by a majority vote of the adult Indians living on the reservation....

§ 478. Acceptance of sections 461 to 479 optional

Sections 461, 462, 463, 464, 465, 466 to 470, 471 to 473, 474, 475, 476 to 478, and 479 of this title shall not apply to any reservation wherein a majority of the adult Indians, voting at a special election duly called by the Secretary of the Interior, shall vote against its application. It shall be the duty of the Secretary of the Interior, within one year after June 18, 1934, to call such an election, which election shall be held by secret ballot upon thirty days' notice.

§ 479. Definitions

The term "Indian" as used in sections 461, 462, 463, 464, 465, 466 to 470, 471 to 473, 474, 475, 476 to 478, and 479 of this title shall include all persons of Indian descent who are members of any recognized Indian tribe now under Federal jurisdiction, and all persons who are descendants of such members who were, on June 1, 1934, residing within the present boundaries of any Indian reservation, and shall further include all other persons of one-half or more Indian blood. For the purposes of said sections, Eskimos and other aboriginal peoples of Alaska shall be considered Indians. The term "tribe" wherever used in said sections shall be construed to refer to any Indian tribe, organized band, pueblo, or the Indians residing on one reservation. The words "adult Indians" wherever used in said sections shall be construed to refer to Indians who have attained the age of twenty-one years.

THE INDIAN CLAIMS COMMISSION ACT OF 1946

25 U.S.C. § 70a

The Commission shall hear and determine ... (1) claims in law or equity arising under the Constitution, laws, treaties of the United States, and Executive orders of the President; (2) all other claims in law or equity, including those sounding in tort, with respect to which the claimant would have been entitled to sue in a court of the United States if the United States was subject to suit; (3) claims which would result if the treaties, contracts, and agreements between the claimant and the United States were revised on the ground of fraud, duress, unconscionable consideration, mutual or unilateral mistake, whether of law or fact, or any other ground cognizable by a court of equity; (4) claims arising from the taking by the United States, whether as the result of a treaty of cession or otherwise, of lands owned or occupied by the claimant without the payment for such lands of compensation agreed to by the claimant; and (5) claims based upon fair and honorable dealings that are not recognized by any existing rule of law or equity.

THE INDIAN COUNTRY STATUTE OF 1948
18 U.S.C. § 1151

§ 1151. Indian country defined

Except as otherwise provided in sections 1154 and 1156 of this title, the term "Indian country," as used in this chapter, means (a) all land within the limits of any Indian reservation under the jurisdiction of the United States Government, notwithstanding the issuance of any patent, and, including rights-of-way running through the reservation, (b) all dependent Indian communities within the borders of the United States whether within the original or subsequently acquired territory thereof, and whether within or without the limits of a state, and (c) all Indian allotments, the Indian titles to which have not been extinguished, including rights-of-way running through the same.

HOUSE CONCURRENT RESOLUTION 108 OF 1953
67 Stat. B132

Whereas it is the policy of Congress, as rapidly as possible, to make the Indians within the territorial limits of the United States subject to the same laws and entitled to the same privileges and responsibilities as are applicable to other citizens of the United States, to end their status as wards of the United States, and to grant them all of the rights and prerogatives pertaining to American citizenship; and whereas the Indians within the territorial limits of the United States should assume their full responsibilities as American citizens: Now, therefore, be it

Resolved by the House of Representatives (the Senate concurring), That it is declared to be the sense of Congress that, at the earliest possible time, all of the Indian tribes and the individual members thereof....

PUBLIC LAW 280 OF 1953
18 U.S.C. § 1162, 25 U.S.C. §§ 1321-1326, 28 U.S.C. §§ 1360, 1360 note

18 U.S.C. § 1162. State jurisdiction over offenses committed by or against Indians in the Indian country

(a) Each of the States or Territories listed in the following table shall have jurisdiction over offenses committed by or against Indians in the areas of Indian country listed opposite the name of the State or Territory to the same extent that such State or Territory has jurisdiction over offenses committed elsewhere within the State or Territory, and the criminal laws of such State or Territory shall have the same force and effect within such Indian country as they have elsewhere within the State or Territory:

State or Territory of	*Indian country affected*
Alaska	All Indian country within the State, except that on Annette Islands, the Metlakatla Indian community may exercise jurisdiction over offenses committed by Indians in the same manner in which such jurisdiction may be exercised by Indian tribes in Indian country over which State jurisdiction has not been extended.
California	All Indian country within the State.
Minnesota	All Indian country within the State, except the Red Lake Reservation.
Nebraska	All Indian country within the State.
Oregon	All Indian country within the State, except the Warm Springs Reservation.
Wisconsin	All Indian country within the State.

(b) Nothing in this section shall authorize the alienation, encumbrance, or taxation of any real or personal property, including water rights, belonging to any Indian or any Indian tribe, band, or community that is held in trust by the United States or is subject to a restriction against alienation imposed by the United States; or shall authorize regulation of the use of such property in a manner inconsistent with any Federal treaty, agreement, or statute or with any regulation made pursuant thereto; or shall deprive any Indian or any Indian tribe, band, or community of any right, privilege, or immunity afforded under Federal treaty, agreement, or statute with respect to hunting, trapping, or fishing or the control, licensing, or regulation thereof.

....

[*The original Act also provided that* "[t]itle 28, United States Code, is hereby amended by inserting ... a new section, to be designated as section 1360." *The new section, in language virtually identical to that of 18 U.S.C. § 1162 above, conferred to the listed states* "jurisdiction over civil causes of action between Indians or to which Indians are parties which arise in the [listed] areas of Indian country." *Jurisdiction was granted* "to the same extent that such State has jurisdiction over other civil causes of action, and those civil laws of such State that are of general application to private persons or private property" *were given* "the same force and effect within such Indian country as they have elsewhere within the State."]

25 U.S.C. §§ 1321, 1322.

[*Enacted as part of the Indian Civil Rights Act of 1968, these two statutes modified Public Law 280 to require, before any other state may assume civil or criminal jurisdiction over Indian country*, "the consent of the Indian tribe ... affected by such assumption."]

25 U.S.C. § 1323. Retrocession of jurisdiction by State

(a) The United States is authorized to accept a retrocession by any State of all or any measure of the criminal or civil jurisdiction, or both, acquired by such State pursuant to the provisions of section 1162 of Title 18, section 1360 of Title 28, or section 7 of the Act of August 15, 1953 (67 Stat. 588), as it was in effect prior to its repeal by subsection (b) of this section.

(b) Section 7 of the Act of August 15, 1953 (67 Stat. 588), is hereby repealed, but such repeal shall not affect any cession of jurisdiction made pursuant to such section prior to its repeal.

25 U.S.C. § 1324. Amendment of state constitutions or statutes to remove legal impediment; effective date

Notwithstanding the provisions of any Enabling Act for the admission of a State, the consent of the United States is hereby given to the people of any State to amend, where necessary, their State constitution or existing statutes, as the case may be, to remove any legal impediment to the assumption of civil or criminal jurisdiction in accordance with the provisions of this subchapter. The provisions of this subchapter shall not become effective with respect to such assumption of jurisdiction by any such State until the people thereof have appropriately amended their State constitution or statutes, as the case may be.

THE MENOMINEE TERMINATION ACT OF 1954

Ch. 303, 68 Stat. 250 (1954)

(Repealed 1973)

AN ACT

To provide for a per capita distribution of Menominee tribal funds and authorize the withdrawal of the Menominee Tribe from Federal jurisdiction.

Be it enacted by the Senate and House of Representatives of the United States of America in Congress assembled, That the purpose of this Act is to provide for orderly termination of Federal supervision over the property and members of the Menominee Indian Tribe of Wisconsin.

....

SEC. 3. At midnight of the date of enactment of this Act the roll of the tribe maintained pursuant to the Act of June 15, 1934 (48 Stat. 965), as amended by the Act of July 14, 1939 (53 Stat. 1003), shall be closed and no child born thereafter shall be eligible for enrollment:

....

SEC. 5. The Secretary is authorized and directed, as soon as practicable after the passage of this Act, to pay from such funds as are deposited to the credit of the tribe in the Treasury of the United States $1,500 to each member of the tribe on the rolls of the tribe on the date of this Act.

....

SEC. 8. The Secretary is hereby authorized and directed to transfer to the tribe, on December 31, 1958, or on such earlier date as may be agreed upon by the tribe and the Secretary, the title to all property, real and personal, held in trust by the United States for the tribe:

....

SEC. 10. When title to the property of the tribe has been transferred, as provided in section 8 of this Act, the Secretary shall publish in the Federal Register an appropriate proclamation of that fact. Thereafter individual members of the tribe shall not be entitled to any of the services performed by the United States for Indians because of their status as Indians, all statutes of the United States which affect Indians because of their status as Indians shall no longer be applicable to the members of the tribe, and the laws of the several States shall apply to the tribe and its members in the same manner as they apply to other citizens or persons within their jurisdiction. Nothing in this Act shall affect the status of the members of the tribe as citizens of the United States.

....

THE INDIAN CIVIL RIGHTS ACT OF 1968

25 U.S.C. §§ 1301-1341

§ 1301. Definitions

For purposes of this subchapter, the term—

(1) "Indian tribe" means any tribe, band, or other group of Indians subject to the jurisdiction of the United States and recognized as possessing powers of self-government;

(2) "powers of self-government" means and includes all governmental powers possessed by an Indian tribe, executive, legislative, and judicial, and all offices, bodies, and tribunals by and through which they are executed, including courts of Indian offenses; and means the inherent power of Indian tribes, hereby recognized and affirmed, to exercise criminal jurisdiction over all Indians;

(3) "Indian court" means any Indian tribal court or court of Indian offense; and

(4) "Indian" means any person who would be subject to the jurisdiction of the United States as an Indian under section 1153, Title 18, if that person were to commit an offense listed in that section in Indian country to which that section applies.

§ 1302. Constitutional rights

No Indian tribe in exercising powers of self-government shall —

(1) make or enforce any law prohibiting the free exercise of religion, or abridging the freedom of speech, or of the press, or the right of the people peaceably to assemble and to petition for a redress of grievances;

(2) violate the right of the people to be secure in their persons, houses, papers, and effects against unreasonable search and seizures, nor issue warrants, but upon probable cause, supported by oath or affirmation, and particularly describing the place to be searched and the person or thing to be seized;

(3) subject any person for the same offense to be twice put in jeopardy;

(4) compel any person in any criminal case to be a witness against himself;

(5) take any private property for a public use without just compensation;

(6) deny to any person in a criminal proceeding the right to a speedy and public trial, to be informed of the nature and cause of the accusation, to be confronted with the witnesses against him, to have compulsory process for obtaining witnesses in his favor, and at his own expense to have the assistance of counsel for his defense;

(7) require excessive bail, impose excessive fines, inflict cruel and unusual punishments, and in no event impose for conviction of any one offense any penalty or punishment greater than imprisonment for a term of one year or a fine of $5000, or both;

(8) deny to any person within its jurisdiction the equal protection of its laws or deprive any person of liberty or property without due process of law;

(9) pass any bill of attainder or ex post facto law; or

(10) deny to any person accused of an offense punishable by imprisonment the right, upon request, to a trial by jury of not less than six persons.

§ 1303. Habeas corpus

The privilege of the writ of habeas corpus shall be available to any person, in a court of the United States, to test the legality of his detention by order of an Indian tribe.

....

(As amended Pub. L. 99-570, Title IV, § 4217, Oct. 27, 1986, 100 Stat. 3207-146.)

CLEAN WATER ACT OF 1972

33 U.S.C. §§ 1251-1377

§ 1377. Indian tribes

(a) Policy

Nothing in this section shall be construed to affect the application of section 1251(g) of this title, and all of the provisions of this section shall be carried out in accordance with the provisions of such section 1251(g) of this title. Indian tribes shall be treated as States for purposes of such section 1251(g) of this title.

(b) Assessment of sewage treatment needs; report

The Administrator, in cooperation with the Director of the Indian Health Service, shall assess the need for sewage treatment works to serve Indian tribes, the degree to which such needs will be met through funds allotted to States under section 1285 of this title and priority lists under section 1296 of this title, and any obstacles which prevent such needs from being met. Not later than one year after February 4, 1987, the Administrator shall submit a report to Congress on the assessment under this subsection, along with recommendations specifying (1) how the Administrator intends to provide assistance to Indian tribes to develop waste treatment management plans and to construct treatment works under this chapter, and (2) methods by which the participation in and administration of programs under this chapter by Indian tribes can be maximized.

. . . .

(d) Cooperative agreements

In order to ensure the consistent implementation of the requirements of this chapter, an Indian tribe and the State or States in which the lands of such tribe are located may enter into a cooperative agreement, subject to the review and approval of the Administrator, to jointly plan and administer the requirements of this chapter.

(e) Treatment as States

The Administrator is authorized to treat an Indian tribe as a State for purposes of subchapter II of this chapter and sections 1254, 1256, 1313, 1315, 1318, 1319, 1324, 1329, 1341, 1342, 1344, and 1346 of this title to the degree necessary to carry out the objectives of this section, but only if—

(1) the Indian tribe has a governing body carrying out substantial governmental duties and powers;

(2) the functions to be exercised by the Indian tribe pertain to the management and protection of water resources which are held by an Indian tribe, held by the United States in trust for Indians, held by a member of an Indian tribe if such property interest is subject to a trust restriction on alienation, or otherwise within the borders of an Indian reservation; and

(3) the Indian tribe is reasonably expected to be capable, in the Administrator's judgment, of carrying out the functions to be exercised in a manner consistent with the terms and purposes of this chapter and of all applicable regulations.

Such treatment as a State may include the direct provision of funds reserved under subsection (c) of this section to the governing bodies of Indian tribes, and the determination of priorities by Indian tribes, where not determined by the Administrator in cooperation with the Director of the Indian Health Service. The Administrator, in cooperation with the Director of the Indian Health Service, is authorized to make grants under subchapter II of this chapter in an amount not to exceed 100 percent of the cost of a project. Not later than 18 months after February 4, 1987, the Administrator shall, in consultation with Indian tribes, promulgate final regulations which specify how Indian tribes shall be treated as States for purposes of this chapter. The Administrator shall, in promulgating such regulations, consult affected States sharing common water bodies and provide a mechanism for the resolution of any unreasonable consequences that may arise as a result of differing water quality standards that may be set by States and Indian tribes located on common bodies of water. Such mechanism shall provide for explicit consideration of relevant factors including, but not limited to, the effects of differing water quality permit requirements on upstream and downstream dischargers, economic impacts, and present and historical uses and quality of the waters subject to such standards. Such mechanism should provide for the avoidance of such unreasonable consequences in a manner consistent with the objective of this chapter.

(f) Grants for nonpoint source programs

The Administrator shall make grants to an Indian tribe under section 1329 of this title as though such tribe was a State....

(g) Alaska Native organizations

No provision of this chapter shall be construed to—

(1) grant, enlarge, or diminish, or in any way affect the scope of the governmental authority, if any, of any Alaska Native organization, including any federally-recognized tribe, traditional Alaska Native council, or Native council organized pursuant to the Act of June 18, 1934 (48 Stat. 987), over lands or persons in Alaska;

(2) create or validate any assertion by such organization or any form of governmental authority over lands or persons in Alaska; or

(3) in any way affect any assertion that Indian country, as defined in section 1151 of Title 18, exists or does not exist in Alaska.

THE MENOMINEE RESTORATION ACT OF 1973

25 U.S.C. §§ 903-903f

§ 903a. Federal recognition
(a) Extension; laws applicable

Notwithstanding the provisions of subchapter XL of this chapter, or any other law, Federal recognition is hereby extended to the Menominee Indian Tribe of Wisconsin and the provisions of the sections 461, 462, 463, 464, 465, 466 to 470, 471 to 473, 474, 475, 476 to 478, and 479 of this title are made applicable to it.

(b) Repeal of provisions terminating Federal supervision; reinstatement of tribal rights and privileges

Subchapter XL of this chapter is hereby repealed and there are hereby reinstated all rights and privileges of the tribe or its members under Federal treaty, statute, or otherwise which may have been diminished or lost pursuant to such subchapter.

....

THE INDIAN SELF-DETERMINATION AND EDUCATION ASSISTANCE ACT OF 1975

25 U.S.C. §§ 450-451n, 455-458e

§ 450a. Congressional declaration of policy

(a) The Congress hereby recognizes the obligation of the United States to respond to the strong expression of the Indian people for self-determination by assuring maximum Indian participation in the direction of educational as well as other Federal services to Indian communities so as to render such services more responsive to the needs and desires of those communities.

(b) The Congress declares its commitment to the maintenance of the Federal Government's unique and continuing relationship with and responsibility to the Indian people through the establishment of a meaningful Indian self-determination policy which will permit an orderly transition from Federal domination of programs for and services to Indians to effective and meaningful participation by the Indian people in the planning, conduct, and administration of those programs and services.

(c) The Congress declares that a major national goal of the United States is to provide the quantity and quality of educational services and opportunities which will permit Indian children to compete and excel in the life areas of their choice, and to achieve the measure of self-determination essential to their social and economic well-being.

. . . .

§ 450f. Contracts by Secretary of the Interior with tribal organizations

(a) Request by tribe for contract by Secretary to plan, conduct and administer education, etc., programs; refusal of request

The Secretary of the Interior is directed, upon the request of any Indian tribe, to enter into a contract or contracts with any tribal organization of any such Indian tribe to plan, conduct, and administer programs, or portions thereof, provided for in sections 452 to 457 of this title, any other program or portion thereof which the Secretary of the Interior is authorized to administer for the benefit of Indians under sections 13 and 52a of this title, and any Act subsequent thereto: *Provided, however,* That the Secretary may initially decline to enter into any contract requested by an Indian tribe if he finds that: (1) the service to be rendered to the Indian beneficiaries of the particular program or function to be contracted will not be satisfactory; (2) adequate protection of trust resources is not assured, or (3) the proposed project or function to be contracted for cannot be properly completed or maintained by the proposed contract: *Provided further,* That in arriving at his finding, the Secretary shall consider whether the tribe or tribal organization would be deficient in performance under the contract with respect to (A) equipment, (B) bookkeeping and accounting procedures, (C) substantive knowledge of the program to be contracted for, (D) community support for the contract, (E) adequately trained personnel, or (F) other necessary components of contract performance.

(b) Procedure upon refusal of request to contract

Whenever the Secretary declines to enter into a contract or contracts pursuant to subsection (a) of this section, he shall (1) state his objections in writing to the tribe within sixty days, (2) provide to the extent practicable assistance to the tribe or tribal organization to overcome his stated objections, and (3) provide the tribe with a hearing, under such rules and regulations as he may promulgate, and the opportunity for appeal on the objections raised.

(c) Procurement of liability insurance by tribe as prerequisite to exercise of contracting authority by Secretary; required policy provisions

The Secretary is authorized to require any tribe requesting that he enter into a contract pursuant to the provisions of this subchapter to obtain adequate liability insurance: *Provided, however,* That each such policy of insurance shall contain a provision that the insurance carrier shall waive any right it may have to raise as a defense the tribe's sovereign immunity from suit, but that such waiver shall extend only to claims the amount and nature of which are within the coverage and limits of the policy and shall not authorize or empower such insurance carrier to waive or otherwise limit the tribe's sovereign immunity outside or beyond the coverage and limits of the policy of insurance.

.....

§ 450h. Grants to tribal organizations or tribes

(a) Request by tribe for contract or grant by Secretary of the Interior for improving, etc., tribal governmental, contracting, and program planning activities

The Secretary of the Interior is authorized, upon the request of any Indian tribe (from funds appropriated for the benefit of Indians pursuant to sections 13 and 52a of this title, and any Act subsequent thereto) to contract with or make a grant or grants to any tribal organization for—

(1) the strengthening or improvement of tribal government (including, but not limited to, the development, improvement, and administration of planning, financial management, or merit personnel systems; the improvement of tribally funded programs or activities; or the development, construction, improvement, maintenance, preservation, or operation of tribal facilities or resources);

(2) the planning, training, evaluation of other activities designed to improve the capacity of a tribal organization to enter into a contract or contracts pursuant to section 450f of this title and the additional costs associated with the initial years of operation under such a contract or contracts;

(3) the acquisition of land in connection with items (1) and (2) above: *Provided,* That in the case of lands within reservation boundaries or which adjoins on at least two sides land held in trust by the United States for the tribe or for individual Indians, the Secretary of Interior may (upon request of the tribe) acquire such land in trust for the tribe; or

(4) the planning, designing, monitoring, and evaluating of Federal programs serving the tribe.

(b) Grants by Secretary of Health and Human Services for development, maintenance, etc., of health facilities or services and improvement of contract capabilities implementing hospital and health facility functions

The Secretary of Health and Human Services may, in accordance with regulations adopted pursuant to section 450k of this title, make grants to any Indian tribe or tribal organization for—

(1) the development, construction, operation, provision, or maintenance of adequate health facilities or services including the training of personnel for such work, from funds appropriated to the Indian Health Service for Indian health services or Indian health facilities; or

(2) planning, training, evaluation or other activities designed to improve the capacity of a tribal organization to enter into a contract or contracts pursuant to section 450g of this title.

(c) Use as matching shares for other similar Federal grant programs

The provisions of any other Act notwithstanding, any funds made available to a tribal organization under grants pursuant to this section may be used as matching shares for any other Federal grant programs which contribute to the purposes for which grants under this section are made.

....

THE INDIAN CHILD WELFARE ACT OF 1978

25 U.S.C. §§ 1901-1963

§ 1901. Congressional findings

Recognizing the special relationship between the United States and the Indian tribes and their members and the Federal responsibility to Indian people, the Congress finds—

(1) that clause 3, section 8, article I of the United States Constitution provides that "The Congress shall have Power ... To regulate Commerce ... with Indian tribes" and, through this and other constitutional authority, Congress has plenary power over Indian affairs;

(2) that Congress, through statutes, treaties, and the general course of dealing with Indian tribes, has assumed the responsibility for the protection and preservation of Indian tribes and their resources;

(3) that there is no resource that is more vital to the continued existence and integrity of Indian tribes than their children and that the United States has a direct interest, as trustee, in protecting Indian children who are members of or are eligible for membership in an Indian tribe;

(4) that an alarmingly high percentage of Indian families are broken up by the removal, often unwarranted, of their children from them by nontribal public and private agencies and that an alarmingly high percentage of such children are placed in non-Indian foster and adoptive homes and institutions; and

(5) that the States, exercising their recognized jurisdiction over Indian child custody proceedings through administrative and judicial bodies, have often failed to recognize the essential tribal relations of Indian people and the cultural and social standards prevailing in Indian communities and families.

§ 1902. Congressional declaration of policy

The Congress hereby declares that it is the policy of this Nation to protect the best interests of Indian children and to promote the stability and security of Indian tribes and families by the establishment of minimum Federal standards for the removal of Indian children from their families and the placement of such children in foster or adoptive homes which will reflect the unique values of Indian culture, and by providing for assistance to Indian tribes in the operation of child and family service programs.

....

§ 1911. Indian tribe jurisdiction over Indian child custody proceedings— Exclusive jurisdiction

(a) An Indian tribe shall have jurisdiction exclusive as to any State over any child custody proceeding involving an Indian child who resides or is domiciled within the reservation of such tribe, except where such jurisdiction is otherwise vested in the State by existing Federal law. Where an Indian child is a ward of a tribal court, the Indian tribe shall retain exclusive jurisdiction, notwithstanding the residence or domicile of the child.

....

(d) The United States, every State, every territory or possession of the United States, and every Indian tribe shall give full faith and credit to the public acts, records, and judicial proceedings of any Indian tribe applicable to Indian child custody proceedings to the same extent that such entities give full faith and credit to the public acts, records, and judicial proceedings of any other entity.

....

§ 1915. Placement of Indian children—Adoptive placements; preferences

(a) In any adoptive placement of an Indian child under State law, a preference shall be given, in the absence of good cause to the contrary, to a placement with (1) a member of the child's extended family; (2) other members of the Indian child's tribe; or (3) other Indian families.

....

(d) The standards to be applied in meeting the preference requirements of this section shall be the prevailing social and cultural standards of the Indian community in which the parent or extended family resides or with which the parent or extended family members maintain social and cultural ties.

THE AMERICAN INDIAN RELIGIOUS FREEDOM ACT OF 1978

92 Stat. 469 (1978)

(codified in part at 42 U.S.C. § 1996)

Whereas the freedom of religion for all people is an inherent right, fundamental to the democratic structure of the United States and is guaranteed by the First Amendment of the United States Constitution;

Whereas the United States has traditionally rejected the concept of a government denying individuals the right to practice their religion and, as a result, has benefited from a rich variety of religious heritages in this country;

Whereas the religious practices of the American Indian (as well as Native Alaskan and Hawaiian) are an integral part of their culture, tradition and heritage, such practices forming the basis of Indian identity and value systems;

Whereas the traditional American Indian religions, as an integral part of Indian life, are indispensable and irreplaceable;

Whereas the lack of a clear, comprehensive, and consistent Federal policy has often resulted in the abridgement of religious freedom for traditional American Indians;

Whereas such religious infringements result from the lack of knowledge or the insensitive and inflexible enforcement of Federal policies and regulations premised on a variety of laws;

Whereas such laws were designed for such worthwhile purposes as conservation and preservation of natural species and resources but were never intended to relate to Indian religious practices and, therefore, were passed without consideration of their effect on traditional American Indian religions;

Whereas such laws and policies often deny American Indians access to sacred sites required in the religions, including cemeteries;

Whereas such laws at times prohibit the use and possession of sacred objects necessary to the exercise of religious rites and ceremonies;

Whereas traditional American Indian ceremonies have been intruded upon, interfered with, and in a few instances banned: …

42 U.S.C. § 1196. Protection and preservation of traditional religions of Native Americans

On and after August 11, 1978, it shall be the policy of the United States to protect and preserve for American Indians their inherent right of freedom to believe, express, and exercise the traditional religions of the American Indian, Eskimo, Aleut, and Native Hawaiians, including but not limited to access to sites, use and possession of sacred objects, and the freedom to worship through ceremonials and traditional rites.

INDIAN GAMING REGULATORY ACT OF 1988
25 U.S.C. §§ 2701-2721.

§ 2701. Findings
The Congress finds that—

(1) numerous Indian tribes have become engaged in or have licensed gaming activities on Indian lands as a means of generating tribal governmental revenue;

(2) Federal courts have held that section 81 of this title requires Secretarial review of management contracts dealing with Indian gaming, but does not provide standards for the approval of such contracts;

(3) existing Federal law does not provide clear standards or regulations for the conduct of gaming on Indian lands;

(4) a principal goal of Federal Indian policy is to promote tribal economic development, tribal self-sufficiency, and strong tribal government; and

(5) Indian tribes have the exclusive right to regulate gaming activity on Indian lands if the gaming activity is not specifically prohibited by Federal law and is

conducted within a State which does not, as a matter of criminal law and public policy, prohibit such gaming activity.

....

§ 2703. Definitions

For the purposes of this chapter—

....

(6) The term "class I gaming" means social games solely for prizes of minimal value or traditional forms of Indian gaming engaged in by individuals as a part of, or in connection with, tribal ceremonies or celebrations.

(7)(A) The term "class II gaming" means—

(i) the game of chance commonly known as bingo (whether or not electronic, computer, or other technologic aids are used in connection therewith)

(ii) card games that—

(I) are explicitly authorized by the laws of the State, or

(II) are not explicitly prohibited by the laws of the State and are played at any location in the State, but only if such card games are played in conformity with those laws and regulations (if any) of the State regarding hours or periods of operation ... or limitations on wagers or pot sizes in such card games.

(8) The term "class III gaming" means all forms of gaming that are not class I gaming or class II gaming.

§ 2704. National Indian Gaming Commission

(a) Establishment

There is established within the Department of the Interior a Commission to be known as the National Indian Gaming Commission.

§ 2705. Powers of Chairman

(a) The Chairman, on behalf of the Commission, shall have power, subject to an appeal to the Commission, to—

(1) issues orders of temporary closure of gaming activities as provided in section 2713(b) of this title;

(2) levy and collect civil fines as provided in section 2713(a) of this title;

(3) approve tribal ordinances or resolutions regulating class II gaming and class III gaming as provided in section 2710 of this title;

(4) approve management contracts for class II gaming and class III gaming as provided in section 2710(d)(9) and 2711 of this title.

....

§ 2710. Tribal gaming ordinances

(a) Exclusive jurisdiction of class I and class II gaming activity

(1) Class I gaming on Indian lands is within the exclusive jurisdiction of the Indian tribes and shall not be subject to the provisions of this chapter.

(2) Any class II gaming on Indian lands shall continue to be within the jurisdiction of Indian tribes, but shall be subject to the provisions of this chapter.

(b) Regulation of class II gaming activity; net revenue allocation; audits; contracts

(1) An Indian tribe may engage in, or license and regulate, class II gaming on Indian lands with such tribe's jurisdiction, if—

    (A) such Indian gaming is located within a State that permits such gaming for any purpose by any person, organization or entity (and such gaming is not otherwise specifically prohibited in Indian lands by Federal law).

    ....

(d) Class II gaming activities; authorization; revocation; Tribal-State compact

(1) Class II gaming activities shall be lawful on Indian lands only if such activities are—

    (A) authorized by an ordinance or resolution that—

    (i) is adopted by the governing body of the Indian tribe having jurisdiction over such lands,

    (ii) meets the requirements of subsection (b) of this section, and

    (iii) is approved by the Chairman.

    (B) located in a State that permits such gaming for any purpose by any person, organization, or entity, and

    (C) conducted in conformance with a Tribal-State compact entered into by the Indian tribe and the State....

    ....

(3)(A) Any Indian tribe having jurisdiction over the Indian lands upon which a class III gaming activity is being conducted, or is to be conducted, shall request the State in which such lands are located to enter into negotiations for the purpose of entering into a Tribal-State compact governing the conduct of gaming activities. Upon receiving such a request, the State shall negotiate with the Indian tribe in good faith to enter into such a compact.

(B) Any State and any Indian tribe may enter into a Tribal-State compact governing gaming activities on the Indian lands of the Indian tribe, but such compact shall take effect only when notice of approval by the Secretary of such compact has been published by the Secretary in the Federal Register.

NATIVE AMERICAN GRAVES PROTECTION AND REPATRIATION ACT OF 1990

25 U.S.C. §§ 3001-3013

§ 3002. Ownership

(a) Native American human remains and objects

The ownership or control of Native American cultural items which are excavated or discovered on Federal or tribal lands after November 16, 1990, shall be (with priority given in the order listed)—

(**1**) in the case of Native American human remains and associated funerary objects, in the lineal descendants of the Native American; or

(**2**) in any case in which such lineal descendants cannot be ascertained, and in the case of unassociated funerary objects, sacred objects, and objects of cultural patrimony—

(**A**) in the Indian tribe or Native Hawaiian organization on whose tribal land such objects or remains were discovered;

(**B**) in the Indian tribe or Native Hawaiian organization which has the closest cultural affiliation with such remains or objects and which, upon notice, states a claim for such remains or objects; or

(**C**) if the cultural affiliation of the objects cannot be reasonably ascertained and if the objects were discovered on Federal land that is recognized by a final judgment of the Indian Claims Commission or the United States Court of Claims as the aboriginal land of some Indian tribe—

(**1**) in the Indian tribe that is recognized as aboriginally occupying the area in which the objects were discovered, if upon notice, such tribe states a claim for such remains or objects, or

(**2**) if it can be shown by a preponderance of the evidence that a different tribe has a stronger cultural relationship with the remains or objects than the tribe or organization specified in paragraph (1), in the Indian tribe that has the strongest demonstrated relationship, if upon notice, such tribe states a claim for such remains or objects.

....

(c) Intentional excavation and removal of Native American human remains and objects

The intentional removal from or excavation of Native American cultural items from Federal or tribal lands for purposes of discovery, study, or removal of such items is permitted only if—

(**1**) such items are excavated or removed pursuant to a permit issued under section 470cc of Title 16 which shall be consistent with this Chapter;

(**2**) such items are excavated or removed after consultation with or, in the case of tribal lands, consent of the appropriate (if any) Indian tribe or Native Hawaiian organization;

....

(**d**) Inadvertent discovery of Native American remains and objects

(**1**) Any person who knows, or has reason to know, that such person has discovered Native American cultural items on Federal or tribal lands after November 16, 1990, shall notify, in writing, the Secretary of the Department, or head of any other agency or instrumentality of the United States, having primary management authority with respect to Federal lands and the appropriate Indian tribe or Native Hawaiian organization with respect to tribal lands, if known or readily ascertainable, and, in the case of lands that have been selected by an Alaska Native Corporation or group organized pursuant to the Alaska Native Claims Settlement Act of 1971 [43 U.S.C. § 1601 et seq.], the appropriate corporation or group. If the discovery occurred in connection with an activity, including (but not limited to) construction, mining, logging, and agriculture, the person shall cease the activity in the area of the discovery, make a reasonable effort to protect the items discovered before resuming such activity, and provide notice under this subsection. Following the notification under this subsection, and upon certification by the Secretary of the department or the head of any agency or instrumentality of the United States or the appropriate Indian tribe or Native Hawaiian organization that notification has been received, the activity may resume after 30 days of such certification.

....

§ 3003. Inventory for human remains and associated funerary objects
(a) In general

Each Federal agency and each museum which has possession or control over holdings or collections of Native American human remains and associated funerary objects shall compile an inventory of such items and, to the extent possible based on information possessed by such museum or Federal agency, identify the geographical and cultural affiliation of such item.

....

(d) Notification

(1) If the cultural affiliation of any particular Native American human remains or associated funerary objects is determined pursuant to this section, the Federal agency or museum concerned shall, not later than 6 months after the completion of the inventory, notify the affected Indian tribes or Native Hawaiian organizations.

§ 3005. Repatriation

(a) Repatriation of Native American human remains and objects possessed or controlled by Federal agencies and museums

(1) If, pursuant to section 3003 of this title, the cultural affiliation of Native American human remains and associated funerary objects with a particular Indian tribe or Native Hawaiian organization is established, then the Federal agency or museum, upon the request of a known lineal descendant of the Native American or of the tribe or organization and pursuant to subsections (b) and (e) of this section, shall expeditiously return such remains and associated funerary objects.

(2) If, pursuant to section 3004 of this title, the cultural affiliation with a particular Indian tribe or Native Hawaiian organization is shown with respect to unassociated funerary objects, sacred objects or objects of cultural patrimony, then the Federal agency or museum, upon the request of the Indian tribe or Native Hawaiian organization ... shall expeditiously return such objects.

....

(4) Where cultural affiliation of Native American human remains and funerary objects has not been established ... such Native American human remains and funerary objects shall be expeditiously returned where the requesting Indian tribe or Native Hawaiian organization can show cultural affiliation by a preponderance of the evidence based upon geographical, kinship, biological, archaeological, anthropological, linguistic, folkloric, oral traditional, historical, or other relevant information or expert opinion.

PART FOUR

SELECTED UNITED STATES
SUPREME COURT DECISIONS
(Edited)

INTRODUCTION

Federal Indian law has been shaped by court decisions stemming back to the early days of the Supreme Court when John Marshall was Chief Justice. In recent years the Court has been more active in Indian law than in many other areas, including anti-trust, securities, international, and environmental law. The extent of the reference notes that conclude the text in Part One give some indication of the number of decisions that have shaped the field. Part Four includes some of the key decisions that have shaped the law that has established Indian tribes as sovereign governments. Following are excerpts of the full decisions, edited to highlight the portions of the decisions that deal most directly with the topics covered in Part One. Footnotes have been omitted, as have many citations to other cases mentioned in the full texts of the decisions presented. In some instances the facts that underlie individual cases are summarized in italicized text within brackets.

JOHNSON v. M'INTOSH

21 U.S. (8 Wheat.) 543, 5 L. Ed. 681 (U.S. Sup. Ct. 1823)

CHIEF JUSTICE MARSHALL delivered the opinion of the Court.

The plaintiffs in this cause claim the land, in their declaration mentioned, under two grants, purporting to be made, the first in 1773, and the last in 1775, by the chiefs of certain Indian tribes, constituting the Illinois and the Piankeshaw nations; and the question is, whether this title can be recognized in the Courts of the United States?

The facts, as stated in the case agreed, show the authority of the chiefs who executed this conveyance, so far as it could be given by their own people; and likewise show, that the particular tribes for whom these chiefs acted were in rightful possession of the land they sold. [*In 1795 the tribes ceded the land in question to the United States by treaty. In 1818 defendant, William McIntosh, received a grant of the land from the United States. The land was located in the State of Illinois.*] … The inquiry, therefore, is, in a great measure, confined to the power of Indians to give, and of private individuals to receive, a title which can be sustained in the Courts of this country.…

On the discovery of this immense continent, the great nations of Europe were eager to appropriate to themselves so much of it as they could respectively acquire. Its vast extent offered an ample field to the ambition and enterprise of all; and the character and religion of its inhabitants afforded an apology for considering them as a people over whom the superior genius of Europe might claim an ascendancy. The potentates of the old world found no difficulty in convincing themselves that they made ample compensation to the inhabitants of the new, by bestowing on them civilization and Christianity, in exchange for unlimited independence. But, as they were all in pursuit of nearly the same object, it was necessary, in order to avoid conflicting settlements, and consequent war with each other, to establish a principle, which all shall acknowledge as the law by which the right of acquisition, which they all asserted, should be regulated as between themselves. This principle was, that discovery gave title to the government by whose subjects, or by whose authority, it was made, against all other European governments, which title might be consummated by possession.

The exclusion of all other Europeans, necessarily gave to the nation making the discovery the sole right of acquiring the soil from the natives, and establishing settlements upon it. It was a right with which no Europeans could interfere.…

Those relations which were to exist between the discoverer and the natives, were to be regulated by themselves. The rights thus acquired being exclusive, no other power could interpose between them.

In the establishment of these relations, the rights of the original inhabitants were, in no instance, entirely disregarded; but were necessarily, to a considerable extent, impaired. They were admitted to be the rightful occupants of the soil, with a legal as well as just claim to retain possession of it, and to use it according to their own discretion; but their rights to complete sovereignty, as independent nations, were necessarily diminished, and their power to dispose of the soil at their own will, to whomsoever they pleased, was denied by the original fundamental principle, that discovery gave exclusive title to those who made it.

While the different nations of Europe respected the right of the natives, as occupants, they asserted the ultimate dominion to be in themselves; and claimed and exercised, as a consequence of this ultimate dominion, a power to grant the soil, while yet in possession of the natives. These grants have been understood by all, to convey a title to the grantees, subject only to the Indian right of occupancy....

No one of the powers of Europe gave its full assent to this principle, more unequivocally than England. The documents upon this subject are ample and complete. So early as the year 1496, her monarch granted a commission to the Cabots, to discover countries then unknown to *Christian people*, and to take possession of them in the name of the king of England. Two years afterwards, Cabot proceeded on this voyage, and discovered the continent of North America, along which he sailed as far south as Virginia. To this discovery the English trace their title.

In this first effort made by the English government to acquire territory on this continent, we perceive a complete recognition of the principle which has been mentioned. The right of discovery given by this commission, is confined to countries "then unknown to all Christian people;" and of these countries Cabot was empowered to take possession in the name of the king of England. Thus asserting a right to take possession, notwithstanding the occupancy of the natives, who were heathens, and, at the same time, admitting the prior title of any Christian people who may have made a previous discovery....

Thus has our whole country been granted by the crown while in the occupation of the Indians. These grants purport to convey the soil as well as the right of dominion to the grantees....

Further proofs of the extent to which this principle has been recognized, will be found in the history of the wars, negotiations, and treaties, which the different nations, claiming territory in America, have carried on, and held with each other....

[A]ll the nations of Europe, who have acquired territory on this continent, have asserted in themselves, and have recognized in others, the exclusive right of the discoverer to appropriate the lands occupied by the Indians. Have the American States rejected or adopted this principle?

By the treaty which concluded the war of our revolution, Great Britain relinquished all claim, not only to the government, but to the "property and territorial rights of the United States," whose boundaries were fixed in the second article. By this treaty, the powers of government, and the right to soil, which had previously been in Great Britain, passed definitively to these States. We had before taken possession of them, by declaring independence; but neither the declaration of independence, nor the treaty confirming it, could give us more than that which we before possessed, or to which Great Britain was before entitled. It has never been doubted, that either the United States, or the several states, had a clear title to all the lands within the boundary lines described in the treaty, subject only to the Indian right of occupancy, and that the exclusive power to extinguish that right, was vested in that government which might constitutionally exercise it....

The United States, then, have unequivocally acceded to that great and broad rule by which its civilized inhabitants now hold this country. They hold, and assert in themselves, the title by which it was acquired....

[*Prior to this case, title to newly discovered lands was acquired, and recognized, as a result of either purchase or conquest. The new continent was vast, however, and its inhabitants independent. By the time this opinion was written, much of the land claimed by the United States had been neither purchased nor conquered.*]

....

That law which regulates, and ought to regulate in general, the relations between the conqueror and conquered, was incapable of application to a people under such circumstances. The resort to some new and different rule, better adapted to the actual state of things, was unavoidable. Every rule which can be suggested will be found to be attended with great difficulty.

However extravagant the pretension of converting the discovery of an inhabited country into conquest may appear; if the principle has been asserted in the first instance, and afterwards sustained; if a country has been acquired and held under it; if the property of the great mass of the community originates in it, it becomes the law of the land, and cannot be questioned. So, too, with respect to the concomitant principle, that the Indian inhabitants are to be considered merely as occupants, to be protected, indeed, while in peace, in the possession of their lands, but to be deemed incapable of transferring the absolute title to others. However this restriction may be opposed to natural right, and to the usages of civilized nations, yet, if it be indispensable to that system under which the country has been settled, and be adapted to the actual condition of the two people, it may, perhaps, be supported by reason, and certainly cannot be rejected by Courts of justice....

[*The judgment of the District Court of Illinois in favor of defendant McIntosh was affirmed.*]

CHEROKEE NATION v. GEORGIA

30 U.S. (5 Pet.) 1, 8 L. Ed. 25 (U.S. Sup. Ct. 1831)

Chief Justice Marshall delivered the opinion of the Court.

This bill is brought by the Cherokee nation, praying an injunction to restrain the state of Georgia from the execution of certain laws of that state, which, as is alleged, go directly to annihilate the Cherokees as a political society, and to seize, for the use of Georgia, the lands of the nation which have been assured to them by the United States in solemn treaties repeatedly made and still in force.

If courts were permitted to indulge their sympathies, a case better calculated to excite them can scarcely be imagined. A people once numerous, powerful, and truly independent, found by our ancestors in the quiet and uncontrolled possession of an ample domain, gradually sinking beneath our superior policy, our arts and our arms, have yielded their lands by successive treaties, each of which contains a solemn guarantee of the residue, until they retain no more of their formerly extensive territory than is deemed necessary to their comfortable subsistence. To preserve this remnant, the present application is made.

Before we can look into the merits of the case, a preliminary inquiry presents itself. Has this court jurisdiction of the cause?

The third article of the constitution describes the extent of the judicial power. The second section closes an enumeration of the cases to which it is extended, with "controversies" "between a state or the citizens thereof, and foreign states, citizens, or subjects." A subsequent clause of the same section gives the supreme court original jurisdiction in all cases in which a state shall be a party. The party defendant may then unquestionably be sued in this court. May the plaintiff sue in it? Is the Cherokee nation a foreign state in the sense in which that term is used in the constitution?

The counsel for the plaintiffs have maintained the affirmative of this proposition with great earnestness and ability. So much of the argument as was intended to prove the character of the Cherokees as a state, as a distinct political society, separated from others, capable of managing its own affairs and governing itself, has, in the opinion of a majority of the judges, been completely successful. They have been uniformly treated as a state from the settlement of our country. The numerous treaties made with them by the United States recognize them as a people capable of maintaining the relations of peace and war, of being responsible in their political character for any violation of their engagements, or for any aggression committed on the citizens of the United States by any individual of their community. Laws have been enacted in the spirit of these treaties. The acts of our government plainly recognize the Cherokee nation as a state, and the courts are bound by those acts.

A question of much more difficulty remains. Do the Cherokees constitute a foreign state in the sense of the constitution?

    . . . .

In the general, nations not owing a common allegiance are foreign to each other. The term *foreign nation* is, with strict propriety, applicable by either to the other. But the relation of the Indians to the United States is marked by peculiar and cardinal distinctions which exist no where else.

    . . . .

Though the Indians are acknowledged to have an unquestionable, and, heretofore, unquestioned right to the lands they occupy, until that right shall be extinguished by a voluntary cession to our government; yet it may well be doubted whether those tribes which reside within the acknowledged boundaries of the United States can, with strict accuracy, be denominated foreign nations. They may, more correctly, perhaps, be denominated domestic dependent nations. They occupy a territory to which we assert a title independent of their will, which must take effect in point of possession when their right of possession ceases. Meanwhile they are in a state of pupilage. Their relation to the United States resembles that of a ward to his guardian.

They look to our government for protection; rely upon its kindness and its power; appeal to it for relief to their wants; and address the president as their great father. They and their country are considered by foreign nations, as well as by ourselves, as being so completely under the sovereignty and dominion of the United States, that any attempt to acquire their lands, or to form a political connexion with them, would be considered by all as an invasion of our territory, and an act of hostility.

These considerations go far to support the opinion, that the framers of our constitution had not the Indian tribes in view, when they opened the courts of the union to controversies between a state or the citizens thereof, and foreign states.

....

[T]he peculiar relations between the United States and the Indians occupying our territory are such, that we should feel much difficulty in considering them as designated by the term *foreign state*, were there no other part of the constitution which might shed light on the meaning of these words. But we think that in construing them, considerable aid is furnished by that clause in the eighth section of the third article; which empowers congress to "regulate commerce with foreign nations, and among the several states, and with the Indian tribes."

In this clause they are as clearly contradistinguished by a name appropriate to themselves, from foreign nations, as from the several states composing the union.

....

[*The Court, based on its determination that the tribe was not a "foreign state," but a "domestic dependent nation," denied the motion for an injunction.*]

WORCESTER v. GEORGIA

31 U.S. (6 Pet.) 515, 8 L. Ed. 483 (U.S. Sup. Ct. 1832)

CHIEF JUSTICE MARSHALL delivered the opinion of the Court.

[*The plaintiff in this case, a non-Indian, had been convicted of "residing within the limits of the Cherokee nation" without obtaining a license from Georgia and "without having taken the oath to support and defend the State of Georgia." The issue raised was whether, under the United States Constitution, the State of Georgia has the authority to impose its laws "within the limits of the Cherokee nation."*]

It has been said at the bar, that the acts of the legislature of Georgia seize on the whole Cherokee country, parcel it out among the neighbouring counties of the state, extend her code over the whole country, abolish its institutions and its laws, and annihilate its political existence.

....

The extra-territorial power of every legislature being limited in its action, to its own citizens or subjects, the very passage of this act is an assertion of jurisdiction over the Cherokee nation, and of the rights and powers consequent on jurisdiction.

The first step, then, in the inquiry, which the constitution and laws impose on this court, is an examination of the rightfulness of this claim.

America, separated from Europe by a wide ocean, was inhabited by a distinct people, divided into separate nations, independent of each other and of the rest of the world, having institutions of their own, and governing themselves by their own laws. It is difficult to comprehend the proposition, that the inhabitants of either quarter of the globe could have rightful original claims of dominion over the inhabitants of the other, or over the lands they occupied; or that the discovery of either by the other should give the discoverer rights in the country discovered, which annulled the pre-existing rights of its ancient possessors.

....

But power, war, conquest, give rights, which, after possession, are conceded by the world; and which can never be controverted by those on whom they descend. We proceed, then, to the actual state of things, having glanced at their origin; because holding it in our recollection might shed some light on existing pretensions.

....

Soon after Great Britain determined on planting colonies in America, the king granted charters to companies of his subjects who associated for the purpose of carrying the views of the crown into effect, and of enriching themselves. The first of these charters was made before possession was taken of any part of the country. They purport, generally, to convey the soil, from the Atlantic to the South Sea. This soil was occupied by numerous and warlike nations, equally willing and able to defend their possessions. The extravagant and absurd idea, that the feeble settlements made on the sea coast, or the companies under whom they were made, acquired legitimate power by them to govern the people, or occupy the lands from sea to sea, did not enter the mind of any man. They were well understood to convey the title which, according to the common law of European sovereigns respecting America, they might rightfully convey, and no more. This was the exclusive right of purchasing such lands as the natives were willing to sell. The crown could not be understood to grant what the crown did not affect to claim; nor was it so understood.

....

Certain it is, that our history furnishes no example, from the first settlement of our country, of any attempt on the part of the crown to interfere with the internal affairs of the Indians, farther than to keep out the agents of foreign powers, who, as traders or otherwise, might seduce them into foreign alliances. The king purchased their lands when they were willing to sell, at a price they were willing to take; but never coerced a surrender of them. He also purchased their alliance and dependence by subsidies; but never intruded into the interior of their affairs, or interfered with their self government, so far as respected themselves only.

....

Such was the policy of Great Britain towards the Indian nations inhabiting the territory from which she excluded all other Europeans; such her claims, and such her practical exposition of the charters she had granted: she considered them as nations capable of maintaining the relations of peace and war; of governing themselves, under her protection; and she made treaties with them, the obligation of which she acknowledged.

This was the settled state of things when the war of our revolution commenced. The influence of our enemy was established; her resources enabled her to keep up that influence; and the colonists had much cause for the apprehension that the Indian nations would, as the allies of Great Britain, add their arms to hers. This, as was to be expected, became an object of great solicitude to congress. Far from advancing a claim to their lands, or asserting any right of dominion over them, congress resolved "that the securing and preserving the friendship of the Indian nations appears to be a subject of the utmost moment to these colonies."

....

During the war of the revolution, the Cherokees took part with the British. After its termination, the United States, though desirous of peace, did not feel its necessity so strongly as while the war continued. Their political situation being changed, they might very well think it advisable to assume a higher tone, and to impress on the Cherokees the same respect for congress which was before felt for the king of Great Britain.

....

When the United States gave peace, did they not also receive it? Were not both parties desirous of it? If we consult the history of the day, does it not inform us that the United States were at least as anxious to obtain it as the Cherokees? We may ask, further: did the Cherokees come to the seat of the American government to solicit peace; or, did the American commissioners go to them to obtain it? The treaty was made at Hopewell, not at New York. The word "give," then, has no real importance attached to it.

....

[*The opinion reviews several provisions of the treaty to show that Cherokee political existence was not extinguished.*]

....

This relation [under the Treaty of Holston] was that of a nation claiming and receiving the protection of one more powerful: not that of individuals abandoning their national character, and submitting as subjects to the laws of a master.

....

This treaty, thus explicitly recognizing the national character of the Cherokees, and their right of self government; thus guarantying their lands; assuming the duty of protection, and of course pledging the faith of the United States for that protection; has been frequently renewed, and is now in full force.

....

The treaties and laws of the United States contemplate the Indian territory as completely separated from that of the states; and provide that all intercourse with them shall be carried on exclusively by the government of the union.

....

Such was the state of things when the confederation was adopted. That instrument surrendered the powers of peace and war to congress, and prohibited them to the states, respectively, unless a state be actually invaded, "or shall have received certain advice of a resolution being formed by some nation of Indians to invade such state, and the danger is so imminent as not to admit of delay till the United States in congress assembled can be consulted." This instrument also gave the United States in congress assembled the sole and exclusive right of "regulating the trade and managing all the affairs with the Indians, not members of any of the states: provided, that the legislative power of any state within its own limits be not infringed or violated."

....

[The constitution] confers on congress the powers of war and peace; of making treaties, and of regulating commerce with foreign nations, and among the several states, and *with the Indian tribes*. These powers comprehend all that is required for the regulation of our intercourse with the Indians. They are not limited by any restrictions on their free actions. The shackles imposed on this power, in the confederation, are discarded.

The Indian nations had always been considered as distinct, independent political communities, retaining their original natural rights, as the undisputed possessors of the soil, from time immemorial, with the single exception of that imposed by irresistible power, which excluded them from intercourse with any other European potentate than the first discoverer of the coast of the particular region claimed: and this was a restriction which those European potentates imposed on themselves, as well as on the Indians. The very term "nation," so generally applied to them, means "a people distinct from others." The constitution, by declaring treaties already made, as well as those to be made, to be the supreme law of the land, has adopted and sanctioned the previous treaties with the Indian nations, and consequently admits their rank among those powers who are capable of making treaties. The words "treaty" and "nation" are words of our own language, selected in our diplomatic and legislative proceedings, by ourselves, having each a definite and well understood meaning. We have applied them to Indians, as we have applied them to the other nations of the earth. They are applied to all in the same sense.

   ....

The very fact of repeated treaties with [*the Indians recognized their entitlement to self-government*]; and the settled doctrine of the law of nations is, that a weaker power does not surrender its independence—its right to self-government, by associating with a stronger, and taking its protection. A weak state, in order to provide for its safety, may place itself under the protection of one more powerful, without stripping itself of the right of government, and ceasing to be a state. Examples of this kind are not wanting in Europe. "Tributary and feudatory states," says Vattel, "do not thereby cease to be sovereign and independent states, so long as self-government and sovereign and independent authority are left in the administration of the state." At the present day, more than one state may be considered as holding its right of self-government under the guarantee and protection of one or more allies.

The Cherokee nation, then, is a distinct community, occupying its own territory, with boundaries accurately described, in which the laws of Georgia can have no force, and which the citizens of Georgia have no right to enter, but with the assent of the Cherokees themselves, or in conformity with treaties, and with the acts of congress. The whole intercourse between the United States and this nation, is, by our constitution and laws, vested in the government of the United States.

The act of the state of Georgia, under which the plaintiff in error was prosecuted, is consequently void, and the judgment is a nullity.

   ....

If the review which has been taken be correct, and we think it is, the acts of Georgia are repugnant to the constitution, laws, and treaties of the United States.

They interfere forcibly with the relations established between the United States and the Cherokee nation, the regulation of which, according to the settled principles of our constitution, are committed exclusively to the government of the union.

They are in direct hostility with treaties, repeated in a succession of years, which mark out the boundary that separates the Cherokee country from Georgia; guaranty to them all the land within their boundary; solemnly pledge the faith of the United States to restrain their citizens from trespassing on it; and recognize the pre-existing power of the nation to govern itself.

They are in equal hostility with the acts of Congress for regulating this intercourse, and giving effect to the treaties.

The forcible seizure and abduction of the plaintiff in error, who was residing in the nation with its permission, and by authority of the president of the United States, is also a violation of the acts which authorize the chief magistrate to exercise this authority.

....

It is the opinion of this court that the judgment of the superior court for the county of Gwinnett, in the state of Georgia, condemning Samuel A. Worcester to hard labour, in the penitentiary of the state of Georgia, for four years, was pronounced by that court under colour of a law which is void, as being repugnant to the constitution, treaties, and laws of the United States, and ought, therefore, to be reversed and annulled.

LONE WOLF v. HITCHCOCK

187 U.S. 553, 23 S. Ct. 216, 47 L. Ed. 299 (U.S. Sup. Ct. 1903)

JUSTICE WHITE delivered the opinion of the Court:

[*The Medicine Lodge Treaty of 1867 set aside a reservation in Oklahoma for the Kiowa and Comanche tribes. A separate treaty located certain Apaches on the reservation and entitled them to share in the benefits of the reservation. They alleged that Congress had unilaterally amended the agreement, to the detriment of the tribes, in the legislation executing the agreement.*]

....

The contention in effect ignores the status of the contracting Indians and the relation of dependency they bore and continue to bear towards the government of the United States. To uphold the claim would be to adjudge that the indirect operation of the treaty was to materially limit and qualify the controlling authority of Congress in respect to the care and protection of the Indians, and to deprive Congress, in a possible emergency, when the necessity might be urgent for a partition and disposal of the tribal lands, of all power to act, if the assent of the Indians could not be obtained.

....

Plenary authority over the tribal relations of the Indians has been exercised by Congress from the beginning, and the power has always been deemed a political one, not subject to be controlled by the judicial department of the government....

The power exists to abrogate the provisions of an Indian treaty, though presumably such power will be exercised only when circumstances arise which will not only justify the government in disregarding the stipulations of the treaty, but may demand, in the interest of the country and the Indians themselves, that it should do so. When, therefore, treaties were entered into between the United States and a tribe of Indians it was never doubted that the *power* to abrogate existed in Congress, and that in a contingency such power might be availed of from considerations of governmental policy, particularly if consistent with perfect good faith towards the Indians. [*The opinion then quoted from United States v. Kagama*, 118 U.S. 375.]

....

Indeed, the controversy which this case presents is concluded by the decision in *Cherokee Nation v. Hitchcock*, 187 U.S. 294 decided at this term, where it was held that full administrative power was possessed by Congress over Indian tribal property. In effect, the action of Congress now complained of was but an exercise of such power, a mere change in the form of investment of Indian tribal property, the property of those who, as we have held, were in substantial effect the wards of the government. We must presume that Congress acted in perfect good faith in the dealings with the Indians of which complaint is made, and that the legislative branch of the government exercised its best judgment in the premises. In any event, as Congress possessed full power in the matter, the judiciary cannot question or inquire into the motives which prompted the enactment of this legislation. If injury was occasioned, which we do not wish to be understood as implying, by the use made by Congress of its power, relief must be sought by an appeal to that body for redress, and not to the courts. The legislation in question was constitutional, and the demurrer to the bill was therefore rightly sustained.

....

Affirmed.

UNITED STATES v. WINANS

198 U.S. 371, 25 S. Ct. 662, 49 L. Ed. 1089 (U.S. Sup. Ct. 1905)

Justice McKenna delivered the opinion of the Court:

[*A treaty was negotiated in 1855 between the Yakima Nation (today known as the Yakama Nation) and the United States. Like many treaties, Article I provided that the tribe would "cede, relinquish, and convey to the United States all their right, title, and interest" in specified land, while Article II "reserved" described land for the "use and occupancy" of the tribe. Article III then provided that the tribe would have the "exclusive right of taking fish" on the reservation. Article III also contained a provision, found in some treaties, that the tribe would have off-reservation fishing rights "at all usual and accustomed places, in common with citizens of the Territory."*

The United States brought this action on behalf of the Yakima Nation to enjoin respondents, Winans and other non-Indians, from obstructing off-reservation fishing at usual and accustomed fishing sites. The sites were located on parcels of land along the Columbia River owned in fee by the non-Indian respondents. The respondents operated fish wheels, pursuant to a license from the State of Washington, which were so efficient that they effectively gained "exclusive possession of the fishing places." In addition, the respondents attempted to exclude tribal members from the fishing sites and refused to permit them to cross over other non-Indian fee land to reach the fishing sites. The lower court dismissed the action, finding that the respondents had acquired "perfect absolute title" to the lands in question and therefore had the right to exclude Yakima tribal members from the land.]

The contention of the respondents was sustained. In other words, it was decided that the Indians acquired no rights but what any inhabitant of the Territory or State would have. Indeed, acquired no rights but such as they would have without the treaty. This is certainly an impotent outcome to negotiations and a convention, which seemed to promise more and give the word of the Nation for more....

The right to resort to the fishing places in controversy was a part of larger rights possessed by the Indians, upon the exercise of which there was not a shadow of impediment, and which were not much less necessary to the existence of the Indians than the atmosphere they breathed. New conditions came into existence, to which those rights had to be accommodated. Only a limitation of them, however, was necessary and intended, not a taking away. In other words, the treaty was not a grant of rights to the Indians, but a grant of rights from them—a reservation of those not granted. And the form of the instrument and its language was adapted to that purpose.... There was an exclusive right of fishing reserved within certain boundaries. There was a right outside of those boundaries reserved "in common with citizens of the Territory." As a mere right, it was not exclusive in the Indians. Citizens might share it, but the Indians were secured in its enjoyment by a special provision of means for its exercise. They were given "the right of taking fish at all usual and accustomed places," and the right "of erecting temporary buildings for curing them." The contingency of the future ownership of the lands, therefore, was foreseen and provided for—in other words, the Indians were given a right in the land—the right of crossing it to the river—the right to occupy it to the extent and for the purpose mentioned. No other conclusion would give effect to the treaty. And the right was intended to be continuing against the United States and its grantees as well as against the State and its grantees....

....

The license from the State, which respondents plead to maintain a fishing wheel, gives no power to them to exclude the Indians, nor was it intended to give such power. It was the permission of the State to use a particular device. What rights the Indians had were not determined or limited....

Decree reversed and the case remanded for further proceedings in accordance with this opinion.

WINTERS v. UNITED STATES

207 U.S. 564, 28 S. Ct. 207, 52 L. Ed. 340 (U.S. Sup. Ct. 1908)

JUSTICE MCKENNA delivered the opinion of the Court.

[*The Fort Belknap Reservation in Montana is part of a much larger area set aside by Congress in 1874 for the Gros Ventre, Piegan, Blood, Blackfeet, and River Crow Indians. In order to open the area for settlement by non-Indians, the government entered into an 1888 agreement with the tribes in which the tribes ceded all the lands set aside for them except the Fort Belknap Reservation. The 1888 agreement described the northern boundary of the reservation as the middle of the Milk River. Settlers came into the ceded area and acquired title under the homestead and desert land laws. In the early 1890s, following Montana water law, they filed and posted their water claims on the Milk River and began diverting and using more than 5,000 miners' inches for agricultural irrigation. This was their only supply of water, without which the lands would be useless. Beginning in 1898 the Indians diverted 10,000 miners' inches for irrigation of reservation lands. Because the upstream diversions deprived the Indians of their asserted rights to Milk River water, the United States sued to enjoin the settlers' diversions. The lower court enjoined the defendants from interfering with water use on the reservation.*]

    ....

The case, as we view it, turns on the agreement of May, 1888, resulting in the creation of Fort Belknap Reservation. In the construction of this agreement there are certain elements to be considered that are prominent and significant. The reservation was a part of a very much larger tract which the Indians had the right to occupy and use and which was adequate for the habits and wants of a nomadic and uncivilized people. It was the policy of the Government, it was the desire of the Indians, to change those habits and to become a pastoral and civilized people. If they should become such the original tract was too extensive, but a smaller tract would be inadequate without a change of conditions. The lands were arid and, without irrigation, were practically valueless. And yet, it is contended, the means of irrigation were deliberately given up by the Indians and deliberately accepted by the Government. The lands ceded were, it is true, also arid; and some argument may be urged, and is urged, that with their cession there was the cession of the waters, without which they would be valueless, and "civilized communities could not be established thereon." And this, it is further contended, the Indians knew, and yet made no reservation of the waters. We realize that there is a conflict of implications, but that which makes for the retention of the waters is of greater force than that which makes for their cession. The Indians had command of the lands and the waters—command of all their beneficial use, whether kept for hunting, "and grazing roving herds of stock," or turned to agriculture and the arts of civilization.... By a rule of interpretation of agreements and treaties with the Indians, ambiguities occurring will be resolved from the standpoint of the Indians. And the rule should certainly be applied to determine between two inferences, one of which would support the purpose of the agreement and the other impair or defeat it. On account of their relations to the Government, it cannot be supposed that the Indians were alert to exclude by formal words every inference which might militate against or defeat the declared purpose of themselves and the Government, even if it could be supposed that they had the intelligence to foresee the "double sense" which might some time be urged against them.

....

[*Employing the same reasoning, the Court also rejected the argument that the reservation of waters*] was repealed by the admission of Montana into the Union ...' upon an equal footing with the original States'.... The power of the Government to reserve the waters and exempt them from appropriation under the state laws is not denied, and could not be. That the Government did reserve them we have decided, and for a use which would be necessarily continued through years. This was done May 1, 1888, and it would be extreme to believe that within a year Congress destroyed the reservation and took from the Indians the consideration of their grant, leaving them a barren waste—took from them the means of continuing their old habits, yet did not leave them the power to change to new ones....

Decree affirmed.

MENOMINEE TRIBE OF INDIANS v. UNITED STATES

391 U.S. 404, 88 S. Ct. 1705, 20 L. Ed. 2d 697 (U.S. Sup. Ct. 1968)

Justice Douglas delivered the opinion of the Court.

[*The Wolf River Reservation was reserved for the Menominee Tribe of Wisconsin pursuant to the 1854 Treaty of Wolf River. Although "[n]othing was said in the 1854 treaty about hunting and fishing rights," the Court concluded that "treaty language requiring reservation lands 'to be held as Indian lands are held' includes the right to fish and hunt." In considering the issue of whether the tribe's fishing and hunting rights had been extinguished, the Court necessarily reviewed both the Menominee Indian Termination Act of 1954 and Public Law 280. At the core of this dispute was the fact that the Termination Act made no express mention of fishing and hunting rights.*]

....

It is ... argued with force that the Termination Act of 1954, which became fully effective in 1961, submitted the hunting and fishing rights of the Indians to state regulation and control. We reach, however, the opposite conclusion. The same Congress that passed the Termination Act also passed Public Law 280, as amended, 18 U.S.C. § 1162. The latter came out of the same committees of the Senate and the House as did the Termination Act; and it was amended in a way that is critical here only two months after the Termination Act became law. As amended, Public Law 280 granted designated States, including Wisconsin, jurisdiction "over offenses committed by or against Indians in the areas of Indian country" named in the Act, which in the case of Wisconsin was described as "All Indian country within the State." But Public Law 280 went on to say that "Nothing in this section ... shall deprive any Indian or any Indian tribe, band, or community of any right, privilege, or immunity afforded under Federal treaty, agreement, or statute *with respect to hunting, trapping, or fishing* or the control, licensing, or regulation thereof." (Emphasis added.) That provision on its face contains no limitation; it protects any hunting, trapping, or fishing right granted by a federal treaty. Public Law 280, as amended, became the law in 1954, nearly seven years *before* the Termination Act became fully effective in 1961. In 1954, when Public Law 280 became effective, the Menominee Reservation was still "Indian country" within the meaning of Public Law 280.

The two Acts read together mean to us that, although federal supervision of the tribe was to cease and all tribal property was to be transferred to new hands, the hunting and fishing rights granted or preserved by the Wolf River Treaty of 1854 survived the Termination Act of 1954.

....

The provision of the Termination Act (25 U.S.C. § 899) that "all statutes of the United States which affect Indians because of their status as Indians shall no longer be applicable to the members of the tribe" plainly refers to the termination of federal supervision. The use of the word "statutes" is potent evidence that no *treaty* was in mind.

We decline to construe the Termination Act as a backhanded way of abrogating the hunting and fishing rights of these Indians. While the power to abrogate those rights exists ... "the intention to abrogate or modify a treaty is not to be lightly imputed to the Congress" ... (citations omitted).

....

We find it difficult to believe that Congress, without explicit statement, would subject the United States to a claim for compensation by destroying property rights conferred by treaty, particularly when Congress was purporting by the Termination Act to settle the Government's financial obligations toward the Indians (footnote omitted).

Accordingly the judgment of the Court of Claims is affirmed.

Affirmed.

McCLANAHAN v. ARIZONA STATE TAX COMMISSION
411 U.S. 164, 93 S. Ct. 1257, 36 L. Ed. 2d 129 (U.S. Sup. Ct. 1973)

Justice Marshall delivered the opinion of the Court.

....

Appellant is an enrolled member of the Navajo tribe who lives on that portion of the Navajo Reservation located within the State of Arizona. Her complaint alleges that all her income earned during 1967 was derived from within the Navajo Reservation. Pursuant to Ariz. Rev. Stat. Ann. § 43-188(f) (Supp. 1972-1973), $16.20 was withheld from her wages for that year to cover her state income tax liability. At the conclusion of the tax year, appellant filed a protest against the collection of any taxes on her income and a claim for a refund of the entire amount withheld from her wages. When no action was taken on her claim, she instituted this action in Arizona Superior Court ... , demanding a return of the money withheld and a declaration that the state tax was unlawful as applied to reservation Indians.

....

[*The Arizona Court of Appeals had ruled that the state tax was a legal exercise of authority because it did not infringe "on the rights of the Navajo tribe of Indians to be self-governing." The Supreme Court therefore began its analysis with a discussion of the doctrine of Indian tribal sovereignty which had its beginnings 141 years earlier in Worcester v. Georgia. In so doing, the Court quoted its "landmark decision" of Williams v. Lee, 358 U.S. 217 (1959).*]

"Over the years this Court has modified [the *Worcester* principle] in cases where essential tribal relations were not involved and where the rights of Indians would not be jeopardized.... Thus, suits by Indians against outsiders in state courts have been sanctioned.... And state courts have been allowed to try non-Indians who committed crimes against each other on a reservation.... But if the crime was by or against an Indian, tribal jurisdiction or that expressly conferred on other courts by Congress has remained exclusive.... Essentially, absent governing Acts of Congress, the question has always been whether the state action infringed on the right of reservation Indians to make their own laws and be ruled by them." *Id.*, at 219-220 (footnote omitted).

[T]he trend has been away from the idea of inherent Indian sovereignty as a bar to state jurisdiction and toward reliance on federal pre-emption. *See Mescalero Apache Tribe v. Jones.* The modern cases thus tend to avoid reliance on platonic notions of Indian sovereignty and to look instead to the applicable treaties and statutes which define the limits of state power. *Compare, e.g., United States v. Kagama*, 118 U.S. 375 (1886), *with Kennerly v. District Court*, 400 U.S. 423 (1971) (footnote omitted).

The Indian sovereignty doctrine is relevant, then, not because it provides a definitive resolution of the issues in this suit, but because it provides a backdrop against which the applicable treaties and federal statutes must be read....

....

[*The Court then reviewed various federal documents, including the 1868 treaty between the Navajo Nation and the United States, Public Law 280, Arizona's enabling statute and the Buck Act, which provides comprehensive federal guidance for state taxation of those living within federal areas. It concluded that these documents evidence "Congress' intent to maintain the tax-exempt status of reservation Indians."*]

....

When Arizona's contentions are measured against these statutory imperatives, they are simply untenable. The State relies primarily upon language in *Williams v. Lee* stating that the test for determining the validity of state action is "whether [it] infringed on the right of reservation Indians to make their own laws and be ruled by them." 358 U.S., at 220. Since Arizona has attempted to tax individual Indians and not the tribe or reservation as such, it argues that it has not infringed on Indian rights of self-government.

[W]e reject the suggestion that the *Williams* test was meant to apply in this situation. It must be remembered that cases applying the *Williams* test have dealt principally with situations involving non-Indians. *See also Organized Village of Kake v. Egan*, 369 U.S., at 75-76. In these situations, both the tribe and the State could fairly claim an interest in asserting their respective jurisdictions. The *Williams* test was designed to resolve this conflict by providing that the State could protect its interest up to the point where tribal self-government would be affected.

The problem posed by this case is completely different. Since appellant is an Indian and since her income is derived wholly from reservation sources, her activity is totally within the sphere which the relevant treaty and statutes leave for the Federal Government and for the Indians themselves. Appellee cites us to no cases holding that this legislation may be ignored simply because tribal self-government has not been infringed (footnote omitted). On the contrary, this Court expressly rejected such a position only two years ago (footnote omitted). In *Kennerly v. District Court*, 400 U.S. 423 (1971), the Blackfoot Indian Tribe had voted to make state jurisdiction concurrent within the reservation. Although the State had not complied with the procedural prerequisites for the assumption of jurisdiction, it argued that it was nonetheless entitled to extend its laws to the reservation since such action was obviously consistent with the wishes of the Tribe and, therefore, with tribal self-government. But we held that the *Williams* rule was inapplicable and that "[t]he unilateral action of the Tribal Council was insufficient to vest Montana with jurisdiction." If Montana may not assume jurisdiction over the Blackfeet by simple legislation even when the Tribe itself agrees to be bound by state law, it surely follows that Arizona may not assume such jurisdiction in the absence of tribal agreement.

    ....

Finally, we cannot accept the notion that it is irrelevant "whether the ... state income tax infringes on [appellant's] rights as an individual Navajo Indian," as the State Court of Appeals maintained. To be sure, when Congress has legislated on Indian matters, it has, most often, dealt with the tribes as collective entities. But those entities are, after all, composed of individual Indians, and the legislation confers individual rights. This Court has therefore held that "the question has always been whether the state action infringed on the right of *reservation Indians* to make their own laws and be ruled by them." *Williams v. Lee, supra*, at 220 (emphasis added). In this case, appellant's rights as a reservation Indian were violated when the state collected a tax from her which it had no jurisdiction to impose. Accordingly, the judgment of the court below must be

Reversed.

OLIPHANT v. SUQUAMISH INDIAN TRIBE

435 U.S. 191, 98 S. Ct. 1011, 55 L. Ed. 2d 209 (U.S. Sup. Ct. 1978)

Justice Rehnquist delivered the opinion of the Court.

[*Pursuant to a law and order code adopted by the Suquamish Indian tribal government, tribal authorities arrested a non-Indian for assaulting a tribal officer and resisting arrest. Tribal court proceedings were stayed pending a decision on the issue of "whether Indian tribal courts have criminal jurisdiction over non-Indians." After reviewing the facts, the Court cited authority from each of the three governmental branches. None of these supported the tribe's "contention that Indian tribes, although fully subordinated to the sovereignty of the United States, retain the power to try non-Indians according to their own customs and procedure."]*

....

Indians do not have criminal jurisdiction over non-Indians absent affirmative delegation of such power by Congress. Indian tribes do retain elements of "quasi-sovereign" authority after ceding their lands to the United States and announcing their dependence on the Federal Government. *See The Cherokee Nation v. Georgia*, 5 Peters 1, 15 (1831). But the tribes' retained powers are not such that they are limited only by specific restrictions in treaties or congressional enactments. As the Court of Appeals recognized, Indian tribes are proscribed from exercising both those powers of autonomous states that are expressly terminated by Congress *and* those powers "*inconsistent with their status.*"

Indian reservations are "a part of the territory of the United States." *United States v. Rogers*, 4 How. 567, 571 (1846). Indian tribes "hold and occupy [the reservations] with the assent of the United States, and under their authority." *Id.*, at 572. Upon incorporation into the territory of the United States, the Indian tribes thereby come under the territorial sovereignty of the United States and their exercise of separate power is constrained so as not to conflict with the interests of this overriding sovereignty. "[T]heir rights of complete sovereignty, as independent nations [are] necessarily diminished." *Johnson v. McIntosh*, 8 Wheat. 543, 574 (1823).

....

Protection of territory within its external political boundaries is, of course, central to the sovereign interests of the United States as it is to any other sovereign nation. But from the formation of the Union and the adoption of the Bill of Rights, the United States has manifested an equally great solicitude that its citizens be protected by the United States from unwarranted intrusions on their personal liberty. The power of the United States to try and criminally punish is an important manifestation of the power to restrict personal liberty. By submitting to the overriding sovereignty of the United States, Indian tribes therefore necessarily give up their power to try non-Indian citizens of the United States except in a manner acceptable to Congress. This principle would have been obvious a century ago when most Indian tribes were characterized by a "want of fixed laws [and] of competent tribunals of justice." H.R. Rep. No. 474, 23d Cong., 1st Sess., at 18 (1834). It should be no less obvious today, even though present day Indian tribal courts embody dramatic advances over their historical antecedents.

....

In summary, respondents' position ignores that
"Indians are within the geographical limits of the United States. The soil and people within these limits are under the political control of the Government of the United States, or of the States of the Union. There exists in the broad domain of sovereignty but these two. There may be cities, counties, and other organized bodies with limited legislative functions, but they . . . exist in subordination to one or the other of these two." *United States v. Kagama*, 118 U.S. 375, 379 (1886).

We recognize that some Indian tribal court systems have become increasingly sophisticated and resemble in many respects their state counterparts. We also acknowledge that with the passage of the Indian Civil Rights Act of 1968, which extends certain basic procedural rights to *anyone* tried in Indian tribal court, many of the dangers that might have accompanied the exercise by tribal courts of criminal jurisdiction over non-Indians only a few decades ago have disappeared. Finally, we are not unaware of the prevalence of non-Indian crime on today's reservations which the tribes forcefully argue requires the ability to try non-Indians. But these are considerations for Congress to weigh in deciding whether Indian tribes should finally be authorized to try non-Indians. They have little relevance to the principles which lead us to conclude that Indian tribes do not have inherent jurisdiction to try and punish non-Indians. The judgments below are therefore reversed.

Reversed.

. . . .

JUSTICE MARSHALL, with whom CHIEF JUSTICE BURGER joins, dissenting.

I agree with the court below that the "power to preserve order on the reservation … is a sine qua non of the sovereignty that the Suquamish originally possessed." In the absence of affirmative withdrawal by treaty or statute, I am of the view that Indian tribes enjoy as a necessary aspect of their retained sovereignty the right to try and punish all persons who commit offenses against tribal law within the reservation. Accordingly, I dissent.

SANTA CLARA PUEBLO v. MARTINEZ

436 U.S. 49, 98 S. Ct. 1670, 56 L. Ed. 2d 106 (U.S. Sup. Ct. 1978)

JUSTICE MARSHALL delivered the opinion of the Court (footnote omitted).

. . . .

Petitioner Santa Clara Pueblo is an Indian tribe that has been in existence for over 600 years. Respondents, a female member of the tribe and her daughter, brought suit in federal court against the tribe and its Governor, petitioner Lucario Padilla, seeking declaratory and injunctive relief against enforcement of a tribal ordinance denying membership in the tribe to children of female members who marry outside the tribe, while extending membership to children of male members who marry outside the tribe. Respondents claimed that this rule discriminates on the basis of both sex and ancestry in violation of Title I of the Indian Civil Rights Act of 1968 (ICRA), 25 U.S.C.A. §§ 1301-1303 (1970), which provides in relevant part that "[n]o Indian tribe in exercising powers of self-government shall … deny to any person within its jurisdiction the equal protection of its laws." *Id.*, § 1302(8).

Title I of the ICRA does not expressly authorize the bringing of civil actions for declaratory or injunctive relief to enforce its substantive provisions. The threshold issue in this case is thus whether the Act may be interpreted to impliedly authorize such actions, against a tribe or its officers, in the federal courts. For the reasons set forth below, we hold that the Act cannot be so read.

[*The Court began its analysis by recognizing that Indian tribes are sovereign entities. As such, they are generally protected from lawsuit unless their sovereign immunity has been expressly waived. In exercising its plenary authority over Indian tribes, Congress provided to individuals the "privilege of the writ of habeas corpus," which allows any person "to test the legality of his detention by order of an Indian tribe" in the courts of the United States. 25 U.S.C. § 1303 (1986). This, the Court found, was merely a limited waiver of immunity, and respondents' request for declaratory and injunctive relief against the tribe was therefore not permitted by the Indian Civil Rights Act. The Court then turned to the issue of whether the Act permitted declaratory and injunctive relief against the tribe's Governor, who was not shielded by tribal sovereign immunity. After first discussing the United States' policy of "self-determination," the Court explained its reluctance to read the Act's language as implying such relief.*]

. . . .

Our reluctance is strongly reinforced by the specific legislative history underlying 25 U.S.C.A. § 1303. This history, extending over more than three years, indicates that Congress' provision for habeas corpus relief, and nothing more, reflected a considered accommodation of the competing goals of "preventing injustices perpetrated by tribal governments, on the one hand, and, on the other, avoiding undue or precipitous interference in the affairs of the Indian people." ... After considering numerous alternatives for review of tribal convictions, Congress apparently decided that review by way of habeas corpus would adequately protect the individual interests at stake while avoiding unnecessary intrusions on tribal governments.

. . . .

By not exposing tribal officials to the full array of federal remedies available to redress actions of federal and state officials, Congress may also have considered that resolution of statutory issues under § 1302, and particularly those issues likely to arise in a civil context, will frequently depend on questions of tribal tradition and custom which tribal forums may be in a better position to evaluate than federal courts.... [E]fforts by the federal judiciary to apply the statutory prohibitions of § 1302 in a civil context may substantially interfere with a tribe's ability to maintain itself as a culturally and politically distinct entity.

As we have repeatedly emphasized, Congress' authority over Indian matters is extraordinarily broad, and the role of courts in adjusting relations between and among tribes and their members correspondingly restrained. *See Lone Wolf v. Hitchcock*, 187 U.S. 553, 565 (1903). Congress retains authority expressly to authorize civil actions for injunctive or other relief to redress violations of § 1302, in the event that the tribes themselves prove deficient in applying and enforcing its substantive provisions. But unless and until Congress makes clear its intention to permit the additional intrusion on tribal sovereignty that adjudication of such actions in a federal forum would represent, we are constrained to find that § 1302 does not impliedly authorize actions for declaratory or injunctive relief against either the tribe or its officers.

The judgment of the Court of Appeals is, accordingly,

Reversed.

———————————————

WASHINGTON v. WASHINGTON STATE COMMERCIAL PASSENGER FISHING VESSEL ASSOCIATION

443 U.S. 658, 99 S. Ct. 3055, 61 L. Ed. 2d 823 (U.S. Sup. Ct. 1978)

JUSTICE STEVENS delivered the opinion of the Court.

To extinguish the last group of conflicting claims to lands lying west of the Cascade Mountains and north of the Columbia River in what is now the State of Washington, the United States entered into a series of treaties with Indian tribes in 1854 and 1855. The Indians relinquished their interest in most of the Territory in exchange for monetary payments. In addition, certain relatively small parcels of land were reserved for their exclusive use, and they were afforded other guarantees, including protection of their "right of taking fish, at all usual and accustomed grounds and stations ... in common with all citizens of the Territory." 10 Stat. 1133.

The principal question presented by this litigation concerns the character of that treaty right to take fish....

....

One hundred and twenty-five years ago when the relevant treaties were signed, anadromous fish were even more important to most of the population of western Washington than they are today. At that time, about three-fourths of the approximately 10,000 inhabitants of the area were Indians. Although in some respects the cultures of the different tribes varied—some bands of Indians, for example, had little or no tribal organization while others, such as the Makah and the Yakima, were highly organized— all of them shared a vital and unifying dependence on anadromous fish. *Id.,* at 350. *See Puyallup Tribe v. Washington Game Dept.,* 433 U.S. 165, 179 (BRENNAN, J., dissenting in part).

Religious rites were intended to insure the continual return of the salmon and the trout; the seasonal and geographic variations in the runs of the different species determined the movements of the largely nomadic tribes. 384 F. Supp., at 343, 351, 382; 459 F. Supp. 1020, 1079; 520 F.2d 676, 682. Fish constituted a major part of the Indian diet, was used for commercial purposes, and indeed was traded in substantial volume. The Indians developed food-preservation techniques that enabled them to store fish throughout the year and to transport it over great distances. 384 F. Supp., at 351. They used a wide variety of methods to catch fish, including the precursors of all modern netting techniques. *Id.,* at 351, 352, 362, 368, 380. Their usual and accustomed fishing places were numerous and were scattered throughout the area, and included marine as well as fresh-water areas. *Id.,* at 353, 360, 368-369.

All of the treaties were negotiated by Isaac Stevens, the first Governor and first Superintendent of Indian Affairs of the Washington Territory, and a small group of advisers. Contemporaneous documents make it clear that these people recognized the vital importance of the fisheries to the Indians and wanted to protect them from the risk that non-Indian settlers might seek to monopolize their fisheries. *Id.,* at 355, 363. There is no evidence of the precise understanding the Indians had of any of the specific English terms and phrases in the treaty. *Id.,* at 356. It is perfectly clear, however, that the Indians were vitally interested in protecting their right to take fish at usual and accustomed places, whether on or off the reservations, *Id.,* at 355, and that they were invited by the white negotiators to rely and in fact did rely heavily on the good faith of the United States to protect that right.

      ....

The Indians understood that non-Indians would also have the right to fish at their off-reservation fishing sites. But this was not understood as a significant limitation on their right to take fish. Because of the great abundance of fish and the limited population of the area, it simply was not contemplated that either party would interfere with the other's fishing rights. The parties accordingly did not see the need and did not intend to regulate the taking of fish by either Indians or non-Indians, nor was future regulation foreseen. *Id.,* at 334, 355, 357.

Indeed, for several decades after the treaties were signed, Indians continued to harvest most of the fish taken from the waters of Washington, and they moved freely about the Territory and later the State in search of that resource. *Id.,* at 334. The size of the fishery resource continued to obviate the need during the period to regulate the taking of fish by either Indians or non-Indians. *Id.,* at 352. Not until major economic developments in canning and processing occurred in the last few years of the 19th century did a significant non-Indian fishery develop. It was as a consequence of these developments, rather than of the treaty, that non-Indians began to dominate the fisheries and eventually to exclude most Indians from participating in it—a trend that was encouraged by the onset of often discriminatory state regulation in the early decades of the 20th century. *Id.,* at 358, 394, 404, 407; 459 F. Supp., at 1032.

In sum, it is fair to conclude that when the treaties were negotiated, neither party realized or intended that their agreement would determine whether, and if so how, a resource that had always been thought inexhaustible would be allocated between the native Indians and the incoming settlers when it later became scarce.

      ....

Unfortunately, that resource has now become scarce, and the meaning of the Indians' treaty right to take fish has accordingly become critical....

... The United States, on its own behalf and as trustee for seven Indian tribes, brought suit against the State of Washington seeking an interpretation of the treaties and an injunction requiring the State to protect the Indians' share of the anadromous fish runs. Additional Indian tribes, the State's Fisheries and Game Departments, and one commercial fishing group, were joined as parties at various stages of the proceedings, while various other agencies and groups, including all of the commercial fishing associations that are parties here, participated as *amici curiae*. 384 F. Supp., at 327, 328, and n.4; 459 F. Supp., at 1028.

During the extensive pretrial proceedings, four different interpretations of the critical treaty language were advanced....

      ....

The District Court [in the "Boldt decision"] agreed with the parties who advocated an allocation to the Indians, and it essentially agreed with the United States as to what that allocation should be. It held that the Indians were then entitled to a 45% to 50% share of the harvestable fish that will at some point pass through recognized tribal fishing grounds in the case area. The share was to be calculated on a river-by-river, run-by-run basis, subject to certain adjustments. Fish caught by Indians for ceremonial and subsistence purposes as well as fish caught within a reservation were excluded from the calculation of the tribes' share. In addition, in order to compensate for fish caught outside of the case area, i.e., beyond the State's jurisdiction, the court made an "equitable adjustment" to increase the allocation to the Indians. The court left it to the individual tribes involved to agree among themselves on how best to divide the Indian share of runs that pass through the usual and accustomed grounds of more than one tribe, and it postponed until a later date the proper accounting for hatchery-bred fish. 384 F. Supp., at 416-417; 459 F. Supp., at 1129. With a slight modification, the Court of Appeals for the Ninth Circuit affirmed, 520 F.2d 676, and we denied certiorari, 423 U.S. 1086.

The injunction entered by the District Court required the Department of Fisheries (Fisheries) to adopt regulations protecting the Indians' treaty rights. 384 F. Supp., at 416-417. After the new regulations were promulgated, however, they were immediately challenged by private citizens in suits commenced in the Washington state courts. The State Supreme Court, in two cases that are here in consolidated form in No. 77-983, ultimately held that Fisheries could not comply with the federal injunction. *Puget Sound Gillnetters Assn. v. Moos,* 88 Wash. 2d 677, 565 P.2d 1151 (1977); *Fishing Vessel Assn. v. Tollefson,* 89 Wash. 2d 276, 571 P.2d 1373 (1977).

As a matter of federal law, the state court first accepted the Game Department's and rejected the District Court's interpretation of the treaties and held that they did not give the Indians a right to a share of the fish runs, and second concluded that recognizing special rights for the Indians would violate the Equal Protection Clause of the Fourteenth Amendment.... Because we are ... satisfied that the constitutional holding is without merit, our review of the state court's judgment will be limited to the treaty issue.

When Fisheries was ordered by the state courts to abandon its attempt to promulgate and enforce regulations in compliance with the federal court's decree—and when the Game Department simply refused to comply—the District Court entered a series of orders enabling it, with the aid of the United States Attorney for the Western District of Washington and various federal law enforcement agencies, directly to supervise those aspects of the State's fisheries necessary to the preservation of treaty fishing rights. 459 F. Supp. 1020. The District Court's power to take such direct action and, in doing so, it enjoin persons who were not parties to the proceeding was affirmed by the United States Court of Appeals for the Ninth Circuit. 573 F.2d 1123.... Subsequently, the District Court entered an enforcement order regarding the salmon fisheries for the 1978 and subsequent seasons....

Because of the widespread defiance of the District Court's orders, this litigation has assumed unusual significance. We [agreed to hear the appeals of] the state and federal cases to interpret this important treaty provision and thereby to resolve the conflict between the state and federal courts regarding what, if any, right the Indians have to a share of the fish, to address the implications of international regulation of the fisheries in the area, and to remove any doubts about the federal court's power to enforce its orders. 439 U.S. 909.

....

The treaties secure a "right of taking fish." The pertinent articles provide:
"The right of taking fish, at all usual and accustomed grounds and stations, is further secured to said Indians, in common with all citizens of the Territory, and of erecting temporary houses for the purpose of curing, together with the privilege of hunting, gathering roots and berries, and pasturing their horses on open and unclaimed lands: *Provided, however,* That they shall not take shell fish from any beds staked or cultivated by citizens."

....

A treaty, including one between the United States and an Indian tribe, is essentially a contract between two sovereign nations. *E.g., Lone Wolf v. Hitchcock,* 187 U.S. 553. When the signatory nations have not been at war and neither is the vanquished, it is reasonable to assume that they negotiated as equals at arm's length. There is no reason to doubt that this assumption applies to the treaties at issue here. *See* 520 F.2d, at 684.

Accordingly, it is the intention of the parties, and not solely that of the superior side, that must control any attempt to interpret the treaties. When Indians are involved, this Court has long given special meaning to this rule. It has held that the United States, as the party with the presumptively superior negotiating skills and superior knowledge of the language in which the treaty is recorded, has a responsibility to avoid taking advantage of the other side. "[T]he treaty must therefore be construed, not according to the technical meaning of its words to learned lawyers, but in the sense in which they would naturally be understood by the Indians." *Jones v. Meehan,* 175 U.S. 1, 11. This rule, in fact, has thrice been explicitly relied on by the Court in broadly interpreting these very treaties in the Indians' favor. *Tulee v. Washington,* 315 U.S. 681; *Seufert Bros. Co. v. United States,* 249 U.S. 194; *United States v. Winans,* 198 U.S. 371. *See also Washington v. Yakima Indian Nation,* 439 U.S. 463, 484.

Governor Stevens and his associates were well aware of the "sense" in which the Indians were likely to view assurances regarding their fishing rights.... It is absolutely clear, as Governor Stevens himself said, that neither he nor the Indians intended that the latter "should be excluded from their ancient fisheries," *see* n.9, *supra,* and it is accordingly inconceivable that either party deliberately agreed to authorize future settlers to crowd the Indians out of any meaningful use of their accustomed places to fish. That each individual Indian would share an "equal opportunity" with thousands of newly arrived individual settlers is totally foreign to the spirit of the negotiations. Such a "right," along with the $207,500 paid the Indians, would hardly have been sufficient to compensate them for the millions of acres they ceded to the Territory.

It is true that the words "in common with" may be read either as nothing more than a guarantee that individual Indians would have the same right as individual non-Indians or as securing an interest in the fish runs themselves. If we were to construe these words by reference to 19th-century property concepts, we might accept the former interpretation, although even "learned lawyers" of the day would probably have offered differing interpretations of the three words. But we think greater importance should be given to the Indians' likely understanding of the other words in the treaties and especially the reference to the "right of *taking* fish"—a right that had no special meaning at common law but that must have had obvious significance to the tribes relinquishing a portion of their pre-existing rights to the United States in return for this promise....

This interpretation is confirmed by additional language in the treaties. The fishing clause speaks of "securing" certain fishing rights, a term the Court has previously interpreted as synonymous with "reserving" rights previously exercised. *Winans,* 198 U.S., at 381. *See also New York ex rel. Kennedy v. Becker,* 241 U.S. 556, 563-564. Because the Indians had always exercised the right to meet their subsistence and commercial needs by taking fish from treaty area waters, they would be unlikely to perceive a "reservation" of that right as merely the chance, shared with millions of other citizens, occasionally to dip their nets into the territorial waters. Moreover, the phrasing of the clause quite clearly avoids placing each individual Indian on an equal footing with each individual citizen of the State. The referent of the "said Indians" who are to share the right of taking fish with "all citizens of the Territory" is not the individual Indians but the various signatory "tribes and bands of Indians" listed in the opening article of each treaty. Because it was the tribes that were given a right in common with non-Indian citizens, it is especially likely that a class right to a share of fish, rather than a personal right to attempt to land fish, was intended.

In our view, the purpose and language of the treaties are unambiguous; they secure the Indians' right to take a share of each run of fish that passes through tribal fishing areas. But our prior decisions provide an even more persuasive reason why this interpretation is not open to question. For notwithstanding the bitterness that this litigation has engendered, the principal issue involved is virtually a "matter decided" by our previous holdings.

The Court has interpreted the fishing clause in these treaties on six prior occasions. In all of these cases the Court placed a relatively broad gloss on the Indians' fishing rights and—more or less explicitly—rejected the State's "equal opportunity" approach; in the earliest and the three most recent cases, moreover, we adopted essentially the interpretation that the United States is reiterating here.

In *United States v. Winans, supra,* the respondent, having acquired title to property on the Columbia River and having obtained a license to use a "fish wheel"—a device capable of catching salmon by the ton and totally destroying a run of fish—asserted the right to exclude the Yakimas from one of their "usual and accustomed" places. The Circuit Court for the District of Washington sustained respondent, but this Court reversed. The Court initially rejected an argument that is analogous to the "equal opportunity" claim now made by the State[.] ... *See also Seufert Bros.,* 249 U.S., at 198, and *Tulee,* 315 U.S., at 684, both of which repeated this analysis, in holding that treaty Indians had rights, "beyond those which other citizens may enjoy," to fish without paying license fees in ceded areas and even in accustomed fishing places lying outside of the lands ceded by the Indians. *See* n.22, *supra.*

But even more significant than the language in *Winans* is its actual disposition. The Court not only upheld the Indians' right of access to respondent's private property but also ordered the Circuit Court on remand to devise some "adjustment and accommodation" that would protect them from total exclusion from the fishery.... In short, it assured the Indians a share of the fish.

In the more recent litigation over this treaty language between the Puyallup Tribe and the Washington Department of Game, the Court in the context of a dispute over rights to the run of steelhead trout on the Puyallup River reaffirmed both of the holdings that may be drawn from *Winans*—the treaty guarantees the Indians more than simply the "equal opportunity" along with all of the citizens of the State to catch fish, and it in fact assures them some portion of each relevant run. But the three *Puyallup* cases are even more explicit; they clearly establish the principle that neither party to the treaties may rely on the State's regulatory powers or on property law concepts to defeat the other's right to a "fairly apportioned" share of each covered run of harvestable anadromous fish.

....

The purport of our cases is clear. Non-treaty fisherman may not rely on property law concepts, devices such as the fish wheel, license fees, or general regulations to deprive the Indians of a fair share of the relevant runs of anadromous fish in the case area. Nor may treaty fisherman rely on their exclusive right of access to the reservations to destroy the rights of other "citizens of the Territory." Both sides have a right, secured by treaty, to take a fair share of the available fish. That, we think, is what the parties to the treaty intended when they secured to the Indians the right of taking fish in common with other citizens.

....

We also agree with the Government that an equitable measure of the common right should initially divide the harvestable portion of each run that passes through a "usual and accustomed" place into approximately equal treaty and non-treaty shares, and should then reduce the treaty share if tribal needs may be satisfied by a lesser amount....

The division arrived at by the District Court is also consistent with our earlier decisions concerning Indian treaty rights to scarce natural resources. In those cases, after determining that at the time of the treaties the resource involved was necessary to the Indians' welfare, the Court typically ordered a trial judge or special master, in his discretion, to devise some apportionment that assured that the Indians' reasonable livelihood needs would be met. *Arizona v. California, supra,* at 600; *Winters, supra. See Winans,* 198 U.S., at 384. This is precisely what the District Court did here, except that it realized that some ceiling should be placed on the Indians' apportionment to prevent their needs from exhausting the entire resource and thereby frustrating the treaty right of "all [other] citizens of the Territory."

Thus, it first concluded that at the time the treaties were signed, the Indians, who comprised three-fourths of the territorial population, depended heavily on anadromous fish as a source of food, commerce, and cultural cohesion. Indeed, it found that the non-Indian population depended on Indians to catch the fish that the former consumed. *See supra,* at 664-669, and n.7. Only then did it determine that the Indians' present-day subsistence and commercial needs should be met, subject, of course, to the 50% ceiling. 384 F. Supp., at 342-343.

It bears repeating, however, that the 50% figure imposes a maximum but not a minimum allocation. As in *Arizona v. California* and its predecessor cases, the central principle here must be that Indian treaty rights to a natural resource that once was thoroughly and exclusively exploited by the Indians secures so much as, but no more than, is necessary to provide the Indians with a livelihood—that is to say, a moderate living. Accordingly, while the maximum possible allocation to the Indians is fixed at 50%, the minimum is not; the latter will, upon proper submissions to the District Court, be modified in response to changing circumstances. If, for example, a tribe should dwindle to just a few members, or if it should find other sources of support that lead it to abandon its fisheries, a 45% or 50% allocation of an entire run that passes through its customary fishing grounds would be manifestly inappropriate because the livelihood of the tribe under those circumstances could not reasonably require an allotment of a large number of fish.

....

So ordered.

JUSTICE POWELL, with whom JUSTICE STEWART and JUSTICE REHNQUIST join, dissenting in part.

I join Parts I-III of the Court's opinion. I am not in agreement, however, with the Court's interpretation of the treaties negotiated in 1854 and 1855 with the Indians of the Washington Territory....

....

In my view, the District Court below—and now this Court—has formulated an apportionment doctrine that cannot be squared with the language or history of the treaties, or indeed with the prior decisions of this Court. The application of this doctrine, and particularly the construction of the term "in common" as requiring a basic 50-50 apportionment, is likely to result in an extraordinary economic windfall to Indian fishermen in the commercial fish market by giving them a substantial position in the market wholly protected from competition from non-Indian fishermen. Indeed, non-Indian fishermen apparently will be required from time to time to stay out of fishing areas completely while Indians catch their court-decreed allotment. In sum, the District Court's decision will discriminate quite unfairly against non-Indians.

....

I would hold that the treaties give to the Indians several significant rights that should be respected. As made clear in *Winans*, the purpose of the treaties was to assure to Indians the right of access over private lands so that they could continue to fish at their usual and accustomed fishing grounds. Indians also have the exclusive right to fish on their reservations, and are guaranteed enough fish to satisfy their ceremonial and subsistence needs. Moreover, as subsequently construed, the treaties exempt Indians from state regulation (including the payment of license fees) except as necessary for conservation in the interest of all fishermen. Finally, under *Puyallup II,* it is settled that even a facially neutral conservation regulation is invalid if its effect is to discriminate against Indian fishermen. These rights, privileges, and exemptions—possessed only by Indians—are quite substantial. I find no basis for according them additional advantages.

WHITE MOUNTAIN APACHE TRIBE v. BRACKER

448 U.S. 136, 100 S. Ct. 2578, 65 L. Ed. 2d 665 (U.S. Sup. Ct. 1980)

Justice Marshall delivered the opinion of the Court:

[*Tribal enterprises, particularly timber operations, provided most of the funding for the White Mountain Apache Tribe's governmental programs. One of these enterprises contracted with Pinetop, a non-Indian logging company who, in fulfilling its contractual obligations, conducted operations on the tribe's reservation. The State of Arizona then sought to impose a state "motor carrier license tax" and an "excise or use fuel tax" on the non-Indian company. The issue thus arose whether state taxes may "lawfully be imposed on logging activities conducted exclusively within the reservation or on hauling activities on Bureau of Indian Affairs and tribal roads." The Court's analysis began with a discussion of the concepts of preemption and infringement, followed by a brief explanation of the "broad power of Congress" over Indian affairs, and the tribal right of self-government. The Court continued with a discussion of the relationship between state, tribal and federal laws.*]

....

When on-reservation conduct involving only Indians is at issue, state law is generally inapplicable, for the State's regulatory interest is likely to be minimal and the federal interest in encouraging tribal self-government is at its strongest. (Citations omitted.) More difficult questions arise where, as here, a State asserts authority over the conduct of non-Indians engaging in activity on the reservation. In such cases we have examined the language of the relevant federal treaties and statutes in terms of both the broad policies that underlie them and the notions of sovereignty that have developed from historical traditions of tribal independence. This inquiry is not dependent on mechanical or absolute conceptions of State or tribal sovereignty, but has called for a particularized inquiry into the nature of the State, Federal, and tribal interests at stake, an inquiry designed to determine whether, in the specific context, the exercise of state authority would violate federal law.... (citations omitted).

[W]e observe that the Federal Government's regulation of the harvesting of Indian timber is comprehensive....

....

In these circumstances we agree with petitioners that the federal regulatory scheme is so pervasive as to preclude the additional burdens sought to be imposed in this case. Respondents seek to apply their motor vehicle license and use fuel taxes on Pinetop for operations that are conducted solely on Bureau and tribal roads within the reservation. There is no room for these taxes in the comprehensive federal regulatory scheme. In a variety of ways, the assessment of state taxes would obstruct federal policies. And equally important, respondents have been unable to identify any regulatory function or service performed by the State that would justify the assessment of taxes for activities on Bureau and tribal roads within the reservation.

....

... Underlying the federal regulatory program rests a policy of assuring that the profits derived from timber sales will inure to the benefit of the Tribe, subject only to administrative expenses incurred by the Federal Government.... The imposition of the taxes at issue would undermine that policy in a context in which the Federal Government has undertaken to regulate the most minute details of timber production and expressed a firm desire that the Tribes should retain the benefits derived from the harvesting and sale of reservation timber.

 ....

 As noted above, this is not a case in which the State seeks to assess taxes in return for governmental functions it performs for those on whom the taxes fall. Nor have respondents been able to identify a legitimate regulatory interest served by the taxes they seek to impose. They refer to a general desire to raise revenue, but we are unable to discern a responsibility or service that justifies the assertion of taxes imposed for on-reservation operations conducted solely on tribal and Bureau of Indian Affairs roads. Pinetop's business in Arizona is conducted solely on the Fort Apache Reservation. Though at least the use fuel tax purports to "compensat[e] the state for the use of its highways," no such compensatory purpose is present here. The roads at issue have been built, maintained, and policed exclusively by the Federal Government, the Tribe, and its contractors. We do not believe that respondents' generalized interest in raising revenue is in this context sufficient to permit its proposed intrusion into the federal regulatory scheme with respect to the harvesting and sale of tribal timber.

 ... The Court has repeatedly emphasized that there is a significant geographical component to tribal sovereignty, a component which remains highly relevant to the pre-emption inquiry; though the reservation boundary is not absolute, it remains an important factor to weigh in determining whether state authority has exceeded the permissible limits.... Moreover, it is undisputed that the economic burden of the asserted taxes will ultimately fall on the Tribe (footnote omitted). Where, as here, the Federal Government has undertaken comprehensive regulation of the harvesting and sale of tribal timber, where a number of the policies underlying the federal regulatory scheme are threatened by the taxes respondents seek to impose, and where respondents are unable to justify the taxes except in terms of a generalized interest in raising revenue, we believe that the proposed exercise of state authority is impermissible.

 ....

 The decision of the Arizona Court of Appeals is Reversed.

MERRION v. JICARILLA APACHE TRIBE

455 U.S. 130, 102 S. Ct. 894, 71 L. Ed. 2d 21 (U.S. Sup. Ct. 1982)

Justice Marshall delivered the opinion of the Court.

 Pursuant to long-term leases with the Jicarilla Apache Tribe, petitioners, 21 lessees, extract and produce oil and gas from the Tribe's reservation lands. In these two consolidated cases, petitioners challenge an ordinance enacted by the Tribe imposing a severance tax on "any oil and natural gas severed, saved and removed from Tribal lands." *See* Oil and Gas Severance Tax No. 77-0-02, App. 38. We granted certiorari to determine whether the Tribe has the authority to impose this tax, and, if so, whether the tax imposed by the Tribe violates the Commerce Clause.

....

The Jicarilla Apache Tribe resides on a reservation in northwestern New Mexico. Established by Executive Order in 1887, the reservation contains 742,315 acres, all of which are held as tribal trust property. The 1887 Executive Order set aside public lands in the Territory of New Mexico for the use and occupation of the Jicarilla Apache Indians, and contained no special restrictions except for a provision protecting pre-existing rights of bona fide settlers....

The Tribe is organized under the Indian Reorganization Act of 1934, ch. 576, 48 Stat. 984, 25 U.S.C. § 461 *et seq.*, which authorizes any tribe residing on a reservation to adopt a constitution and bylaws, subject to the approval of the Secretary of the Interior (Secretary). The Tribe's first Constitution, approved by the Secretary on August 4, 1937, preserved all powers conferred by § 16 of the Indian Reorganization Act of 1934, ch. 576, 48 Stat. 987, 25 U.S.C. § 476. In 1968, the Tribe revised its Constitution.... The Revised Constitution provides that "[t]he tribal council may enact ordinances to govern the development of tribal lands and other resources," Art. XI, § 1(a)(3). It further provides that "[t]he tribal council may levy and collect taxes and fees on tribal members, and may enact ordinances, subject to approval by the Secretary of the Interior, to impose taxes and fees on non-members of the tribe doing business on the reservation," Art. XI, § 1(e). The Revised Constitution was approved by the Secretary on February 13, 1969.

To develop tribal lands, the Tribe has executed mineral leases encompassing some 69% of the reservation land. Beginning in 1953, the petitioners entered into leases with the Tribe....

Pursuant to its Revised Constitution, the Tribal Council adopted an ordinance imposing a severance tax on oil and gas production on tribal land. *See* App. 38. The ordinance was approved by the Secretary, through the Acting Director of the Bureau of Indian Affairs, on December 23, 1976. The tax applies to "any oil and natural gas severed, saved and removed from Tribal lands...." *Ibid.*... Oil and gas consumed by the lessees to develop their leases or received by the Tribe as in-kind royalty payments are exempted from the tax. *Ibid.*; Brief for Respondent Jicarilla Apache Tribe 59, n.42.

In two separate actions, petitioners sought to enjoin enforcement of the tax by either the tribal authorities or the Secretary....

....

In *Washington v. Confederated Tribes of Colville Indian Reservation*, 447 U.S. 134 (1980) (*Colville*), we addressed the Indian tribes' authority to impose taxes on non-Indians doing business on the reservation. We held that "[t]he power to tax transactions occurring on trust lands and significantly involving a tribe or its members is a fundamental attribute of sovereignty which the tribes retain unless divested of it by federal law or necessary implication of their dependent status." *Id.*, at 152. The power to tax is an essential attribute of Indian sovereignty because it is a necessary instrument of self-government and territorial management. This power enables a tribal government to raise revenues for its essential services. The power does not derive solely from the

Indian tribe's power to exclude non-Indians from tribal lands. Instead, it derives from the tribe's general authority, as sovereign, to control economic activity within its jurisdiction, and to defray the cost of providing governmental services by requiring contributions from persons or enterprises engaged in economic activities within that jurisdiction. *See, e.g., Gibbons v. Ogden,* 9 Wheat. 1, 199 (1824).

The petitioners avail themselves of the "substantial privilege of carrying on business" on the reservation. *Mobil Oil Corp. v. Commissioner of Taxes,* 445 U.S. 425, 437 (1980); *Wisconsin v. J. C. Penney Co.,* 311 U.S. 435, 444-445 (1940). They benefit from the provision of police protection and other governmental services, as well as from " 'the advantages of a civilized society' " that are assured by the existence of tribal government. *Exxon Corp. v. Wisconsin Dept. of Revenue,* 447 U.S. 207, 228 (1980) (quoting *Japan Line, Ltd. v. County of Los Angeles,* 441 U.S. 434, 445 (1979)). Numerous other governmental entities levy a general revenue tax similar to that imposed by the Jicarilla Tribe when they provide comparable services. Under these circumstances, there is nothing exceptional in requiring petitioners to contribute through taxes to the general cost of tribal government. *Cf. Commonwealth Edison Co. v. Montana,* 453 U.S. 609, 624-629 (1981); *Id.,* at 647 (BLACKMUN J., dissenting); *Mobil Oil Corp. v. Commissioner of Taxes, supra,* at 436-437.

As we observed in *Colville, supra,* the tribe's interest in levying taxes on nonmembers to raise "revenues for essential governmental programs ... is strongest when the revenues are derived from value generated on the reservation by activities involving the Tribes and when the taxpayer is the recipient of tribal services." 447 U.S., at 156-157. This surely is the case here. The mere fact that the government imposing the tax also enjoys rents and royalties as the lessor of the mineral lands does not undermine the government's authority to impose the tax. *See infra,* at 145-148. The royalty payments from the mineral leases are paid to the Tribe in its role as partner in petitioners' commercial venture. The severance tax, in contrast, is petitioners' contribution "to the general cost of providing governmental services." *Commonwealth Edison Co. v. Montana, supra,* at 623. State governments commonly receive both royalty payments and severance taxes from lessees of mineral lands within their borders.

Viewing the taxing power of Indian tribes as an essential instrument of self-government and territorial management has been a shared assumption of all three branches of the Federal Government....

     ....

Of course, the Tribe's authority to tax nonmembers is subject to constraints not imposed on other governmental entities: the Federal Government can take away this power, and the Tribe must obtain the approval of the Secretary before any tax on nonmembers can take effect. These additional constraints minimize potential concern that Indian tribes will exercise the power to tax in an unfair or unprincipled manner, and ensure that any exercise of the tribal power to tax will be consistent with national policies.

     ....

... Nonmembers who lawfully enter tribal lands remain subject to the tribe's *power* to exclude them. This power necessarily includes the lesser power to place conditions on entry, on continued presence, or on reservation conduct, such as a tax on business activities conducted on the reservation. When a tribe grants a non-Indian the right to be on Indian land, the tribe agrees not to exercise its *ultimate* power to oust the non-Indian as long as the non-Indian complies with the initial conditions of entry. However, it does not follow that the lawful property right to be on Indian land also immunizes the non-Indian from the tribe's exercise of its lesser-included power to tax or to place other conditions on the non-Indian's conduct or continued presence on the reservation. A nonmember who enters the jurisdiction of the tribe remains subject to the risk that the tribe will later exercise its sovereign power. The fact that the tribe chooses not to exercise its power to tax when it initially grants a non-Indian entry onto the reservation does not permanently divest the tribe of its authority to impose such a tax.

Petitioners argue that their leaseholds entitle them to enter the reservation and exempt them from further exercises of the Tribe's sovereign authority. Similarly, the dissent asserts that the Tribe has lost the power to tax petitioners' mining activities because it has leased to them the use of the mineral lands and such rights of access to the reservation as might be necessary to enjoy the leases. *Post,* at 186-190....

[P]etitioners and the dissent confuse the Tribe's role as commercial partner with its role as sovereign. This confusion relegates the powers of sovereignty to the bargaining process undertaken in each of the sovereign's commercial agreements. It is one thing to find that the Tribe has agreed to sell the right to use the land and take from it valuable minerals; it is quite another to find that the Tribe has abandoned its sovereign powers simply because it has not expressly reserved them through a contract.

Confusing these two results denigrates Indian sovereignty. Indeed, the dissent apparently views the tribal power to exclude, as well as the derivative authority to tax, as merely the power possessed by any individual landowner or any social group to attach conditions, including a "tax" or fee, to the entry by a stranger onto private land or into the social group, and not as a sovereign power....

... Indian sovereignty is not conditioned on the assent of a nonmember; to the contrary, the nonmember's presence and conduct on Indian lands are conditioned by the limitations the tribe may choose to impose.

Viewed in this light, the absence of a reference to the tax in the leases themselves hardly impairs the Tribe's authority to impose the tax. Contractual arrangements remain subject to subsequent legislation by the presiding sovereign. *See, e.g., Veix v. Sixth Ward Building & Loan Assn. of Newark,* 310 U.S. 32 (1940); *Home Building & Loan Assn. v. Blaisdell,* 290 U.S. 398 (1934). Even where the contract at issue requires payment of a royalty for a license or franchise issued by the governmental entity, the government's power to tax remains unless it "has been specifically surrendered in terms which admit of no other reasonable interpretation." *St. Louis v. United R.. Co.,* 210 U.S. 266, 280 (1908).

To state that Indian sovereignty is different than that of Federal, State or local Governments, *see post,* at 189, n.50, does not justify ignoring the principles announced by this Court for determining whether a sovereign has waived its taxing authority in cases involving city, state, and federal taxes imposed under similar circumstances. Each of these governments has different attributes of sovereignty, which also may derive from different sources. These differences, however, do not alter the principles for determining whether any of these governments has waived a sovereign power through contract, and we perceive no principled reason for holding that the different attributes of Indian sovereignty require different treatment in this regard. Without regard to its source, sovereign power, even when unexercised, is an enduring presence that governs all contracts subject to the sovereign's jurisdiction, and will remain intact unless surrendered in unmistakable terms.

... We could find a waiver of the Tribe's taxing power only if we inferred it from silence in the leases. To presume that a sovereign forever waives the right to exercise one of its sovereign powers unless it expressly reserves the right to exercise that power in a commercial agreement turns the concept of sovereignty on its head, and we do not adopt this analysis.

....

Finding no defect in the Tribe's exercise of its taxing power, we now address petitioners' contention that the severance tax violates the "negative implications" of the Commerce Clause because it taxes an activity that is an integral part of the flow of commerce, discriminates against interstate commerce, and imposes a multiple burden on interstate commerce....

To date, however, this Court has relied on the Indian Commerce Clause as a shield to protect Indian tribes from state and local interference, and has not relied on the Clause to authorize tribal regulation of commerce without any constitutional restraints. We see no need to break new ground in this area today: even if we assume that tribal action is subject to the limitations of the Interstate Commerce Clause, this tax does not violate the "negative implications" of that Clause.

....

A state tax may violate the "negative implications" of the Interstate Commerce Clause by unduly burdening or discriminating against interstate commerce. *See, e.g., Commonwealth Edison Co. v. Montana,* 453 U.S. 609 (1981); *Complete Auto Transit, Inc. v. Brady,* 430 U.S. 274 (1977). Judicial review of state taxes under the Interstate Commerce Clause is intended to ensure that States do not disrupt or burden interstate commerce when Congress' power remains unexercised: it protects the free flow of commerce, and thereby safeguards Congress' latent power from encroachment by the several States.

... Courts are final arbiters under the Commerce Clause only when Congress has not acted. *See Japan Line, Ltd. v. County of Los Angeles,* 441 U.S., at 454.

Here, Congress has affirmatively acted by providing a series of federal checkpoints that must be cleared before a tribal tax can take effect....

As we noted earlier, the severance tax challenged by petitioners was enacted in accordance with this congressional scheme.... As a result, this tribal tax comes to us in a posture significantly different from a challenged state tax, which does not need specific federal approval to take effect, and which therefore requires, in the absence of congressional ratification, judicial review to ensure that it does not unduly burden or discriminate against interstate commerce. Judicial review of the Indian tax measure, in contrast, would duplicate the administrative review called for by the congressional scheme.

....

[Petitioners] argue that the tax discriminates against interstate commerce. In essence, petitioners argue that the language "sold or transported off the reservation" exempts from taxation minerals sold on the reservation, kept on the reservation for use by individual members of the Tribe, and minerals taken by the Tribe on the reservation as in-kind royalty.... We ... agree with the Tribe, the Solicitor General, and the Court of Appeals that the tax is imposed on minerals sold on the reservation or transported off the reservation before sale. *See* 617 F.2d, at 546. *Cf.* n.22, *supra*. Under this interpretation, the tax does not treat minerals transported away from the reservation differently than it treats minerals that might be sold on the reservation. Nor does the Tribe's tax ordinance exempt minerals ultimately received by individual members of the Tribe. The ordinance does exempt minerals received by the Tribe as in-kind payments on the leases and used for tribal purposes, but this exemption merely avoids the administrative makework that would ensue if the Tribe, as local government, taxed the amount of minerals that the Tribe, as commercial partner, received in royalty payments. Therefore, this exemption cannot be deemed a discriminatory preference for local commerce.

....

In *Worcester v. Georgia,* 6 Pet., at 559, Chief Justice Marshall observed that Indian tribes had "always been considered as distinct, independent political communities, retaining their original natural rights." Although the tribes are subject to the authority of the Federal Government, the "weaker power does not surrender its independence— its right to self-government, by associating with a stronger, and taking its protection." *Id.,* at 561. Adhering to this understanding, we conclude that the Tribe did not surrender its authority to tax the mining activities of petitioners, whether this authority is deemed to arise from the Tribe's inherent power of self-government or from its inherent power to exclude nonmembers. Therefore, the Tribe may enforce its severance tax unless and until Congress divests this power, an action that Congress has not taken to date. Finally, the severance tax imposed by the Tribe cannot be invalidated on the ground that it violates the "negative implications" of the Commerce Clause.

Affirmed.

Justice Stevens, with whom Chief Justice Burger and Justice Rehnquist join, dissenting.

... Indian tribes were afforded no general powers over citizens of the United States. Many tribes, however, were granted a power unknown to any other sovereignty in this Nation: a power to exclude nonmembers entirely from territory reserved for the tribe....

....

The power to exclude petitioners would have supported the imposition of a discriminatory tribal tax on petitioners when they sought to enter the Jicarilla Apache Reservation to explore for minerals. Moreover, even if no tax had been imposed at the time of initial entry, a discriminatory severance tax could have been imposed as a condition attached to the grant of the privilege of extracting minerals from the earth. But the Tribe did not impose any tax prior to petitioners' entry or as a condition attached to the privileges granted by the leases in 1953. As a result, the tax imposed in 1976 is not valid unless the Tribe retained its power either to exclude petitioners from the reservation or to prohibit them from continuing to extract oil and gas from reservation lands.

... Under the leases petitioners clearly have the right to remain on the reservation to do business for the duration of the contracts.

There is no basis for a claim that exercise of the mining rights granted by the leases was subject to an additional, unstated condition concerning the payment of severance taxes. At the time the leases contained in the record were executed, the Jicarilla Apache Constitution contained no taxing authorization whatever; the severance tax ordinance was not enacted until many years after all lessees had been granted an unlimited right to extract oil and gas from the reservation. In addition, the written leases unambiguously stated:

> "[N]o regulation hereafter approved shall effect a change in rate or royalty
> or annual rental herein specified without the written consent of the parties
> to this lease." App. 27.

Nor can it be said that notice of an inherent right to tax could have been gleaned from relevant statutory enactments. When Congress enacted legislation in 1927 granting the Indians the royalty income from oil and gas leases on reservations created by Executive Order, it neither authorized nor prohibited the imposition of any taxes by the tribes. Although the absence of such reference does not indicate that Congress preempted the right of the tribes to impose such a tax, the lack of any mention of tribal severance taxes defeats the argument that all parties were aware as a matter of law that a severance tax could be imposed at any time as a condition to the continued performance of a mineral lease.

....

... Petitioners were granted authority by the Tribe to extract oil and gas from reservation lands. The Tribe now seeks to change retroactively the conditions of that authority.... Moreover, it may be sound policy to find additional sources of revenue to better the economic conditions of many Indian tribes. If this retroactive imposition of a tax on oil companies is permissible, however, an Indian tribe may with equal legitimacy contract with outsiders for the construction of a school or a hospital, or for the rendition of medical or technical services, and then—after the contract is partially performed—change the terms of the bargain by imposing a gross receipts tax on the outsider. If the Court is willing to ignore the risk of such unfair treatment of a local contractor or a local doctor because the Secretary of the Interior has the power to veto a tribal tax, it must equate the unbridled discretion of a political appointee with the protection afforded by rules of law. That equation is unacceptable to me. Neither wealth, political opportunity, nor past transgressions can justify denying any person the protection of the law.

NEW MEXICO v. MESCALERO APACHE TRIBE

462 U.S. 324, 103 S. Ct. 2378, 76 L. Ed. 2d 611 (U.S. Sup. Ct. 1983)

JUSTICE MARSHALL delivered the opinion of the Court.

[*The Mescalero Apache Tribe and the federal government "jointly conduct a comprehensive fish and game management program." The program achieved much success despite the fact that New Mexico neither assisted the tribe in stocking its waters with fish, nor "contributed significantly to the development of the elk herd or the other game on the reservation."*]

We are called upon to decide in this case whether a State may restrict an Indian Tribe's regulation of hunting and fishing on its reservation....

. . . .

Numerous conflicts exist between State and tribal hunting regulations.... The New Mexico Department of Game and Fish has enforced the State's regulations by arresting non-Indian hunters for illegal possession of game killed on the reservation in accordance with tribal ordinances but not in accordance with State hunting regulations.

. . . .

In *White Mountain Apache Tribe v. Bracker*, 448 U.S. 136 (1980),.... [w]e stated that [the] determination [of federal preemption] does not depend "on mechanical or absolute conceptions of state or tribal sovereignty, but calls for a particularized inquiry into the nature of the state, federal, and tribal interests at stake."

[*The Court next discussed the special application the doctrine of preemption has in Indian law analysis.*]

. . . .

We have stressed that Congress' objective of furthering tribal self-government encompasses far more than encouraging tribal management of disputes between members, but includes Congress' overriding goal of encouraging "tribal self-sufficiency and economic development." *Bracker*, supra, 448 U.S., at 143. In part as a necessary implication of this broad federal commitment, we have held that tribes have the power to manage the use of its territory and resources by both members and nonmembers, to undertake and regulate economic activity within the reservation, and to defray the cost of governmental services by levying taxes. Thus, when a tribe undertakes an enterprise under the authority of federal law, an assertion of State authority must be viewed against any interference with the successful accomplishment of the federal purpose....

Our prior decisions also guide our assessment of the state interest asserted to justify State jurisdiction over a reservation. The exercise of State authority which imposes additional burdens on a tribal enterprise must ordinarily be justified by functions or services performed by the State in connection with the on-reservation activity.... A State's regulatory interest will be particularly substantial if the State can point to off-reservation effects that necessitate State intervention.

[*The Court then recognized that the tribe's treaty rights included the "right to regulate the use of its resources by members as well as non-members."*]

. . . .

It is important to emphasize that concurrent jurisdiction [*between the tribe and the state*] would effectively nullify the Tribe's authority to control hunting and fishing on the reservation. Concurrent jurisdiction would empower New Mexico wholly to supplant tribal regulations. The State would be able to dictate the terms on which nonmembers are permitted to utilize the reservation's resources. The Tribe would thus exercise its authority over the reservation only at the sufferance of the State....

Furthermore, the exercise of concurrent State jurisdiction in this case would completely "disturb and disarrange" the comprehensive scheme of federal and tribal management established pursuant to federal law....

Concurrent State jurisdiction would supplant this regulatory scheme with an inconsistent dual system: members would be governed by Tribal ordinances, while non-members would be regulated by general State hunting and fishing laws. This could severely hinder the ability of the Tribe to conduct a sound management program.... Permitting the State to enforce different restrictions simply because they would have been determined to be appropriate for the State as a whole would impose on the Tribe the possibly insurmountable task of ensuring that the patchwork application of State and Tribal regulations remains consistent with sound management of the reservation's resources.

     ....

The assertion of concurrent jurisdiction by New Mexico not only would threaten to disrupt the federal and tribal regulatory scheme, but would also threaten Congress' overriding objective of encouraging tribal self-government and economic development....

     ....

The State has failed to "identify any regulatory function or service ... that would justify" the assertion of concurrent regulatory authority. The hunting and fishing permitted by the Tribe occur entirely on the reservation. The fish and wildlife resources are either native to the reservation or were created by the joint efforts of the Tribe and the Federal Government. New Mexico does not contribute in any significant respect to the maintenance of these resources, and can point to no other "governmental functions it provides," in connection with hunting and fishing on the reservation by nonmembers that would justify the assertion of its authority.

The State also cannot point to any off-reservation effects that warrant State intervention. Some species of game never leave tribal lands, and the State points to no specific interest concerning those that occasionally do....

Given the strong interests favoring exclusive tribal jurisdiction and the absence of State interests which justify the assertion of concurrent authority, we conclude that the application of the State's hunting and fishing laws to the reservation is preempted.

     ....

ARIZONA v. SAN CARLOS APACHE TRIBE

463 U.S. 545, 103 S. Ct. 3201, 77 L. Ed. 2d 837 (U.S. Sup. Ct. 1983)

JUSTICE BRENNAN delivered the opinion of the Court.

....

The two petitions considered here arise out of three separate consolidated appeals that were decided within three days of each other by the same panel of the Court of Appeals for the Ninth Circuit. In each of the underlying cases, either the United States as trustee or certain Indian tribes on their own behalf, or both, asserted the right to have certain Indian water rights in Arizona or Montana adjudicated in federal court.

[*In the 1952 McCarran Amendment, Congress expressly consented to the joinder of the United States in state court water rights adjudications where the federal government has an interest in the river system at issue. 43 U.S.C. § 666 (1986). After briefly discussing the background of the cases before it, the Court determined that, under the McCarran Amendment, no jurisdictional distinction should be drawn between states whose enabling acts disclaimed jurisdiction over Indian affairs, and states whose enabling acts contained no such disclaimer. The Court was then faced with the remaining issue of whether a suit brought in federal court by an Indian tribe to adjudicate Indian water rights may be dismissed in favor of a state court adjudication involving water rights in the same system.*]

....

If the state proceedings have jurisdiction over the Indian water rights at issue here, as appears to be the case, then concurrent federal proceedings are likely to be duplicative and wasteful, generating "additional litigation through permitting inconsistent dispositions of property." Moreover, since a judgment by either court would ordinarily be res judicata in the other, the existence of such concurrent proceedings creates the serious potential for spawning an unseemly and destructive race to see which forum can resolve the same issues first—a race contrary to the entire spirit of the McCarran Amendment and prejudicial, to say the least, to the possibility of reasoned decisionmaking by either forum....

....

[Prior case law,] of course, does not require that a federal water suit must always be dismissed or stayed in deference to a concurrent and adequate comprehensive state adjudication [citing *Colorado River Conservation District v. United States*, 424 U.S. 800 (1976)]. Certainly, the federal courts need not defer to the state proceedings if the state courts expressly agree to stay their own consideration of the issues raised in the federal action pending disposition of that action. Moreover, it may be in a particular case that, at the time a motion to dismiss is filed, the federal suit at issue is well enough along that its dismissal would itself constitute a waste of judicial resources and an invitation to duplicative effort. Finally, we do not deny that, in a case in which the arguments for and against deference to the state adjudication were otherwise closely matched, the fact that a federal suit was brought by Indians on their own behalf and sought only to adjudicate Indian rights should be figured into the balance. But the most important consideration in *Colorado River*, and the most important consideration in any federal water suit concurrent to a comprehensive state proceeding, must be the "policy underlying the

McCarran Amendment," and, despite the strong arguments raised by the respondents, we cannot conclude that water rights suits brought by Indians and seeking adjudication only of Indian rights should be excepted from the application of that policy or from the general principles set out in *Colorado River*. In the cases before us, assuming that the state adjudications are adequate to quantify the rights at issue in the federal suits, and taking into account the McCarran Amendment policies we have discussed, the expertise and administrative machinery available to the state courts, the infancy of the federal suits, the general judicial bias against piecemeal litigation, and the convenience to the parties, we must conclude that the District Courts were correct in deferring to the state proceedings (footnote omitted).

    ....

COUNTY OF ONEIDA v. ONEIDA INDIAN NATION

470 U.S. 226, 105 S. Ct. 1245, 84 L. Ed. 2d 169 (U.S. Sup. Ct. 1985)

JUSTICE POWELL delivered the opinion of the Court (footnote omitted).

These cases present the question whether three Tribes of the Oneida Indians may bring a suit for damages for the occupation and use of tribal land allegedly conveyed unlawfully in 1795.

    ....

The Oneida Indian Nation of New York, the Oneida Indian Nation of Wisconsin, and the Oneida of the Thames Band Council (the Oneidas) instituted this suit in 1970 against the Counties of Oneida and Madison, New York. The Oneidas alleged that their ancestors conveyed 100,000 acres to the State of New York under a 1795 agreement that violated the Trade and Intercourse Act of 1793, 1 Stat. 329, and thus that the transaction was void....

[The case was first brought before the Supreme Court to resolve questions concerning federal court jurisdiction over the Oneida's action against the counties for interference with tribal possessory rights to aboriginal lands. Oneida Indian Nation v. County of Oneida, 414 U.S. 661 (1974) (Oneida I) (upholding federal jurisdiction).]

    ....

[The Trade and Intercourse Act provided] that "no purchase or grant of lands, or of any title or claim thereto, from any Indians or nation or tribe of Indians, within the bounds of the United States, shall be of any validity in law or equity, unless the same be made by a treaty or convention entered into pursuant to the constitution ... [and] in the presence, and with the approbation of the commissioner or commissioners of the United States" appointed to supervise such transactions. 1 Stat. 330, § 8....

Despite Congress' clear policy that no person or entity should purchase Indian land without the acquiescence of the Federal Government, in 1795 the State of New York began negotiations to buy the remainder of the Oneidas' land.... [I]n the summer of 1795 [New York] entered into an agreement with the Oneidas whereby they conveyed virtually all of their remaining land to the State for annual cash payments. It is this transaction that is the basis of the Oneidas' complaint in this case.

    ....

At the outset, we are faced with petitioners' contention that the Oneidas have no right of action for the violation of the 1793 Act....

    ....

[A]s we concluded in *Oneida I*, "the possessory right claimed [by the Oneidas] is a *federal* right to the lands at issue in this case." 414 U.S., at 671 (emphasis in original). Numerous decisions of this Court prior to *Oneida I* recognized at least implicitly that Indians have a federal common-law right to sue to enforce their aboriginal land rights. In *Johnson v. M'Intosh*, ..., the Court declared invalid two private purchases of Indian land that occurred in 1773 and 1775 without the Crown's consent (citation omitted).... [T]he Court's opinion in *Oneida I* implicitly assumed that the Oneidas could bring a common-law action to vindicate their aboriginal rights. Citing *United States v. Santa Fe Pacific R. Co.*, [314 U.S. 349 (1941)], we noted that the Indians' right of occupancy need not be based on treaty, statute, or other formal Government action. We stated that "absent federal statutory guidance, the governing rule of decision would be fashioned by the federal court in the mode of the common law."

In keeping with these well-established principles, we hold that the Oneidas can maintain this action for violation of their possessory rights based on federal common law.

[*The Court also rejected petitioners' argument that the tribe's federal common law cause of action was preempted by the Nonintercourse Acts.*]

    ....

Having determined that the Oneidas have a cause of action under federal common law, we address the question whether there are defenses available to the counties....

    ....

There is no federal statute of limitations governing federal common-law actions by Indians to enforce property rights. In the absence of a controlling federal limitations period, the general rule is that a state limitations period for an analogous cause of action is borrowed and applied to the federal claim, provided that the application of the state statute would not be inconsistent with underlying federal policies (footnote omitted). *See Johnson v. Railway Express Agency, Inc.*, 421 U.S. 454, 465 (1975). We think the borrowing of a state limitations period in these cases would be inconsistent with federal policy. Indeed, on a number of occasions Congress has made this clear with respect to Indian land claims.

In adopting the statute that gave jurisdiction over civil actions involving Indians to the New York courts, Congress included this proviso: "[N]othing herein contained shall be construed as conferring jurisdiction on the courts of the State of New York or making applicable the laws of the State of New York in civil actions involving Indian lands or claims with respect thereto which relate to transactions or events transpiring prior to September 13, 1952." 25 U.S.C. § 233. This proviso was added specifically to ensure that the New York statute of limitations would not apply to pre-1952 land claims. In *Oneida I*, we relied on the legislative history of 25 U.S.C. § 233 in concluding that Indian land claims were exclusively a matter of federal law. 414 U.S. at 680-682. This history also reflects congressional policy against the application of state statutes of limitations in the context of Indian land claims.

[*The Court similarly rejected petitioners' other defenses, including: the doctrine of laches; the abatement of the cause of action upon the expiration of the 1793 Nonintercourse Act; the ratification by the United States of the unlawful 1795 land conveyance, and; the nonjusticiability of the issue presented because it was a political question.*]

....

One would have thought that claims dating back for more than a century and a half would have been barred long ago. As our opinion indicates, however, neither petitioners nor we have found any applicable statute of limitations or other relevant legal basis for holding that the Oneidas' claims are barred or otherwise have been satisfied. The judgment of the Court of Appeals is affirmed with respect to the finding of liability under federal common law....

It is so ordered.

....

KERR-McGEE CORP. v. NAVAJO TRIBE OF INDIANS

471 U.S. 195, 105 S. Ct. 1900, 85 L. Ed. 2d 200 (U.S. Sup. Ct. 1985)

Chief Justice Burger delivered the opinion of the Court.

We granted certiorari to decide whether the Navajo Tribe of Indians may tax business activities conducted on its land without first obtaining the approval of the Secretary of the Interior.

....

In 1978, the Navajo Tribal Council, the governing body of the Navajo Tribe of Indians, enacted two ordinances imposing taxes known as the Possessory Interest Tax and the Business Activity Tax. The Possessory Interest Tax is measured by the value of leasehold interests in tribal lands; the tax rate is 3% of the value of those interests. The Business Activity Tax is assessed on receipts from the sale of property produced or extracted within the Navajo Nation, and from the sale of services within the Nation; a tax rate of 5% is applied after subtracting a standard deduction and specified expenses. The tax laws apply to both Navajo and non-Indian businesses, with dissatisfied taxpayers enjoying the right of appeal to the Navajo Tax Commission and the Navajo Court of Appeals.

The Navajo Tribe, uncertain whether federal approval was required, submitted the two tax laws to the Bureau of Indian Affairs of the Department of the Interior. The Bureau informed the Tribe that no federal statute or regulation required the Department of the Interior to approve or disapprove the taxes.

Before any taxes were collected, petitioner, a substantial mineral lessee on the Navajo Reservation, brought this action seeking to invalidate the taxes. Petitioner claimed in the United States District Court for the District of Arizona that the Navajo taxes were invalid without approval of the Secretary of the Interior. The District Court agreed....

The United States Court of Appeals for the Ninth Circuit reversed. 731 F.2d 597 (1984).... [I]t held that no federal statute or principle of law mandated Secretarial approval.

....

In *Merrion v. Jicarilla Apache Tribe,* 455 U.S. 130 (1982), we held that the "power to tax is an essential attribute of Indian sovereignty because it is a necessary instrument of self-government and territorial management." *Id.,* at 137. Congress, of course, may erect "checkpoints that must be cleared before a tribal tax can take effect." *Id.,* at 155. The issue in this case is whether Congress has enacted legislation requiring Secretarial approval of Navajo tax laws.

Petitioner suggests that the Indian Reorganization Act of 1934, 48 Stat. 984, 25 U.S.C. § 461 *et seq.,* is such a law. Section 16 of the IRA authorizes any tribe on a reservation to adopt a constitution and bylaws, subject to the approval of the Secretary of the Interior. 25 U.S.C. § 476. The Act, however, does not provide that a tribal constitution must condition the power to tax on Secretarial approval. Indeed, the terms of the IRA do not govern tribes, like the Navajo, which declined to accept its provisions. 25 U.S.C. § 478.

Many tribal constitutions written under the IRA in the 1930's called for Secretarial approval of tax laws affecting non-Indians. *See, e.g.,* Constitution and Bylaws of the Rosebud Sioux Tribe of South Dakota, Art. 4, § 1(h) (1935). But there were exceptions to this practice.... Thus the most that can be said about this period of constitution writing is that the Bureau of Indian Affairs, in assisting the drafting of tribal constitutions, had a policy of including provisions for Secretarial approval; but that policy was not mandated by Congress.

Nor do we agree that Congress intended to recognize as legitimate only those tribal taxes authorized by constitutions written under the IRA....

Some tribes that adopted constitutions in the early years of the IRA may be dependent on the Government in a way that the Navajos are not. However, such tribes are free, with the backing of the Interior Department, to amend their constitutions to remove the requirement of Secretarial approval. *See, e.g.,* Revised Constitution and Bylaws of the Mississippi Band of Choctaw Indians, Art. 8, § 1(r) (1975).

Petitioner also argues that the Indian Mineral Leasing Act of 1938, 52 Stat. 347, 25 U.S.C. § 396a *et seq.,* requires Secretarial approval of Navajo tax laws. Section[ ] ... 4 provides that "[a]ll operations under any oil, gas, or other mineral lease issued pursuant to the [Act] shall be subject to the rules and regulations promulgated by the Secretary of the Interior." 25 U.S.C. § 396d. Under this grant of authority, the Secretary has issued comprehensive regulations governing the operation of oil and gas leases. *See* 25 CFR pt. 211 (1984). The Secretary, however, does not demand that tribal laws taxing mineral production be submitted for his approval.

Petitioner contends that the Secretary's decision not to review such tax laws is inconsistent with the statute. In *Merrion,* we emphasized the difference between a tribe's "role as commercial partner," and its "role as sovereign." 455 U.S., at 145-146. The tribe acts as a commercial partner when it agrees to sell the right to the use of its land for mineral production, but the tribe acts as a sovereign when it imposes a tax on economic activities within its jurisdiction. *Id.*, at 146;....

Even assuming that the Secretary could review tribal laws taxing mineral production, it does not follow that he must do so. We are not inclined to impose upon the Secretary a duty that he has determined is not needed to satisfy the 1938 Act's basic purpose—to maximize tribal revenues from reservation lands. *See* S. Rep. No. 985, 75th Cong., 1st Sess., 2-3 (1937). Thus, in light of our obligation to "tread lightly in the absence of clear indications of legislative intent," *Santa Clara Pueblo v. Martinez,* 436 U.S. 49, 60 (1978), we will not interpret a grant of authority to regulate leasing operations as a command to the Secretary to review every tribal tax relating to mineral production.

Finally, we do not believe that statutes requiring Secretarial supervision in other contexts, *see, e.g.,* 25 U.S.C. §§ 81, 311-321, reveal that Congress has limited the Navajo Tribal Council's authority to tax non-Indians. As we noted in *New Mexico v. Mescalero Apache Tribe,* 462 U.S. 324 (1983), the Federal Government is "firmly committed to the goal of promoting tribal self-government." *Id.,* at 334-335; *see, e.g.,* Indian Financing Act of 1974, 88 Stat. 77, 25 U.S.C. § 1451 *et seq.* The power to tax members and non-Indians alike is surely an essential attribute of such self-government; the Navajos can gain independence from the Federal Government only by financing their own police force, schools, and social programs. *See* President's Statement on Indian Policy, 19 Weekly Comp. Pres. Doc. 98, 99 (Jan. 24, 1983).

....

The Navajo Government has been called "probably the most elaborate" among tribes. H.R. Rep. No. 78, 91st Cong., 1st Sess., 8 (1969). The legitimacy of the Navajo Tribal Council, the freely elected governing body of the Navajos, is beyond question. *See, e.g.,* 25 U.S.C. §§ 635(b), 637, 638. We agree with the Court of Appeals that neither Congress nor the Navajos have found it necessary to subject the Tribal Council's tax laws to review by the Secretary of the Interior; accordingly, the judgment is

Affirmed.

JUSTICE POWELL took no part in the consideration or decision of this case.

CALIFORNIA v. CABAZON BAND OF MISSION INDIANS

480 U.S. 202, 107 S. Ct. 1083, 94 L. Ed. 2d 244 (U.S. Sup. Ct. 1987)

JUSTICE WHITE delivered the opinion of the Court.

[*The Cabazon Band of Mission Indians, located in Riverside County, California, conducts on-reservation bingo games, as well as poker and other card games, which are open to the public and are predominantly played by non-Indians. The games are the tribe's sole source of income, and are a major source of tribal employment. The tribe seeks to prevent the*

State of California, a Public Law 280 state, from enforcing its state statute that prohibits bingo games not operated by charitable organizations and sets a $250 per game limit. The tribe further seeks to prevent Riverside County from imposing its gambling ordinance, which would prohibit the tribe from conducting its card games, upon the tribe. The similarly situated Morongo Band of Mission Indians is also a party to this suit.]

....

In § 2 [of Public Law 280], California was granted broad criminal jurisdiction over offenses committed by or against Indians within all Indian country within the State. Section 4's grant of civil jurisdiction was more limited (footnotes omitted).... The Act plainly was not intended to effect total assimilation of Indian tribes into mainstream American society. (Citation omitted.) ... Accordingly, when a State seeks to enforce a law within an Indian reservation under the authority of Pub. L. 280, it must be determined whether the law is criminal in nature, and thus fully applicable to the reservation under § 2, or civil in nature, and applicable only as it may be relevant to private civil litigation in state court.

In [*Barona Group of the Capitan Grande Band of Mission Indians v. Duffy*, 694 F.2d 1185 (9th Cir. 1982), *cert. denied*, 461 U.S. 929 (1983)], applying what it thought to be the civil/criminal dichotomy drawn in *Bryan v. Itasca County*, the Court of Appeals drew a distinction between state "criminal/prohibitory" laws and state "civil/regulatory" laws: if the intent of a state law is generally to prohibit certain conduct, it falls within Pub. L. 280's grant of criminal jurisdiction, but if the state law generally permits the conduct at issue, subject to regulation, it must be classified as civil/regulatory and Pub. L. 280 does not authorize its enforcement on an Indian reservation. The shorthand test is whether the conduct at issue violates the State's public policy....

....

California does not prohibit all forms of gambling.... In light of the fact that California permits a substantial amount of gambling activity, including bingo, and actually promotes gambling through its state lottery, we must conclude that California regulates rather than prohibits gambling in general and bingo in particular (footnote omitted).

[*The Court next determined that, based on the "public policy test," the federal Organized Crime Control Act authorizes neither the application nor enforcement of California's gambling laws in Indian Country.*]

[U]nder certain circumstances a State may validly assert authority over the activities of nonmembers on a reservation, and ... in exceptional circumstances a State may assert jurisdiction over the on-reservation activities of tribal members." *New Mexico v. Mescalero Apache Tribe*, 462 U.S. 324, 331-332 (1983) (footnotes omitted)....

Decision in this case turns on whether state authority is pre-empted by the operation of federal law; and "[s]tate jurisdiction is pre-empted ... if it interferes or is incompatible with federal and tribal interests reflected in federal law, unless the state interests at stake are sufficient to justify the assertion of state authority." *Mescalero*, 462 U.S., at 333, 334. The inquiry is to proceed in light of traditional notions of Indian sovereignty and the congressional goal of Indian self-government, including its "overriding goal" of encouraging tribal self-sufficiency and economic development. *Id.*, at 334-335. (Footnote and citations omitted.)

....

[*The Court proceeded to discuss federal actions which either approved or promoted tribal bingo enterprises.*]

These policies and actions, which demonstrate the Government's approval and active promotion of tribal bingo enterprises, are of particular relevance in this case. The Cabazon and Morongo Reservations contain no natural resources which can be exploited. The tribal games at present provide the sole source of revenues for the operation of tribal governments and the provision of tribal services. They are also the major sources of employment on the reservations. Self-determination and economic development are not within reach if the Tribes cannot raise revenues and provide employment for their members. The Tribes' interests obviously parallel the federal interests.

. . . .

The sole interest asserted by the State to justify the imposition of its bingo laws on the Tribes is in preventing the infiltration of the tribal games by organized crime....

We conclude that the State's interest in preventing the infiltration of the tribal bingo enterprises by organized crime does not justify state regulation of the tribal bingo enterprises in light of the compelling federal and tribal interests supporting them. State regulation would impermissibly infringe on tribal government, and this conclusion applies equally to the county's attempted regulation of the Cabazon card club. We therefore affirm the judgment of the Court of Appeals and remand the case for further proceedings consistent with this opinion.

It is so ordered.

LYNG v. NORTHWEST INDIAN CEMETERY PROTECTIVE ASSOCIATION, et al.

485 U.S. 439, 108 S. Ct. 1319, 99 L. Ed. 2d 534 (U.S. Sup. Ct. 1988)

JUSTICE O'CONNOR delivered the opinion of the Court.

This case requires us to consider whether the First Amendment's Free Exercise Clause prohibits the Government from permitting timber harvesting in, or constructing a road through, a portion of a National Forest that has traditionally been used for religious purposes by members of three American Indian tribes in northwestern California. We conclude that it does not.

. . . .

The Free Exercise Clause of the First Amendment provides that "Congress shall make no law ... prohibiting the free exercise [of religion]." It is undisputed that the Indian respondents' beliefs are sincere and that the Government's proposed actions will have severe adverse effects on the practice of their religion. Those respondents contend that the burden on their religious practices is heavy enough to violate the Free Exercise Clause unless the Government can demonstrate a compelling need to complete the G-O road or to engage in timber harvesting in the Chimney Rock area. We disagree.

In *Bowen v. Roy*, 476 U.S. 693 (1986), we considered a challenge to a federal statute that required the States to use Social Security numbers in administering certain welfare programs. Two applicants for benefits under these programs contended that their religious beliefs prevented them from acceding to the use of a Social Security number for their 2-year-old daughter because the use of a numerical identifier would "'rob the spirit' of [their] daughter and prevent her from attaining greater spiritual power." *Id.*, at 696. Similarly, in this case, it is said that disruption of the natural environment caused by the G-O road will diminish the sacredness of the area in question and create distractions that will interfere with "training and ongoing religious experience of individuals using [sites within] the area for personal medicine and growth ... and as integrated parts of a system of religious belief and practice which correlates ascending degrees of personal power with a geographic hierarchy of power." App. 181. *Cf. Id.*, at 178 ("Scarred hills and mountains, and disturbed rocks destroy the purity of the sacred areas, and [Indian] consultants repeatedly stressed the need of a training doctor to be undistracted by such disturbance"). The Court rejected this kind of challenge in *Roy*....

....

The building of a road or the harvesting of timber on publicly owned land cannot meaningfully be distinguished from the use of a Social Security number in *Roy*. In both cases, the challenged Government action would interfere significantly with private persons' ability to pursue spiritual fulfillment according to their own religious beliefs. In neither case, however, would the affected individuals be coerced by the Government's action into violating their religious beliefs; nor would either governmental action penalize religious activity by denying any person an equal share of the rights, benefits, and privileges enjoyed by other citizens.

....

... This does not and cannot imply that incidental effects of government programs, which may make it more difficult to practice certain religions but which have no tendency to coerce individuals into acting contrary to their religious beliefs, require government to bring forward a compelling justification for its otherwise lawful actions....

....

Even if we assume that we should accept the Ninth Circuit's prediction, according to which the G-O road will "virtually destroy the ... Indians' ability to practice their religion," 795 F.2d, at 693 (opinion below), the Constitution simply does not provide a principle that could justify upholding respondents' legal claims....

... However much we might wish that it were otherwise, government simply could not operate if it were required to satisfy every citizen's religious needs and desires. A broad range of government activities—from social welfare programs to foreign aid to conservation projects—will always be considered essential to the spiritual well-being of some citizens, often on the basis of sincerely held religious beliefs.... The First Amendment must apply to all citizens alike, and it can give to none of them a veto over public programs that do not prohibit the free exercise of religion....

....

... No disrespect for these practices is implied when one notes that such beliefs could easily require *de facto* beneficial ownership of some rather spacious tracts of public property. Even without anticipating future cases, the diminution of the Government's property rights, and the concomitant subsidy of the Indian religion, would in this case be far from trivial....

....

The Constitution does not permit government to discriminate against religions that treat particular physical sites as sacred, and a law prohibiting the Indian respondents from visiting the Chimney Rock area would raise a different set of constitutional questions. Whatever rights the Indians may have to the use of the area, however, those rights do not divest the Government of its right to use what is, after all, *its* land....

....

Nothing in our opinion should be read to encourage governmental insensitivity to the religious needs of any citizen. The Government's rights to the use of its own land, for example, need not and should not discourage it from accommodating religious practices like those engaged in by the Indian respondents. *Cf. Sherbert,* 374 U.S., at 422-423 (HARLAN, J., dissenting). It is worth emphasizing, therefore, that the Government has taken numerous steps in this very case to minimize the impact that construction of the G-O road will have on the Indians' religious activities. First, the Forest Service commissioned a comprehensive study of the effects that the project would have on the cultural and religious value of the Chimney Rock area....

Although the Forest Service did not in the end adopt the report's recommendation that the project be abandoned, many other ameliorative measures were planned. No sites where specific rituals take place were to be disturbed. In fact, a major factor in choosing among alternative routes for the road was the relation of the various routes to religious sites....

Except for abandoning its project entirely, and thereby leaving the two existing segments of the road to deadend in the middle of a national forest, it is difficult to see how the government could have been more solicitous. Such solicitude accords with "the policy of the United States to protect and preserve for American Indians their inherent right of freedom to believe, express, and exercise the traditional religions of the American Indian ... including but not limited to access to sites, use and possession of sacred objects, and the freedom to worship through ceremonials and traditional rites." American Indian Religious Freedom Act (AIRFA), Pub. L. 95-341, 92 Stat. 469, 42 U.S.C. § 1996.

Respondents, however, suggest that AIRFA goes further and in effect enacts their interpretation of the First Amendment into statutory law.... This argument is without merit.... Nowhere in the law is there so much as a hint of any intent to create a cause of action or any judicially enforceable individual rights.

What is obvious from the face of the statute is confirmed by numerous indications in the legislative history. The sponsor of the bill that became AIRFA, Representative Udall, called it "a sense of Congress joint resolution," aimed at ensuring that "the basic right of the Indian people to exercise their traditional religious practices is not infringed without a clear decision on the part of the Congress or the administrators that such religious practices must yield to some higher consideration." 124 Cong. Rec. 21444 (1978). Representative Udall emphasized that the bill would not "confer special religious rights on Indians," would "not change any existing State or Federal law," and in fact "has no teeth in it." *Id.,* at 21444-21445.

....

It is so ordered.

Justice Brennan, with whom Justice Marshall and Justice Blackmun join, dissenting.

"'[T]he Free Exercise Clause,'" the Court explains today, "'is written in terms of what the government cannot do to the individual, not in terms of what the individual can exact from the government.'" *Ante,* at 1326 (quoting *Sherbert v. Verner,* 374 U.S. 398, 412 (1963) (Douglas, J., concurring)). Pledging fidelity to this unremarkable constitutional principle, the Court nevertheless concludes that even where the Government uses federal land in a manner that threatens the very existence of a Native American religion, the Government is simply not "*doing*" anything to the practitioners of that faith. Instead, the Court believes that Native Americans who request that the Government refrain from destroying their religion effectively seek to exact from the Government *de facto* beneficial ownership of federal property. These two astonishing conclusions follow naturally from the Court's determination that federal land-use decisions that render the practice of a given religion impossible do not burden that religion in a manner cognizable under the Free Exercise Clause, because such decisions neither coerce conduct inconsistent with religious belief nor penalize religious activity.... Because the Court today refuses even to acknowledge the constitutional injury respondents will suffer, and because this refusal essentially leaves Native Americans with absolutely no constitutional protection against perhaps the gravest threat to their religious practices, I dissent.

STRATE v. A-1 CONTRACTORS

520 U.S. 438, 117 S. Ct. 1404, 137 L. Ed. 2d 661 (U.S. Sup. Ct. 1997)

Justice Ginsburg delivered the opinion of the Court.

This case concerns the adjudicatory authority of tribal courts over personal injury actions against defendants who are not tribal members. Specifically, we confront this question: When an accident occurs on a portion of a public highway maintained by the State under a federally granted right-of-way over Indian reservation land, may tribal courts entertain a civil action against an allegedly negligent driver and the driver's employer, neither of whom is a member of the tribe?

Such cases, we hold, fall within state or federal regulatory and adjudicatory governance; tribal courts may not entertain claims against nonmembers arising out of accidents on state highways, absent a statute or treaty authorizing the tribe to govern the conduct of nonmembers on the highway in question....

I

.... [P]etitioner ... and respondent ... were involved in a traffic accident on a portion of a North Dakota state highway running through the Fort Berthold Indian Reservation. The highway strip crossing the reservation is a 6.59-mile stretch of road, open to the public, affording access to a federal water resource project. North Dakota maintains the road under a right-of-way granted by the United States to the State's Highway Department; the right-of-way lies on land held by the United States in trust for the Three Affiliated Tribes (Mandan, Hidatsa, and Arikara) and their members.

....

II

Our case law establishes that, absent express authorization by federal statute or treaty, tribal jurisdiction over the conduct of nonmembers exists only in limited circumstances. In *Oliphant v. Suquamish Tribe,* 435 U.S. 191 (1978), the Court held that Indian tribes lack criminal jurisdiction over non-Indians. [Footnote omitted.] *Montana v. United States,* decided three years later, is the pathmarking case concerning tribal civil authority over nonmembers.... In the main, the Court explained, "the inherent sovereign powers of an Indian tribe"—those powers a tribe enjoys apart from express provision by treaty or statute—"do not extend to the activities of nonmembers of the tribe." [450 U.S., at 565.] The *Montana* opinion added, however, that in certain circumstances, even where Congress has not expressly authorized it, tribal civil jurisdiction may encompass nonmembers:

> "To be sure, Indian tribes retain inherent sovereign power to exercise some forms of civil jurisdiction over non-Indians on their reservations, even on non-Indian fee lands. A tribe may regulate, through taxation, licensing, or other means, the activities of nonmembers who enter consensual relationships with the tribe or its members, through commercial dealing, contracts, leases, or other arrangements. A tribe may also retain inherent power to exercise civil authority over the conduct of non-Indians on fee lands within its reservation when that conduct threatens or has some direct effect on the political integrity, the economic security, or the health or welfare of the tribe." *Id.,* at 565-566 (citations and footnote omitted).

....

Montana thus described a general rule that, absent a different congressional direction, Indian tribes lack civil authority over the conduct of nonmembers on non-Indian land within a reservation, subject to two exceptions: The first exception relates to nonmembers who enter consensual relationships with the tribe or its members; the second concerns activity that directly affects the tribe's political integrity, economic security, health, or welfare....

....

Petitioners and the United States refer to no treaty or statute authorizing the Three Affiliated Tribes to entertain highway-accident tort suits of the kind ... commenced against A-1 Contractors.... Rather, petitioners and the United States ground their defense of tribal-court jurisdiction exclusively on the concept of retained or inherent sovereignty. *Montana,* we have explained, is the controlling decision for this case. To prevail here, petitioners must show that ... [the] tribal-court action against nonmembers qualifies under one of *Montana's* two exceptions.

The first exception to the *Montana* rule covers "activities of nonmembers who enter consensual relationships with the tribe or its members, through commercial dealing, contracts, leases, or other arrangements." 450 U.S., at 565. The tortious conduct alleged in Fredericks' complaint does not fit that description. The dispute, as the Court of Appeals said, is "distinctly non-tribal in nature." 76 F.3d, at 940.... Although A-1 was engaged in subcontract work on the Fort Berthold Reservation, and therefore had a "consensual relationship" with the Tribes, "Gisela Fredericks was not a party to the subcontract, and the [T]ribes were strangers to the accident." *Ibid.*

   ....

The second exception to *Montana's* general rule concerns conduct that "threatens or has some direct effect on the political integrity, the economic security, or the health or welfare of the tribe." 450 U.S., at 566. Undoubtedly, those who drive carelessly on a public highway running through a reservation endanger all in the vicinity, and surely jeopardize the safety of tribal members. But if *Montana's* second exception requires no more, the exception would severely shrink the rule....

   ....

Read in isolation, the *Montana* rule's second exception can be misperceived. Key to its proper application, however, is the Court's preface: "Indian tribes retain their inherent power [to punish tribal offenders,] to determine tribal membership, to regulate domestic relations among members, and to prescribe rules of inheritance for members.... But [a tribe's inherent power does not reach] beyond what is necessary to protect tribal self-government or to control internal relations." 450 U.S., at 564. Neither regulatory nor adjudicatory authority over the state highway accident at issue is needed to preserve "the right of reservation Indians to make their own laws and be ruled by them." *Williams,* 358 U.S., at 220. The *Montana* rule, therefore, and not its exceptions, applies to this case.

Affirmed.

ALASKA v. NATIVE VILLAGE OF VENETIE TRIBAL GOVERNMENT

522 U.S. 520, 118 S. Ct. 948, 140 L. Ed. 2d 30 (U.S. Sup. Ct. 1998)

Justice Thomas delivered the opinion of the Court.

In this case, we must decide whether approximately 1.8 million acres of land in northern Alaska, owned in fee simple by the Native Village of Venetie Tribal Government pursuant to the Alaska Native Claims Settlement Act, is "Indian country." We conclude that it is not....

I

The Village of Venetie, which is located in Alaska above the Arctic Circle, is home to the Neets'aii Gwich'in Indians. In 1943, the Secretary of the Interior created a reservation for the Neets'aii Gwich'in out of the land surrounding Venetie and another nearby tribal village, Arctic Village. *See* App. to Pet. for Cert. 2a. This land, which is about the size of Delaware, remained a reservation until 1971, when Congress enacted the Alaska Native Claims Settlement Act (ANCSA), a comprehensive statute designed to settle all land claims by Alaska Natives. *See* 85 Stat. 688, as amended, 43 U.S.C. § 1601 *et seq.*

In enacting ANCSA, Congress sought to end the sort of federal supervision over Indian affairs that had previously marked federal Indian policy....

....

To this end, ANCSA revoked "the various reserves set aside ... for Native use" by legislative or Executive action, except for the Annette Island Reserve inhabited by the Metlakatla Indians, and completely extinguished all aboriginal claims to Alaska land. §§ 1603, 1618(a). In return, Congress authorized the transfer of $962.5 million in state and federal funds and approximately 44 million acres of Alaska land to state-chartered private business corporations that were to be formed pursuant to the statute; all of the shareholders of these corporations were required to be Alaska Natives. §§ 1605, 1607, 1613. The ANCSA corporations received title to the transferred land in fee simple, and no federal restrictions applied to subsequent land transfers by them.

....

[*This action arose from the Tribe's attempt to levy taxes on a private contractor who conducted business on the tribes' land. The issue is whether the tribal lands constitute "Indian country" under 18 U.S.C. § 1151(b), and are thus subject to tribal regulatory jurisdiction.*]

II
A

"Indian country" is currently defined at 18 U.S.C. § 1151. In relevant part, the statute provides:

> "[T]he term 'Indian country' ... means (a) all land within the limits of any Indian reservation under the jurisdiction of the United States Government ..., (b) all dependent Indian communities within the borders of the United States whether within the original or subsequently acquired territory thereof, and whether within or without the limits of a state, and (c) all Indian allotments, the Indian titles to which have not been extinguished, including rights-of-way running through the same."

....

Because ANCSA revoked the Venetie Reservation, and because no Indian allotments are at issue, whether the Tribe's land is Indian country depends on whether it falls within the "dependent Indian communities" prong of the statute, § 1151(b). Since 18 U.S.C. § 1151 was enacted in 1948, we have not had an occasion to interpret the term "dependent Indian communities." We now hold that it refers to a limited category of Indian lands that are neither reservations nor allotments, and that satisfy two requirements—first, they must have been set aside by the Federal Government for the use of the Indians as Indian land; second, they must be under federal superintendence. Our holding is based on our conclusion that in enacting § 1151, Congress codified these two requirements, which previously we had held necessary for a finding of "Indian country" generally.

Before § 1151 was enacted, we held in three cases that Indian lands that were not reservations could be Indian country and that the Federal Government could therefore exercise jurisdiction over them. *See United States v. Sandoval*, 231 U.S. 28 (1913); *United States v. Pelican*, 232 U.S. 442 (1914); *United States v. McGowan*, 302 U.S. 535 (1938)....

In each of these cases, therefore, we relied upon a finding of both a federal set-aside and federal superintendence in concluding that the Indian lands in question constituted Indian country and that it was permissible for the Federal Government to exercise jurisdiction over them. Section 1151 does not purport to alter this definition of Indian country, but merely lists the three different categories of Indian country mentioned in our prior cases....

We therefore must conclude that in enacting § 1151(b), Congress indicated that a federal set-aside *and* a federal superintendence requirement must be satisfied for a finding of a "dependent Indian community"—just as those requirements had to be met for a finding of Indian country before 18 U.S.C. § 1151 was enacted....

The Tribe's ANCSA lands do not satisfy either of these requirements. After the enactment of ANCSA, the Tribe's lands are neither "validly set apart for the use of the Indians as such," nor are they under the superintendence of the Federal Government.

With respect to the federal set-aside requirement, it is significant that ANCSA, far from designating Alaskan lands for Indian use, revoked the existing Venetie Reservation, and indeed revoked all existing reservations in Alaska "*set aside* by legislation or by Executive or Secretarial Order *for Native use*," save one. 43 U.S.C. § 1618(a) (emphasis added). In no clearer fashion could Congress have departed from its traditional practice of setting aside Indian lands....

....

... By ANCSA's very design, Native corporations can immediately convey former reservation lands to non-Natives, and such corporations are not restricted to using those lands for Indian purposes. Because Congress contemplated that non-Natives could own the former Venetie Reservation, and because the Tribe is free to use it for non-Indian purposes, we must conclude that the federal set-aside requirement is not met....

Equally clearly, ANCSA ended federal superintendence over the Tribe's lands.... Congress stated explicitly that ANCSA's settlement provisions were intended to avoid a "lengthy wardship or trusteeship." § 1601(b). After ANCSA, federal protection of the Tribe's land is essentially limited to a statutory declaration that the land is exempt from adverse possession claims, real property taxes, and certain judgments as long as it has not been sold, leased, or developed. *See* § 1636(d). These protections, if they can be called that, simply do not approach the level of superintendence over the Indians' land that existed in our prior cases. In each of those cases, the Federal Government actively controlled the lands in question, effectively acting as a guardian for the Indians....

....

... Whether the concept of Indian country should be modified is a question entirely for Congress.

The judgment of the Court of Appeals is reversed.

It is so ordered.

MINNESOTA v. MILLE LACS BAND OF CHIPPEWA

526 U.S. 172, 119 S. Ct. 1187, 143 L. Ed. 2d 270 (U.S. Sup. Ct. 1999)

JUSTICE O'CONNOR delivered the opinion of the Court.

In 1837, the United States entered into a Treaty with several Bands of Chippewa Indians. Under the terms of this Treaty, the Indians ceded land in present-day Wisconsin and Minnesota to the United States, and the United States guaranteed to the Indians certain hunting, fishing, and gathering rights on the ceded land. We must decide whether the Chippewa Indians retain these usufructuary rights today. The State of Minnesota argues that the Indians lost these rights through an Executive Order in 1850, an 1855 Treaty, and the admission of Minnesota into the Union in 1858. After an examination of the historical record, we conclude that the Chippewa retain the usufructuary rights guaranteed to them under the 1837 Treaty.

....

... The United States ... in the fifth article of the Treaty, guaranteed to the Chippewa the right to hunt, fish, and gather on the ceded lands:

"The privilege of hunting, fishing, and gathering the wild rice, upon the lands, the rivers and the lakes included in the territory ceded, is guarantied [sic] to the Indians, during the pleasure of the President of the United States." 1837 Treaty with the Chippewa, 7 Stat. 537.

....

In the late 1840's, pressure mounted to remove the Chippewa to their unceded lands in the Minnesota Territory....

....

... President Taylor responded to this pressure by issuing an Executive Order on February 6, 1850. The order provided:

"The privileges granted temporarily to the Chippewa Indians of the Mississippi, by the Fifth Article of the Treaty made with them on the 29th of July 1837, 'of hunting, fishing and gathering the wild rice, upon the lands, the rivers and the lakes included in the territory ceded' by that treaty to the United States; and the right granted to the Chippewa Indians of the Mississippi and Lake Superior, by the Second Article of the treaty with them of October 4th 1842, of hunting on the territory which they ceded by that treaty, 'with the other usual privileges of occupancy until required to remove by the President of the United States,' are hereby revoked; and all of the said Indians remaining on the lands ceded as aforesaid, are required to remove to their unceded lands." App. to Pet. for Cert. 565.

....

In 1849, white lumbermen built a dam on the Rum River (within the Minnesota portion of the 1837 ceded Territory), and the Mille Lacs Band of Chippewa protested that the dam interfered with its wild rice harvest.... In February 1855, the Governor of the Minnesota Territory, Willis Gorman, who also served as the ex officio superintendent of Indian affairs for the Territory, wrote to Commissioner Manypenny about this dispute. In his letter, he noted that "[t]he lands occupied by the timbermen have been surveyed and sold by the United States and the Indians have no other treaty interests *except hunting and fishing.*" *Id.*, at 295-296 (letter of Feb. 16, 1855) (emphasis added).... Thus, as of 1855, the federal official responsible for Indian affairs in the Minnesota Territory acknowledged and recognized Chippewa rights to hunt and fish in the 1837 ceded Territory.

. . . .

Although the United States abandoned its removal policy, it did not abandon its attempts to acquire more Chippewa land. To this end, in the spring of 1854, Congress began considering legislation to authorize additional treaties for the purchase of Chippewa lands....

. . . .

When the Senate finally passed the authorizing legislation in December 1854, Minnesota's territorial delegate to Congress recommended to Commissioner Manypenny that he negotiate a treaty with the Mississippi, Pillager, and Lake Winnibigoshish Bands of Chippewa Indians. App. 286-287 (letter from Rice to Manypenny, Dec. 17, 1854). Commissioner Manypenny summoned representatives of those Bands to Washington, D.C., for the treaty negotiations.... The purpose and result of these negotiations was the sale of Chippewa lands to the United States. To this end, the first article of the 1855 Treaty contains two sentences:

"The Mississippi, Pillager, and Lake Winnibigoshish bands of Chippewa Indians hereby cede, sell, and convey to the United States all their right, title, and interest in, and to, the lands now owned and claimed by them, in the Territory of Minnesota, and included within the following boundaries, viz: [describing territorial boundaries]. And the said Indians do further fully and entirely relinquish and convey to the United States, any and all right, title, and interest, of whatsoever nature the same may be, which they may now have in, and to any other lands in the Territory of Minnesota or elsewhere." 10 Stat. 1165- 1166.

... The Treaty, however, makes no mention of hunting and fishing rights, whether to reserve new usufructuary rights or to abolish rights guaranteed by previous treaties....

A little over three years after the 1855 Treaty was signed, Minnesota was admitted to the Union. *See* Act of May 11, 1858, 11 Stat. 285. The admission Act is silent with respect to Indian treaty rights.

. . . .

We are first asked to decide whether President Taylor's Executive Order of February 6, 1850, terminated Chippewa hunting, fishing, and gathering rights under the 1837 Treaty....

. . . .

... We agree that the Removal Act did not forbid the President's removal order, but as noted by the Court of Appeals, it also did not authorize that order.

Because the Removal Act did not authorize the 1850 removal order, we must look elsewhere for a constitutional or statutory authorization for the order. In this Court, only the landowners argue for an alternative source of authority; they argue that the President's removal order was authorized by the 1837 Treaty itself.... There is no support for this proposition, however. The Treaty makes no mention of removal, and there was no discussion of removal during the Treaty negotiations.... Because the parties have pointed to no colorable source of authority for the President's removal order, we agree with the Court of Appeals' conclusion that the 1850 removal order was unauthorized.

[*The Court then went on to reject the State's proposition that the Tribe's 1837 Treaty privileges were still revoked because the removal portion of the Executive Order could be severed from the portion revoking their usufructuary rights. The Court looked to the President's intent when issuing the order and found that "President Taylor intended the 1850 order to stand or fall as a whole.*]

....

We conclude that President Taylor's 1850 Executive Order was ineffective to terminate Chippewa usufructuary rights under the 1837 Treaty. The State has pointed to no statutory or constitutional authority for the President's removal order, and the Executive Order, embodying as it did one coherent policy, is inseverable. We do not mean to suggest that a President, now or in the future, cannot revoke Chippewa usufructuary rights in accordance with the terms of the 1837 Treaty. All we conclude today is that the President's 1850 Executive Order was insufficient to accomplish this revocation because it was not severable from the invalid removal order.

....

The State argues that the Mille Lacs Band of Chippewa Indians relinquished its usufructuary rights under the 1855 Treaty with the Chippewa. Specifically, the State argues that the Band unambiguously relinquished its usufructuary rights by agreeing to the second sentence of Article 1 in that Treaty:

> "And the said Indians do further fully and entirely relinquish and convey to
> the United States, any and all right, title, and interest, of whatsoever nature
> the same may be, which they may now have in, and to any other lands in the
> Territory of Minnesota or elsewhere." 10 Stat. 1166.

This sentence, however, does not mention the 1837 Treaty, and it does not mention hunting, fishing, and gathering rights. The entire 1855 Treaty, in fact, is devoid of any language expressly mentioning—much less abrogating—usufructuary rights. Similarly, the Treaty contains no language providing money for the abrogation of previously held rights. These omissions are telling because the United States treaty drafters had the sophistication and experience to use express language for the abrogation of treaty rights. In fact, just a few months after Commissioner Manypenny completed the 1855 Treaty, he negotiated a Treaty with the Chippewa of Sault Ste. Marie that expressly revoked fishing rights that had been reserved in an earlier Treaty. *See* Treaty with the Chippewa of Sault Ste. Marie, Art. 1, 11 Stat. 631....

....

[*The Court then points out that an examination into the historical record of the 1855 Treaty demonstrates that the Treaty was designed to transfer lands from the Chippewa to the United States, not to terminate Chippewa usufructuary rights.*]

....

Finally, the State argues that the Chippewa's usufructuary rights under the 1837 Treaty were extinguished when Minnesota was admitted to the Union in 1858. In making this argument, the State faces an uphill battle. Congress may abrogate Indian treaty rights, but it must clearly express its intent to do so. *United States v. Dion*, 476 U.S. 734, 738-740 (1986); *see also Washington v. Washington State Commercial Passenger Fishing Vessel Assn.*, 443 U.S., at 690; *Menominee Tribe v. United States*, 391 U.S. 404, 413 (1968). There must be "clear evidence that Congress actually considered the conflict between its intended action on the one hand and Indian treaty rights on the other, and chose to resolve that conflict by abrogating the treaty." *United States v. Dion, supra,* at 740. There is no such "clear evidence" of congressional intent to abrogate the Chippewa Treaty rights here. The relevant statute—Minnesota's enabling Act—provides in relevant part:

> "[T]he State of Minnesota shall be one, and is hereby declared to be one, of the United States of America, and admitted into the Union on an equal footing with the original States in all respects whatever." Act of May 11, 1858, 11 Stat. 285.

This language, like the rest of the Act, makes no mention of Indian treaty rights; it provides no clue that Congress considered the reserved rights of the Chippewa and decided to abrogate those rights when it passed the Act....

With no direct support for its argument, the State relies principally on this Court's decision in *Ward v. Race Horse*, 163 U.S. 504 (1896). In *Race Horse*, we held that a Treaty reserving to a Tribe "'the right to hunt on the unoccupied lands of the United States, so long as game may be found thereon, and so long as peace subsists among the whites and Indians on the borders of the hunting districts'" terminated when Wyoming became a State in 1890. *Id.,* at 507 (quoting Art. 4 of the Treaty). This case does not bear the weight the State places on it, however, because it has been qualified by later decisions of this Court.

The first part of the holding in *Race Horse* was based on the "equal footing doctrine," the constitutional principle that all States are admitted to the Union with the same attributes of sovereignty (*i.e.,* on equal footing) as the original 13 States. *See Coyle v. Smith*, 221 U.S. 559 (1911). As relevant here, it prevents the Federal Government from impairing fundamental attributes of state sovereignty when it admits new States into the Union. *Id.,* at 573. According to the *Race Horse* Court, because the treaty rights conflicted irreconcilably with state regulation of natural resources—"an essential attribute of its governmental existence," 163 U.S., at 516—the treaty rights were held an invalid impairment of Wyoming's sovereignty. Thus, those rights could not survive Wyoming's admission to the Union on "equal footing" with the original States.

But *Race Horse* rested on a false premise. As this Court's subsequent cases have made clear, an Indian tribe's treaty rights to hunt, fish, and gather on state land are not irreconcilable with a State's sovereignty over the natural resources in the State. *See, e.g.,*

Washington v. Washington State Commercial Passenger Fishing Vessel Assn., [443 U.S. 658 (1979)].... Although States have important interests in regulating wildlife and natural resources within their borders, this authority is shared with the Federal Government when the Federal Government exercises one of its enumerated constitutional powers, such as treaty making. U.S. Const., Art. VI, cl. 2.... Here, the 1837 Treaty gave the Chippewa the right to hunt, fish, and gather in the ceded territory free of territorial, and later state, regulation, a privilege that others did not enjoy. Today, this freedom from state regulation curtails the State's ability to regulate hunting, fishing, and gathering by the Chippewa in the ceded lands....

[*The Court goes on to explain that the State may impose reasonable and nondiscriminatory regulations on off-reservation treaty hunting and fishing rights in the "interest of conservation."*]

Accordingly, the judgment of the United States Court of Appeals for the Eighth Circuit is affirmed.

ATKINSON TRADING COMPANY v. SHIRLEY

532 U.S. 645, 121 S. Ct. 1825, 149 L. Ed. 2d 889 (U.S. Sup. Ct. 2001)

CHIEF JUSTICE REHNQUIST delivered the opinion of the Court.

....

In 1916, Hubert Richardson, lured by the possibility of trading with wealthy Gray Mountain Navajo cattlemen, built the Cameron Trading Post just south of the Little Colorado River near Cameron, Arizona.... Richardson purchased the land directly from the United States, but the Navajo Nation Reservation, which had been established in 1868, ... was later extended eight miles south so that the Cameron Trading Post fell within its exterior boundaries.... It is, like millions of acres throughout the United States, non-Indian fee land within a tribal reservation.

Richardson's "drafty, wooden store building and four small, one-room-shack cabins overlooking the bare river canyon," ... have since evolved into a business complex consisting of a hotel, restaurant, cafeteria, gallery, curio shop, retail store, and recreational vehicle facility. The current owner, petitioner Atkinson Trading Company, Inc., benefits from the Cameron Trading Post's location near the intersection of Arizona Highway 64 (which leads west to the Grand Canyon) and United States Highway 89 (which connects Flagstaff on the south with Glen Canyon Dam to the north). A significant portion of petitioner's hotel business stems from tourists on their way to or from the Grand Canyon National Park.

In 1992, the Navajo Nation enacted a hotel occupancy tax, which imposes an 8 percent tax upon any hotel room located within the exterior boundaries of the Navajo Nation Reservation.... Although the legal incidence of the tax falls directly upon the guests, the owner or operator of the hotel must collect and remit it to respondents, members of the Navajo Tax Commission.... The nonmember guests at the Cameron Trading Post pay approximately $84,000 in taxes to respondents annually.

Petitioner's challenge under *Montana* to the Navajo Nation's authority to impose the hotel occupancy tax was rejected by both the Navajo Tax Commission and the Navajo Supreme Court. Petitioner then sought relief in the United States District Court for the District of New Mexico, which also upheld the tax. A divided panel of the Court of Appeals for the Tenth Circuit affirmed....

We granted certiorari, ... and now reverse.

Tribal jurisdiction is limited: For powers not expressly conferred them by federal statute or treaty, Indian tribes must rely upon their retained or inherent sovereignty. In *Montana*, the most exhaustively reasoned of our modern cases addressing this latter authority, we observed that Indian tribe power over nonmembers on non-Indian fee land is sharply circumscribed....

Although we extracted from our precedents "the general proposition that the inherent sovereign powers of an Indian tribe do not extend to the activities of nonmembers of the tribe," ... we nonetheless noted in *Montana* two possible bases for tribal jurisdiction over non-Indian fee land. First, "[a] tribe may regulate, through taxation, licensing, or other means, the activities of nonmembers who enter consensual relationships with the tribe or its members, through commercial dealings, contracts, leases, or other arrangements."... Second, "[a] tribe may ... exercise civil authority over the conduct of non-Indians on fee lands within its reservation when that conduct threatens or has some direct effect on the political integrity, the economic security, or the health or welfare of the tribe." ... Applying these precepts, we found that the nonmembers at issue there had not subjected themselves to "tribal civil jurisdiction" through any agreements or dealings with the Tribe and that hunting and fishing on non-Indian fee land did not "imperil the subsistence or welfare of the Tribe."....

....

Citing our decision in *Merrion*, respondents submit that *Montana* and *Strate* do not restrict an Indian tribe's power to impose revenue-raising taxes. In *Merrion*, ... we upheld a severance tax imposed by the Jicarilla Apache Tribe upon non-Indian lessees authorized to extract oil and gas from tribal land. In so doing, we noted that the power to tax derives not solely from an Indian tribe's power to exclude non-Indians from tribal land, but also from an Indian tribe's "general authority, as sovereign, to control economic activity within its jurisdiction." ... Such authority, we held, was incident to the benefits conferred upon nonmembers.

Merrion, however, was careful to note that an Indian tribe's inherent power to tax only extended to "'transactions occurring on trust lands and significantly involving a tribe or its members.'" ... *Merrion* involved a tax that only applied to activity occurring on the reservation, and its holding is therefore easily reconcilable with the *Montana-Strate* line of authority, which we deem to be controlling.... An Indian tribe's sovereign power to tax—whatever its derivation—reaches no further than tribal land.

We therefore do not read *Merrion* to exempt taxation from *Montana*'s general rule that Indian tribes lack civil authority over nonmembers on non-Indian fee land. Accordingly, as in *Strate*, we apply *Montana* straight up. Because Congress has not authorized the Navajo Nation's hotel occupancy tax through treaty or statute, and because the incidence of the tax falls upon nonmembers on non-Indian fee land, it is incumbent upon the Navajo Nation to establish the existence of one of *Montana*'s exceptions.

... [R]espondents note that the Cameron Trading Post benefits from the numerous services provided by the Navajo Nation. The record reflects that the Arizona State Police and the Navajo Tribal Police patrol the portions of United States Highway 89 and Arizona Highway 64 traversing the reservation; that the Navajo Tribal Police and the Navajo Tribal Emergency Medical Services Department will respond to an emergency call from the Cameron Trading Post; and that local Arizona Fire Departments and the Navajo Tribal Fire Department provide fire protection to the area. Although we do not question the Navajo Nation's ability to charge an appropriate fee for a particular service actually rendered, we think the generalized availability of tribal services patently insufficient to sustain the Tribe's civil authority over nonmembers on non-Indian fee land.

The consensual relationship must stem from "commercial dealing, contracts, leases, or other arrangements," ... and a nonmember's actual or potential receipt of tribal police, fire, and medical services does not create the requisite connection.... Such a result does not square with our precedents; indeed, we implicitly rejected this argument in *Strate*, where we held that the nonmembers had not consented to the Tribes' adjudicatory authority by availing themselves of the benefit of tribal police protection while traveling within the reservation.... We therefore reject respondents' broad reading of *Montana*'s first exception, which ignores the dependent status of Indian tribes and subverts the territorial restriction upon tribal power.

    ....

Montana's consensual relationship exception requires that the tax or regulation imposed by the Indian tribe have a nexus to the consensual relationship itself.... The hotel occupancy tax at issue here is grounded in petitioner's relationship with its nonmember hotel guests, who can reach the Cameron Trading Post on United States Highway 89 and Arizona Highway 64, non-Indian public rights-of-way. Petitioner cannot be said to have consented to such a tax by virtue of its status as an "Indian trader."

Although the Court of Appeals did not reach *Montana*'s second exception, both respondents and the United States argue that the hotel occupancy tax is warranted in light of the direct effects the Cameron Trading Post has upon the Navajo Nation.... [W]e fail to see how petitioner's operation of a hotel on non-Indian fee land "threatens or has some direct effect on the political integrity, the economic security, or the health or welfare of the tribe."

    ....

Indian tribes are "unique aggregations possessing attributes of sovereignty over both their members and their territory," but their dependent status generally precludes extension of tribal civil authority beyond these limits.... The Navajo Nation's imposition of a tax upon nonmembers on non-Indian fee land within the reservation is, therefore, presumptively invalid. Because respondents have failed to establish that the hotel occupancy tax is commensurately related to any consensual relationship with petitioner or is necessary to vindicate the Navajo Nation's political integrity, the presumption ripens into a holding. The judgment of the Court of Appeals for the Tenth Circuit is accordingly Reversed.

NEVADA v. HICKS

533 U.S. 353, 121 S. Ct. 2304, 150 L. Ed. 2d 398 (U.S. Sup. Ct. 2001)

JUSTICE SCALIA delivered the opinion of the Court.

This case presents the question whether a tribal court may assert jurisdiction over civil claims against state officials who entered tribal land to execute a search warrant against a tribe member suspected of having violated state law outside the reservation.

....

Respondent Hicks ... is one of about 900 members of the Fallon Paiute-Shoshone Tribes of western Nevada. He resides on the Tribes' reservation of approximately 8000 acres.... In 1990 Hicks came under suspicion of having killed, off the reservation, a California bighorn sheep, a gross misdemeanor under Nevada law.... A state game warden obtained from state court a search warrant "SUBJECT TO OBTAINING APPROVAL FROM THE FALLON TRIBAL COURT IN AND FOR THE FALLON PAIUTE-SHOSHONE TRIBES." According to the issuing judge, ... tribal-court authorization was necessary because "[t]his Court has no jurisdiction on the Fallon Paiute-Shoshone Indian Reservation." ... A search warrant was obtained from the tribal court, and the warden, accompanied by a tribal police officer, searched respondent's yard....

Approximately one year later, ... [t]he warden again obtained a search warrant from state court; though this warrant did not explicitly require permission from the Tribes, ... a tribal-court warrant was nonetheless secured, and respondent's home was again (unsuccessfully) searched by three wardens and additional tribal officers.

Respondent, claiming that his sheep-heads had been damaged, and that the second search exceeded the bounds of the warrant, brought suit against the Tribal Judge, the tribal officers, the state wardens in their individual and official capacities, and the State of Nevada in the Tribal Court in and for the Fallon Paiute-Shoshone Tribes. (His claims against all defendants except the state wardens and the State of Nevada were dismissed by directed verdict and are not at issue here.) ... Respondent later voluntarily dismissed his case against the State and against the state officials in their official capacities, leaving only his suit against those officials in their individual capacities....

....

The principle of Indian law central to this aspect of the case is our holding in *Strate v. A-1 Contractors*: "As to nonmembers ... a tribe's adjudicative jurisdiction does not exceed its legislative jurisdiction.... " We first inquire, ... whether the Fallon Paiute-Shoshone Tribes—either as an exercise of their inherent sovereignty, or under grant of federal authority—can regulate state wardens executing a search warrant for evidence of an off-reservation crime.

Indian tribes' regulatory authority over nonmembers is governed by the principles set forth in *Montana v. United States*, ... which we have called the "pathmarking case" on the subject....

Both *Montana* and *Strate* rejected tribal authority to regulate nonmembers' activities on land over which the tribe could not "assert a landowner's right to occupy and exclude." ... Respondents ... argue that since Hicks's home and yard are on tribe-owned land within the reservation, the Tribe may make its exercise of regulatory authority over nonmembers a condition of nonmembers' entry. Not necessarily. While it is certainly true that the non-Indian ownership status of the land was central to the analysis in both *Montana* and *Strate*, the reason that was so was not that Indian ownership suspends the "general proposition" derived from *Oliphant* that "the inherent sovereign powers of an Indian tribe do not extend to the activities of nonmembers of the tribe" except to the extent "necessary to protect tribal self-government or to control internal relations." ... *Oliphant* itself drew no distinctions based on the status of land. And *Montana*, after announcing the general rule of no jurisdiction over nonmembers, cautioned that "[t]o be sure, Indian tribes retain inherent sovereign power to exercise some forms of civil jurisdiction over non-Indians on their reservations, even on non-Indian fee lands," ...—clearly implying that the general rule of *Montana* applies to both Indian and non-Indian land. The ownership status of land, in other words, is only one factor to consider in determining whether regulation of the activities of nonmembers is "necessary to protect tribal self-government or to control internal relations." It may sometimes be a dispositive factor. Hitherto, the absence of tribal ownership has been virtually conclusive of the absence of tribal civil jurisdiction; with one minor exception, we have never upheld under *Montana* the extension of tribal civil authority over nonmembers on non-Indian land....

    ....

In *Strate*, we explained that what is necessary to protect tribal self-government and control internal relations can be understood by looking at the examples of tribal power to which *Montana* referred: tribes have authority "[to punish tribal offenders,] to determine tribal membership, to regulate domestic relations among members, and to prescribe rules of inheritance for members." ... Indians have "'the right ... to make their own laws and be ruled by them.'" ... Tribal assertion of regulatory authority over nonmembers must be connected to that right of the Indians to make their own laws and be governed by them....

Our cases make clear that the Indians' right to make their own laws and be governed by them does not exclude all state regulatory authority on the reservation. State sovereignty does not end at a reservation's border. Though tribes are often referred to as "sovereign" entities, it was "long ago" that "the Court departed from Chief Justice Marshall's view that 'the laws of [a State] can have no force' within reservation boundaries....

That is not to say that States may exert the same degree of regulatory authority within a reservation as they do without. To the contrary, the principle that Indians have the right to make their own laws and be governed by them requires "an accommodation between the interests of the Tribes and the Federal Government, on the one hand, and those of the State, on the other." ... When, however, state interests outside the reservation are implicated, States may regulate the activities even of tribe members on tribal land, as exemplified by our decision in [*Washington v.*] *Confederated Tribes* [*of Colville Reservation*]. In that case, ... [w]e held that the State could require the Tribes to collect [state cigarette] tax from nonmembers, and could "impose at least 'minimal' burdens on the Indian retailer to aid in enforcing and collecting the tax." ... It is also well established in our precedent that States have criminal jurisdiction over reservation Indians for crimes committed (as was the alleged poaching in this case) off the reservation....

We conclude today, in accordance with ... prior statements, that tribal authority to regulate state officers in executing process related to the violation, off reservation, of state laws is not essential to tribal self-government or internal relations—to "the right to make laws and be ruled by them." The State's interest in execution of process is considerable, and even when it relates to Indian-fee lands it no more impairs the tribe's self-government than federal enforcement of federal law impairs state government. Respondents argue that, even conceding the State's general interest in enforcing its off-reservation poaching law on the reservation, Nevada's interest in this suit is minimal, because it is a suit against state officials in their individual capacities. We think, however, that the distinction between individual and official capacity suits is irrelevant....

    ....

We turn next to the contention of respondent ... that the tribal court, as a court of general jurisdiction, has authority to entertain federal claims.... under [42 U.S.C.] § 1983.... Th[e] historical and constitutional assumption of concurrent state-court jurisdiction over federal-law cases is completely missing with respect to tribal courts.

Respondents' contention that tribal courts are courts of "general jurisdiction" is also quite wrong. ... Tribal courts, it should be clear, cannot be courts of general jurisdiction ..., for a tribe's inherent adjudicative jurisdiction over nonmembers is at most only as broad as its legislative jurisdiction....

    ....

The last question before us is whether petitioners were required to exhaust their jurisdictional claims in Tribal Court before bringing them in Federal District Court.... Since it is clear, ... that tribal courts lack jurisdiction over state officials for causes of action relating to their performance of official duties, adherence to the tribal exhaustion requirement in such cases "would serve no purpose other than delay," and is therefore unnecessary.

    ....

Because the Fallon Paiute-Shoshone Tribes lacked legislative authority to restrict, condition, or otherwise regulate the ability of state officials to investigate off-reservation violations of state law, they also lacked adjudicative authority to hear respondent's claim that those officials violated tribal law in the performance of their duties. Nor can the Tribes identify any authority to adjudicate respondent's § 1983 claim. And since the lack of authority is clear, there is no need to exhaust the jurisdictional dispute in tribal court. State officials operating on a reservation to investigate off-reservation violations of state law are properly held accountable for tortious conduct and civil rights violations in either state or federal court, but not in tribal court.

The judgment of the Court of Appeals is reversed, and the case remanded for further proceedings consistent with our opinion.

UNITED STATES v. LARA

541 U.S. _____, 124 S. Ct. 1628, _____ L. Ed. 2d _____ (U.S. Sup. Ct. 2004)

Justice Breyer delivered the opinion of the Court.

This case concerns a congressional statute "recogniz[ing] and affirm[ing]" the "inherent" authority of a tribe to bring a criminal misdemeanor prosecution against an Indian who is not a member of that tribe—authority that this Court previously held a tribe did not possess. *Compare* 25 U.S.C. § 1301(2) with *Duro v. Reina*, 495 U.S. 676 (1990). We must decide whether Congress has the constitutional power to relax restrictions that the political branches have, over time, placed on the exercise of a tribe's inherent legal authority. We conclude that Congress does possess this power [*to reverse Duro v. Reina and expressly affirm the inherent sovereign authority of tribes to exercise criminal jurisdiction over members of other tribes*].

I.

Respondent Billy Jo Lara is an enrolled member of the Turtle Mountain Band of Chippewa Indians.... He married a member of a different tribe, the Spirit Lake Tribe, and lived with his wife and children on the Spirit Lake Reservation.... After several incidents of serious misconduct, the Spirit Lake Tribe issued an order excluding him from the reservation. Lara ignored the order; federal officers stopped him; and he struck one of the arresting officers....

The Spirit Lake Tribe subsequently prosecuted Lara in the Spirit Lake Tribal Court for "violence to a policeman." ... Lara pleaded guilty and, in respect to that crime, served 90 days in jail....

After Lara's tribal conviction, the Federal Government charged Lara in the Federal District Court for the District of North Dakota with the federal crime of assaulting a federal officer.... Key elements of this federal crime mirror elements of the tribal crime of "violence to a policeman." ... And this similarity between the two crimes would *ordinarily* have brought Lara within the protective reach of the Double Jeopardy Clause. ... ([T]he Government may not "subject" any person "for the same offense to be twice put in jeopardy of life or limb")…. But the Government, responding to Lara's claim of double jeopardy, pointed out that the Double Jeopardy Clause does not bar successive prosecutions brought by *separate sovereigns,* and it argued that this "dual sovereignty" doctrine determined the outcome here….

… The Government recognized, of course, that Lara is not one of the Spirit Lake Tribe's *own* members; it also recognized that, in *Duro v. Reina, supra,* this Court had held that a tribe no longer possessed *inherent or sovereign authority* to prosecute a "nonmember Indian." *Id.,* at 679. But it pointed out that, soon after this Court decided *Duro,* Congress enacted new legislation specifically authorizing a tribe to prosecute Indian members of a different tribe. *See [25 U.S.C. § 1301(2)]….*

In the Government's view, given this statute, the Tribe, in prosecuting Lara, had exercised its own inherent *tribal* authority, not delegated *federal* authority; hence the "dual sovereignty" doctrine applies, … and since the two prosecutions were brought by two different sovereigns, the second, federal, prosecution does not violate the Double Jeopardy Clause.

The Federal Magistrate Judge accepted the Government's argument and rejected Lara's double jeopardy claim…. But the [Eighth Circuit] … held the Tribal Court, in prosecuting Lara, was exercising a *federal* prosecutorial power; hence the "dual sovereignty" doctrine does not apply; and the Double Jeopardy Clause bars the second prosecution….

Because the Eighth Circuit and Ninth Circuit have reached different conclusions about the new statute, we granted certiorari. *Compare United States v. Enas,* 255 F.3d 662….We now reverse the Eighth Circuit.

II

We assume, as do the parties, that Lara's double jeopardy claim turns on the answer to the "dual sovereignty" question. What is "the source of [the] power to punish" nonmember Indian offenders, "inherent *tribal* sovereignty" or delegated *federal* authority? *See [U.S. v.] Wheeler* … (emphasis added).

We also believe that Congress intended the former answer. The statute says that it "recognize[s] and affirm[s]" in each tribe the *"inherent" tribal* power (not delegated federal power) to prosecute nonmember Indians for misdemeanors … (emphasis added). And the statute's legislative history confirms that such was Congress' intent. *See, e.g.,* H.R. Conf. Rep. No. 102-261, pp. 3-4 (1991) ("The Committee of the Conference notes that … this legislation is not a delegation of this jurisdiction but a clarification of the status of tribes as domestic dependent nations"); *accord,* H.R. Rep. No. 102-61, p.7 (1991) ("recogniz[ing] and reaffirm[ing] the inherent authority of tribal governments to exercise criminal jurisdiction over all Indians"); 137 Cong. Rec. 9446 (1991) (statement of Sen. Inouye) (the "premise [of the legislation] is that the Congress affirms the *inherent* jurisdiction of tribal governments over nonmember Indians" (emphasis added)); *id.,* at 10712-10714 (statement of Rep. Miller, House manager of the bill) (the statute "is not a delegation of authority but an affirmation that tribes retain all rights not expressly taken away" and the bill "recognizes an inherent tribal right which always existed"); *id.,* at 10713 (statement of Rep. Richardson, a sponsor of the amendment) (the legislation "reaffirms" tribes' power).

Thus the statute seeks to adjust the tribes' status. It relaxes the restrictions, recognized in *Duro*, that the political branches had imposed on the tribes' exercise of inherent prosecutorial power. The question before us is whether the Constitution authorizes Congress to do so. Several considerations lead us to the conclusion that Congress does possess the constitutional power to lift the restrictions on the tribes' criminal jurisdiction over nonmember Indians as the statute seeks to do.

First, the Constitution grants Congress broad general powers to legislate in respect to Indian tribes, powers that we have consistently described as "plenary and exclusive." *E.g.*, W. Canby, American Indian Law 2 (3d ed. 1998) (hereinafter Canby) ("[T]he independence of the tribes is subject to exceptionally great powers of Congress to regulate and modify the status of the tribes").

This Court has traditionally identified the Indian Commerce Clause ... and the Treaty Clause ... as sources of that power *E.g., Morton v. Mancari*, 417 U.S. 535, 552 (1974); *McClanahan v. Arizona Tax Comm'n*, 411 U.S. 164, 172, n.7 (1973); *see also* Canby 11-12; F. Cohen, Handbook of Federal Indian Law 209-210 (1982 ed.) (hereinafter Cohen) (also mentioning, *inter alia*, the Property Clause). The "central function of the Indian Commerce Clause," we have said, "is to provide Congress with plenary power to legislate in the field of Indian affairs."....

    ....

We recognize that in 1871 Congress ended the practice of entering into treaties with the Indian tribes. 25 U.S.C. § 71 (stating that tribes are not entities "with whom the United States may contract by treaty"). But the statute saved existing treaties from being "invalidated or impaired," ... and this Court has explicitly stated that the statute "in no way affected Congress' plenary powers to legislate on problems of Indians." *Antoine v. Washington*, 420 U.S. 194, 203 (1975) (emphasis deleted).

Moreover, "at least during the first century of America's national existence ... Indian affairs were more an aspect of military and foreign policy than a subject of domestic or municipal law." Cohen 208.... Insofar as that is so, Congress' legislative authority would rest in part, not upon "affirmative grants of the Constitution," but upon the Constitution's adoption of preconstitutional powers necessarily inherent in any Federal Government, namely powers that this Court has described as "necessary concomitants of nationality." ... *Worcester v. Georgia*, 6 Pet. 515, 557 (1832) ("The treaties and laws of the United States contemplate ... that all intercourse with [Indians] shall be carried on exclusively by the government of the union").

Second, Congress, with this Court's approval, has interpreted the Constitution's "plenary" grants of power as authorizing it to enact legislation that both restricts and, in turn, relaxes those restrictions on tribal sovereign authority. From the Nation's beginning Congress' need for such legislative power would have seemed obvious. After all, the Government's Indian policies, applicable to numerous tribes with diverse cultures, affecting billions of acres of land, of necessity would fluctuate dramatically as the needs of the Nation and those of the tribes changed over time. *See, e.g.*, Cohen 48. And Congress has in fact authorized at different times very different Indian policies (some with beneficial results but many with tragic consequences). Congressional policy, for example, initially favored "Indian removal," then "assimilation" and the break-up of tribal lands, then protection of the tribal land base (interrupted by a movement toward greater state involvement and "termination" of recognized tribes); and it now seeks greater tribal autonomy within the framework of a "government-to-government relationship" with federal agencies. 59 Fed. Reg. 22951 (1994); *see also* 19 Weekly Comp. of Pres. Doc. 98 (1983) (President Reagan reaffirming the rejection of termination as a policy and announcing the goal of decreasing tribal dependence on the Federal Government); *see* 25 U.S.C. § 450a(b) (congressional commitment to "the development of strong and stable tribal governments"). *See generally*, Cohen 78-202 (describing this history); Canby 13-32 (same)....

Such major policy changes inevitably involve major changes in the metes and bounds of tribal sovereignty. The 1871 statute, for example, changed the status of an Indian tribe from a "powe[r] ... capable of making treaties" to a "power with whom the United States may [not] contract by treaty." *Compare Worcester, supra*, at 559, with 25 U.S.C. § 71.

One can readily find examples in congressional decisions to recognize, or to terminate, the existence of individual tribes. *See United States v. Holliday*, 3 Wall. 407, 419 (1866) ("If by [the political branches] those Indians are recognized as a tribe, this court must do the same"); *Menominee Tribe v. United States*, 391 U.S. 404 (1968) (examining the rights of Menominee Indians following the termination of their Tribe). Indeed, Congress has restored previously extinguished tribal status—by re-recognizing a Tribe whose tribal existence it previously had terminated. 25 U.S.C. §§ 903-903f (restoring the Menominee Tribe)....

Third, Congress' statutory goal—to modify the degree of autonomy enjoyed by a dependent sovereign that is not a State—is not an unusual legislative objective. The political branches, drawing upon analogous constitutional authority, have made adjustments to the autonomous status of other such dependent entities—sometimes making far more radical adjustments than those at issue here. *See, e.g.,* Hawaii—*Hawaii v. Mankichi*, 190 U.S. 197, 209-210 (1903) (describing annexation of Hawaii by joint resolution of Congress and the maintenance of a "Republic of Hawaii" until formal incorporation by Congress)....

....

We concede that *Duro*, like several other cases, referred only to the need to obtain a congressional statute that "*delegated*" power to the tribes.... But in so stating, *Duro* (like the other cases) simply did not consider whether a statute, like the present one, could constitutionally achieve the same end by removing restrictions on the tribes' inherent authority. Consequently we do not read any of these cases as holding that the Constitution forbids Congress to change "judicially made" federal Indian law through this kind of legislation.... *Oliphant [v. Suquamish Tribe, 435 U.S. 191] ...; cf. County of Oneida v. Oneida Indian Nation of N.Y.*, 470 U.S. 226 (1985) (recognizing the "federal common law" component of Indian rights, which "common law" federal courts develop as "a 'necessary expedient' when Congress has not 'spoken to a *particular* issue'" ...).

Wheeler, *Oliphant*, and *Duro*, then, are not determinative because Congress has enacted a new statute, relaxing restrictions on the bounds of the inherent tribal authority that the United States recognizes. And that fact makes all the difference.

....

IV

For these reasons, we hold, with the reservations set forth in Part III, ... that the Constitution authorizes Congress to permit tribes, as an exercise of their inherent tribal authority, to prosecute nonmember Indians. We hold that Congress exercised that authority in writing this statute. That being so, the Spirit Lake Tribe's prosecution of Lara did not amount to an exercise of federal power, and the Tribe acted in its capacity of a separate sovereign. Consequently, the Double Jeopardy Clause does not prohibit the Federal Government from proceeding with the present prosecution for a discrete *federal* offense....

The contrary judgment of the Eighth Circuit is Reversed.

INDEX

TABLE OF CASES
Boldface page numbers indicate locations of case excerpts in Part Four.